MW00453213

LIVING IN THE CHILDREN OF GOD

BP
605
.C38
V36
1991

LIVING IN THE
CHILDREN OF GOD

David E. Van Zandt

PRINCETON UNIVERSITY PRESS

PRINCETON, NEW JERSEY

WITHDRAWN

GOSHEN COLLEGE LIBRARY
GOSHEN, INDIANA

COPYRIGHT © 1991 BY PRINCETON UNIVERSITY PRESS

PUBLISHED BY PRINCETON UNIVERSITY PRESS, 41 WILLIAM STREET,
PRINCETON, NEW JERSEY 08540

IN THE UNITED KINGDOM: PRINCETON UNIVERSITY PRESS, OXFORD

ALL RIGHTS RESERVED

LIBRARY OF CONGRESS CATALOGING-IN-PUBLICATION DATA

VAN ZANDT, DAVID E., 1953-

LIVING IN THE CHILDREN OF GOD / DAVID E. VAN ZANDT.

P. CM.

INCLUDES BIBLIOGRAPHICAL REFERENCES AND INDEX.

ISBN 0-691-09463-2

1. CHILDREN OF GOD (MOVEMENT) 2. VAN ZANDT, DAVID E., 1953-

I. TITLE.

BP605.C38V36 1991 305.6'89—DC20 91-10453 CIP

THIS BOOK HAS BEEN COMPOSED IN LINOTRON PALATINO

PRINCETON UNIVERSITY PRESS BOOKS ARE PRINTED ON ACID-FREE PAPER,
AND MEET THE GUIDELINES FOR PERMANENCE AND DURABILITY OF THE
COMMITTEE ON PRODUCTION GUIDELINES FOR BOOK LONGEVITY OF THE
COUNCIL ON LIBRARY RESOURCES

PRINTED IN THE UNITED STATES OF AMERICA BY PRINCETON UNIVERSITY PRESS,
PRINCETON, NEW JERSEY

1 3 5 7 9 10 8 6 4 2

CONTENTS

ACKNOWLEDGMENTS   vii

INTRODUCTION
Studying the Children of God   3

ONE
Ideology and Proselytization   18

TWO
A Short History of the Children of God   30

THREE
The Organizational Setting of Everyday Life   56

FOUR
Social Relations in Everyday Life   72

FIVE
Litnessing: Street Proselytization as an Access Strategy   83

SIX
Witnessing: Techniques for Conversion   98

SEVEN
Reading Religious Literature   117

EIGHT
Practical Religious Activity: Creating and Maintaining the Children
of God Reality   133

NINE
Socialization and Role Negotiation   149

POSTSCRIPT
January 1991   166

APPENDIX A
The Life History of the Research and Ethical Considerations   173

APPENDIX B
Sample Mo Letters   197

BIBLIOGRAPHY   213

INDEX   225

ACKNOWLEDGMENTS

I WISH to thank friends and family, particularly Lisa Huestis and my parents, for their support during both the research and writing of this book. I owe special debts of gratitude to Rex Davis for his introduction to the Children of God and to numerous members and ex-members of the Children of God for their help during the research.

LIVING IN THE CHILDREN OF GOD

INTRODUCTION

STUDYING THE CHILDREN OF GOD

O F THE cultish religious groups that blossomed in the late 1960s and 1970s, the Children of God (the COG, also the "Family of Love" or the "Family")[1] was certainly one of the most radical and controversial. Its requirement that members "drop out" of conventional society to "serve God" on a full-time basis drew the ire of parents and more mainline religious leaders, as did its later advocacy of sex as a method to attract converts. It was constantly cited by the press as a symptom of some darker strain in American culture, and it spawned a thriving business in "deprogramming," the forceful abduction of young adherents in an often vain attempt to reverse the supposed consequences of "religious brainwashing."[2]

The Family was the cutting edge of the branch of the youth movement in the late 1960s that took a religious turn. That branch, known generically as the Jesus Revolution or the Jesus People, adopted an apocalyptic vision that mixed oldtime evangelical fervor with more modern attitudes toward social mores (Enroth et al. 1972:161–220; Richardson and Davis 1983). To these ingredients, the COG added the organizational traits of a second religious phenomenon that was appearing at the same time; groups such as the Unification Church (Barker 1984; Bromley and Shupe 1979; Cozin 1973; Lofland 1966; Robbins et al. 1976) and the Hare Krsna (Daner 1976; Johnson 1976) were organized as authoritarian, communal bodies led by charismatic prophets or teachers. While the religious doctrines of each of these organizations differed, each, including the COG, demanded and enforced the total commitment and obedience of its members to the life and the work of the group.

---

[1] Although the COG do not draw the connection, the name evokes the Anabaptists of Munster, led by Jan Matthys and later by Jan Bockelson, who in 1534 also referred to themselves as the Children of God. Both Matthys and Bockelson considered themselves prophets of God leading the last remnant of true believers in a doomed world. They organized the Anabaptist citizens of Munster communally, doing away with private property and distributing excess goods to the poor. The movement was anti-intellectual and extremely authoritarian. Over time, sexual behavioral norms moved from a rigorous asceticism to institutionalized polygamy and promiscuousness (Cohn 1970:261–74).

[2] Ted Patrick (1976) began deprogramming after one of his children had a proselytization encounter with a member of the COG.

Much has been written and said about the COG and similar groups. Their radical life-styles, odd beliefs, and authoritarian structure are magnets for the public spotlight. To the outsider, these groups have the appeal of a modern morality play, in which young, impressionable individuals are lured into psychological bondage by seemingly well-meaning but essentially evil masters. These victims either are liberated forcefully by concerned family and community members or, through a process of self-realization, free themselves after grueling ordeals.

When I began the research that led to this book I also was attracted by that appeal. I wanted to get inside the COG to see for myself how these young people were attracted and held by a set of religious ideas that seemed so strange. I therefore initially "joined" the COG and lived as a member for a short time. Subsequently, I gained the approval of the COG hierarchy to live full-time within their communes for an extended period. Once inside, I began to see things that were not observable from the outside. The world of the COG is more complicated and interesting than the plot of the standard morality play. This book is therefore quite different from much else written on these groups; instead of focusing on the sensational history and radical doctrines of the COG, I try to view the COG from the perspective of the average member living within the cult. *Living in the Children of God* tackles the phenomenon of the cults from a different angle.

Overview of the Children of God

The COG was formed in the late 1960s by David Berg, an itinerant evangelical preacher. With a message of the imminent end of the world and the necessity for total commitment to God, Berg attracted a small group of young people with whom he and his family established a communal life-style in Huntington Beach, California. The movement quickly grew, and by 1971 it had spread from the United States into western Europe. For most of the 1970s, its organizational center was in Europe, although members continued their geographical dispersion into Latin America and the Far East. As of 1984, the Family was a worldwide organization in over eighty countries claiming over nine thousand full-time members.

After the early years, Berg (known within the Family as Moses David, Father Love, or simply Dad) led the movement from self-imposed exile. Although he did not do so initially, Moses David now claims to be God's last prophet and God's vessel for messages to the world. According to the Family ideology, the revelations received by

Moses David fill out and often replace God's previous revelations in the bible, and they are transmitted to members and to the world through missives called "Mo letters."[3] The religious ideology contained in these Mo letters emphasizes personal salvation and evangelism, the necessity of total commitment to God's work, utopian socialistic critiques of capitalist society—referred to as the "System"— and the imminent introduction of the millennium on earth.

The members, who adopt new "bible names" upon joining,[4] live in colonies or "Homes" scattered throughout the world. Colonies, which typically consist of a dozen adult members plus children, are for the most part self-supporting. Unlike the Unification Church, the Family does not engage in large-scale economic projects, and its finances remain decentralized and unsophisticated; colonies depend on the money members collect through the street sale of COG literature and through donations from the public. The colonies are communally organized, and internal mores have changed through the Family's history: early strict asceticism, in which sexual relations were limited to marriage relationships, has given way to complete sexual freedom.

As with many total commitment groups, proselytization efforts are central to the Family. The Family's roots in the American southern evangelical tradition predispose it toward the belief that conversion of nonbelievers is the goal of the true religion. Members work at all times to propagate the group's message and to convert and recruit the uninitiated. Almost every activity of a member is at least tangentially affected by this fact. In its proselytization efforts, the Family has developed a number of strategies—"access strategies" (Lofland 1966)—both for proclaiming its message to the world and for initiating conversion or "witnessing" interactions with potential converts. The preeminent access strategy is "litnessing": street proselytization through the sale or distribution of COG literature. Conversion or witnessing interactions follow successful performances of access strategies and are intended to cause an evangelical or "born-again" conversion experience in the potential convert that may or may not lead

[3] In citing these letters, I provide the COG number for the letter followed by a reference, if any, to a specific paragraph within the letter. The bibliography contains the titles and dates of issuance of each letter cited.

[4] Although the new name is the only name used in the Family, the old, legal name (referred to as the member's "System name") is used whenever necessary for activities such as opening a bank account, using a postal box, or applying for a passport. Usually, one member does not know another's System name. For the most part, the names are biblical, but some members adopt other names that they believe are inspirational, such as "Happy," "Sunflower," "Black Simon," and "Windy."

to affiliation with the group. In the late 1970s, a more controversial access strategy developed. Called "Flirty Fishing," it involves members' approaching potential converts on the pretense of sexual or romantic attraction. If necessary to make a witnessing interaction successful, the Family member may engage in sexual relations with the prospect.[5]

Studying the Children of God

I first met the Family on a wet Saturday evening in New York City's Greenwich Village in December 1974, when a smiling teenager handed me a COG leaflet. Only later did I read it and realize that it was from the COG, a name I recognized from *Time* magazine. The leaflet, entitled *Holy Holes!* (Mo letter 237; hereafter, Mo letters are cited by number and internal paragraph reference if any) was a whimsical play on the words "holy" and "hole," contained fairly explicit sexual references, and called on the reader to empty themselves to let God work. I was fascinated by these religious ideas and the effect they would have on members. This was a group whose strong ideology, I thought, determined all aspects of the members' lives.

I was not alone in this initial reaction. As a rule, sociologists and anthropologists of religion have been overly impressed by the exotic nature of extreme religious beliefs (Bloch 1977:285). They tend to see the beliefs of a social group, its "ideology," as its chief constituting fact; they ignore religious practice unless it is in an extremely ideological form, such as ritual. Consistent with this methodological orientation, modern sociological studies of specific religious groups typically portray members as the necessary but unimportant bearers of the ideology and as placeholders in organizational roles.[6] The ideology of the religious group is treated as a phenomenon independent of the everyday practice of religion, and it is studied as a systematic set of ideas that provide members with an overarching worldview.[7]

---

[5] Because my period of research finished before Flirty Fishing became a substantial practice among local members, I devote little detailed attention to the phenomenon (see Richardson and Davis 1983; Wallis 1978; Wallis 1979).

[6] The massive literature on conversion is the exception that proves the rule: for the most part, the literature addresses the question, why does an individual adopt the organizational role? It confronts a problem at the boundary of religious activity, rather than the problem of religious activity itself. In Chapter 6, I examine a different aspect of the conversion process: members' activity in converting.

[7] The "interpretive anthropology" of Clifford Geertz is a good example of this approach (Geertz 1973; Geertz 1983). Geertz examines a social group's "symbol system" and asserts that members of the group express that system in a variety of ways. It has

With the ideology so delineated and explained, the analyst then describes the relation between the abstracted ideology and the abstracted organizational activity,[8] and argues that the ideology influences or is influenced by the configuration of social relations among members.

Studies of this type have their place: properly formulated abstractions are essential to institutional analyses of broad social processes. The belief that animates my approach, however, is that studies with overly formalized views of the ideology may have little to say about actual religious activity.[9] The fact is that the sociologist's reconstruction of the ideology is often alien to the beliefs held by the members themselves in everyday life. What is written in group texts (and read by sociologists) and what practiced group ideologists are able to articulate in interviews (with sociologists) may be far more explicit and systematic than the individual member's understanding. Viewing the ideology itself as the problematic and most significant aspect of religious activity leads to analyses with little connection to the reality of participating in a religious group.

Emphasizing and explaining the ideological also causes the sociologist to ignore an important and resistant fact of members' everyday lives: for believers, religious ideas are simply empirical facts that they employ in social activity (Gellner 1970:19, 37–38). Moral prescriptions are valid because they are "true" empirical conclusions—the moral and the empirical are melded in everyday life (Van Zandt 1987:916–17). This observation holds true for Family members: God, for example, is an empirical reality, a formidable being who intervenes in human affairs. For members, God is not a symbolic expression of so-

---

been argued that the coherence or systematicity that Geertz finds is imposed by Geertz himself (Lieberson 1984). To his credit, Geertz's more empirical work shows greater sensitivity to the messiness of the world (e.g., Geertz 1960).

[8] Whether the studies are based in the Durkheimian tradition that asserts that the ideology expresses social relations and that social relations buttress the ideology (Douglas 1973; Erikson 1966; Kanter 1972; Nelsen 1972; Pope 1942; Sommerfeld 1968; Swanson 1960; see also Radcliffe-Brown 1952), or in more Weberian approaches that examine the role of the ideology in institutional change such as the evolution from sect to church or the increasing secularization of modern society (Beckford 1975; Gerlach and Hine 1970; O'Dea 1957; Pope 1942; Schwartz 1970; Smelser 1962; Wallis 1976b; Wilson 1961; Wilson 1973), the ideology is an overarching, normative-regulative structure for institutional behavior, a massive sacred canopy (Berger 1967:25–28).

[9] Such studies seem to argue that some correlation between the variables of ideology and of social structure is causal. Max Weber referred to this connection obliquely as "elective affinity" (Weber 1958:91–92; see Hill 1973:104–5). As Schutz and others suggest, the microsociological study of social relations and everyday practices may supply the unarticulated link (Collins 1975; Collins 1981; Garfinkel 1967; Giddens 1979:117; Zimmerman 1976:11n.9).

cial structures or a symbol for the expression of an inexpressible social reality; the beliefs are empirical propositions, just like many others that the members rely on in everyday life.

My point is not the timeworn proposition that the analyst should take the believer's beliefs "seriously" or respect those beliefs. It is not the sociologist's task to "cover up" for believers—to demonstrate somehow that their beliefs are "rational" (e.g., Winch 1958:19–20; see Wuthnow 1981:20)—any more than it is a proper sociological goal to debunk their beliefs. Instead, the task is to observe and explain "social facts"; that is, the analyst should investigate the role these beliefs play in everyday social interaction and how that interaction affects the beliefs. The ideology should be studied as it naturally occurs, embedded in social life.

In pursuing this sociological task, I analyze religion and religious ideas as a feature of everyday social interaction. My working hypothesis is that social interaction is thoroughly socially structured: religious practice and belief, as are any social activities, are products of sets of socially given rules of interpretation and practice employed by members in everyday life. Such rules are constitutive rules (Rawls 1955:26) of social life: they prescribe or provide guidelines for the successful accomplishment of tasks in everyday life. Living in the COG "makes sense" to members because, by following these rules, members create or produce a form of social order—they render their world explainable and their action in it efficacious. These rules form the social infrastructure of everyday life.

Throughout this book, I identify certain patterns in the behavior of COG members that suggest the presence of these constitutive rules. The rules have remained relatively stable in COG interactions despite the radical institutional and historical changes affecting the Family or the different environments that host the interactions. Members belong to the Family because they are capable of applying these rules in social interactions, thus making the interactions recognizable to other members as orderly or appropriate. For example, as I discuss in Chapter 6, "witnessing"—or attempting to convert outsiders—is an activity governed by a specific set of socially provided rules, and a competent COG witnesser is able to conduct a witnessing interaction according to these rules.

Even though I argue that COG members routinely employ these rules in everyday life, members are only rarely conscious of them in an abstract and systematic way. Members are not generally "theologians." Moreover, the understanding they do have differs from my formalistic sociological formulation of these rules. My analysis requires a certain level of systemization and coherence, whereas the members' understanding is at a different level of abstraction (Garfinkel 1960:74–76; Habermas 1971:174–78; Schutz 1943:145)—theirs is the pragmatic understanding needed to get through the day.

In addition to defining the competence of COG members, these recurrent rules define the COG as a subculture residing in the wider social context of modern society. An essential element of my analysis, and one neglected by other studies, is the fact that the social rules or structures peculiar to the Family do not completely define members' equipment or competence for negotiating the tasks they face in everyday life. All COG members also have at their disposal general commonsense knowledge and ways of doing things that all competent members of society possess: they share with the rest of us certain assumptions about the world and practices that help them to make sense of their world and to operate in it. Despite their allegiance to the COG subculture, members are far more like us than they are different. In going through their daily lives, COG members employ both sets of rules: the subcultural religious set and the more general commonsensical set.

This view poses a new problem for analysis. In addition to the examination of the subcultural rules, a significant aspect of my study, elaborated on in Chapters 5, 6, 7, and 8, is the daily interaction of those rules with the more general, commonsense rules: how these two sets of guidelines are drawn on in distinctive ways to produce social interactions that exhibit a compost of the subcultural and ideological mixed with the pragmatic.

Methodology: The Role of the Participant Observer

Because I wanted to understand everyday life within the Family, I thought intensive participant observation was essential. Although I supplemented the research with interviews with members, ex-members, and outsiders, the bulk of my efforts involved interjecting myself into the stream of social relations in the Family in order to understand daily processes and activities through ethnographic methods. Although rare in modern sociological studies,[10] this is the

---

[10] There are some studies of this type (Anderson 1975; Jules-Rosette 1975; Whyte 1961; Zablocki 1980), but rarely do sociologists observe a community by round-the-clock participant observation. More commonly, sociologists engage in participant observation for short periods arranged around their other pursuits (e.g., Bainbridge 1978; Daner 1976:4; Festinger et al. 1964:245; Heilman 1983:9–21; Lofland 1966:273; Neitz 1987:8–14).

only technique that permits the analyst of modern religious groups access to the texture of interactions in their social context.

The research proceeded through two somewhat complementary phases. From May 15 through June 5, 1976, I feigned membership in the Family[11] and lived full-time in a COG colony in Bradford, England. Although this provided substantial data pertaining to the everyday life of members, it was a shorter stay than I had originally planned. My research continued when I met several high-level Family leaders who permitted me to overtly observe a colony in Arnhem, Holland, for a two-month period beginning June 24, 1977. Again, my method was complete immersion in colony life: I lived, slept, and worked in the colony twenty-four hours a day. In addition, I visited and lived in numerous other COG colonies in the Netherlands, as well as colonies in Belgium, France, Italy, and Germany.

While essential to my study, intensive participant observation, even in its overt form, poses certain obstacles. First, religious groups such as the COG are often hostile to outsiders or at least highly conscious of their own deviance. Attempts by an outsider to penetrate the social life are made difficult. In most cases, a group's willingness to permit such research is not based on devotion to the goals of science or altruistic concern for a young academic's career: deviant religious groups often cooperate out of more self-promoting motives than these (Daner 1976:4; Lofland 1966:274). In my case, the COG hoped for both good publicity and the chance to gain a new member. Members frequently told me that "the Lord was using" me to provide the world with an "objective" account of the group, and that when the study was disseminated He would make me a member. By "objective," members meant "favorable": in their view, any objective observer would have to agree that the group's way of life was correct and desirable.[12]

The second obstacle is that long-term complete immersion in such groups is also highly stressful. Deviant or religious subcultures, which are strongly conversionistic and frequently feel attacked by wider society, make the management of the role of the observer, whether overt or covert, a particularly precarious endeavor. At some point the group will want to know why the overt observer has not

[11] In Appendix A, I describe the research in more detail and discuss some of the ethical issues raised by my covert observation.

[12] Although I showed early versions of Chapters 5 and 7 to members, the Family's expectations of gain from my research involved no commitment on my part to provide those gains. They found the chapters factually accurate, but were puzzled by the approach.

converted, and will often attempt to manipulate the observer's views to guarantee a favorable report.

Because of these problems, I had to adjust my presentation of self to the group to develop a relationship of trust and confidence with the members. Moreover, this relationship had to develop quickly because of the limited observation period. As a result, I developed special ways of interacting with members. While this may seem obvious in covert participant observation, it was hardly less true when I observed Family activities with their permission.

In *covert* participant observation, the goal is to appear to be a trustworthy and reliable member. Such a presentation must reach basic levels of competence as measured by group standards: the covert participant observer, who is viewed by members as incompetent, may collect only data on members' interactions with a troublesome or incompetent member.[13] In so doing, however, the sociologist must attempt to be only competent, not overcompetent or innovative; again, the innovative participant observer may do much to alter the phenomena under examination (e.g., Festinger et al. 1964:238–39). The existence of a range of competence among members in most groups permits a covert participant observer to find a niche near the passive end of the continuum. This range is inevitably sufficiently wide to include the irrepressible eccentricities (Matza 1969:10–14) of most members (Hilbert 1980:59).

During the initial period of covert participant observation, I fashioned a self for presentation to members. I kept alterations in my biography to a minimum (e.g., Lofland 1966:271) to prevent inadvertent slips that might belie my claim to be a member: I told members that I was a graduate student in sociology studying sociological theory. I described my life accurately, including my prior religious history. The area of alteration was my dissatisfaction with my studies and the attractiveness I claimed that the Family had for me. Therefore, the only fabrications involved the events immediately preceding my infiltration.

Within the Family, I quickly learned what was necessary to pass as

[13] In the Family there were always some members deemed to have a "weird spirit." Those members I met who fell in this category were deficient in their ability to get along with others. Their violation of norms and etiquette were not sufficient to expel them; they were simply slightly "off" in their attempts to interact. While other members did not question these members' sincerity, they were acknowledged to be difficult to deal with. Colony leaders made a point of managing around these "problem" members to reduce interpersonal tensions. Although such members were entitled to participate fully in Family activities, they rarely were completely accepted by other members in the full range of both formal and informal interactions.

a reasonably competent member and to avoid the suspicions of others. First and foremost, I adopted the Family argot and timing in the use of the argot. A carefully placed "Praise the Lord" or "Thank you, Jesus," I learned, did much to cement my putative identity. I also became a follower in interactions: after determining the topic and direction of conversation from my partner, I consciously attempted to produce correct utterances based on my growing knowledge of Family practice.

A second important factor in feigning membership was a willingness to participate in Family activities such as street proselytization ("litnessing"), reading, and group devotionals. Despite my qualms, I was ready to litness when necessary, and attempted to appear willing to do so. When called upon to pray in a group prayer, I produced nondescript, but unobjectionable, prayer fragments. I had fewer objections to participating in more secular activities such as cleaning, washing dishes, and cooking. In fact, I probably compensated in these areas to balance out my hidden reticence over more ideological activities.

Members quickly accepted me as an authentic, if new, member who was eager to learn. My sociological interest in the Mo letters dovetailed with the "thirst for the Word" expected of new members. Although my participation in interactions might have been in some respects naive or inartful, those failings could be overlooked as those of a "young brother." My eagerness to volunteer for projects was interpreted as a sign of commitment to the Family. Certain research activities I conducted were left unchallenged apparently because they were interpreted as legitimate activities of a neophyte (Hilbert 1980:60–61). Notetaking by new members, for example, was encouraged—we were to write down our daily experiences and "victories" over the Devil or other weaknesses—and served as a cover for my recording of events and impressions. I carefully kept my notetaking within reasonable bounds, taking more than other members, but not an excessive amount.

During my subsequent period of *overt* participant observation, surprisingly little changed in my day-to-day comportment. While my methods of assimilation were slightly different, my main objective remained the same: to establish a relationship of trust and confidence with members that would offer me entree into their normal interactions. As an overt observer I occupied a highly ambiguous postion: the members—being part of a group that claims that "there are no neutrals"—had no category for an extremely interested nonbeliever.

I worked hard at reducing the ambiguity, attempting to pass as a member in most situations.

Only if, when meeting a member for the first time, it was clear that the member believed I was also a member would I inform him or her of my research. In most cases, members were vaguely aware of my special status, and I felt no need to highlight that by starting off a conversation with a disclaimer. I used Family language; I employed and even initiated typical topics of conversation; I rarely asked directly "sociological" questions; I participated in all nonproselytizing activities, including prayer, laying on of hands for healing, group readings; and I expressed interest in members' testimony about successful witnessing ventures. I enjoyed no special treatment: I ate what other members ate; I slept in the same room with other unmarried males; if visitors arrived and beds were at a premium, I slept in the living room. Although members knew that I was not part of the Family, in almost all situations it was easier to treat me as a member, and it made no practical difference.

A significant aspect of this was the development of individual relationships with members. As in the covert period, the relationships were artifices, established for research purposes, even though their putative foundation differed from those of the covert period. In the covert period, my relationships were based on assumed common membership; the relationships of the overt period were often constructed on feigned personal interest in the members.[14] Generally, a relationship with a member went through three discrete stages. First, a newly met member would be interested in my endeavor and status as a nonbeliever, and they might attempt a conversion or witnessing interaction with me. After a very short period, the new acquaintance would grow cooler and observe me from a distance, checking on others' reactions to me, particularly those of leaders who served as my sponsors in the colonies. The final stage was the establishment of a stable relationship in which my ambiguous status was hardly ever mentioned. I was spoken to and treated as a member; I was admitted to personal confidences vis-à-vis other members, and was occasionally asked for advice about organizational concerns and problems. Jokes were sometimes made about my status as a sociologist, but their exaggerated nature indicated some disbelief on the part of members that I really was an outsider.

[14] In most cases, these relationships were artificial in the sense that, outside of my research, I would not have entered into them. I frequently found the members' bubbling enthusiasm naive and unattractive (Lofland 1971:99–100).

Managing Role Stress

Although I did develop some closer relationships, particularly with leaders of the COG, for the most part I presented a self to which I felt little "attachment" (Goffman 1961b:89). Because of this, the problem of role stress became a factor: the demands of an insincere role often cause fatigue and attempts to distance the self from the role (see Festinger et al. 1964:12–15). In most social situations, actors may express their displeasure with a particular role they are playing by "role distancing" (Goffman 1961b:108). The participant-observation research context, however, reduces the availability of role distancing as a device for dealing with the stress: the participant observer, whether overt or covert, must at least appear to "embrace" the role he or she presents.

In my covert observation, I consistently engaged in acts that expressed my lack of embracement of the role I was presenting. I found the most difficult part of my act to be litnessing. Most of my time was spent on the streets of industrial English towns attempting to sell Family literature to members of the public—people with whom I otherwise identified—and I was embarrassed to be associated with religious ideas I myself found unacceptable.

Fortunately, the structure of litnessing permitted me to develop a number of techniques to avoid these unpleasant interactions. Chief among these was to reduce my activity to the minimum acceptable limit: I litnessed very slowly and approached only a small number of people; I litnessed furiously for a very short time. I took a deep breath, attempted to desensitize my feelings, and rapidly approached people with the same statement. After such a period, I would slip out of view of my litnessing partner and take a rest. Another technique I used was to claim that I needed more "Word Time" or devotional time, and request that we take a break to read a Mo letter together. I drew on my status as a neophyte as an excuse to take more and longer breaks than most competent members.

Although on most occasions I faithfully attempted to complete a proper litnessing interaction, I did in some instances use the interaction as a way to lessen role stress. When approaching someone, I sometimes tried obliquely to communicate that I was really more like him or her than I seemed at first. One way was to engage the person in a conversation on mundane topics, whether politics or sports. This could go on for some time until my partner came over to see if I was having "trouble." In many interactions I used facial expressions—

"Can you believe I'm doing this? I can't."—to indicate that somehow I was different from fellow litnessers.

Finally, on two occasions, I did the ultimate in role distancing: I confessed that I was really a sociologist conducting a covert study. The first recipient of this information was skeptical and moved on saying nothing. The second interaction occurred when a litnessing target told me that he had a cousin who had joined the Family, but had left. I then told him of my true identity, and asked for the address of the cousin. He, of course, found my approach slightly unbelievable, even threatening. I had to speak more concretely of my academic association, including offering the name of my tutor to enable him to check my credentials, in order to convince him that my second presentation of self was truly sincere. He finally gave me the address and moved on. I never did contact that ex-member; the interaction functioned as a form of role distancing, not of information gathering.

Problems of role stress were less within the colony itself, but there was always an underlying tension that expressed itself through my irritation with minor acts of other members. To "get by" within the colony during the covert period, I tried to isolate myself occasionally from interaction with others. I consciously attempted to keep my activity within the research perspective by reminding myself about the "good data" I was collecting. When I found interactions especially oppressive, I tried to redirect the conversation to less religious topics. Sometimes, in an act of reckless self-assertion, I would snap at members who irritated me.[15] These techniques all helped me maintain, in my own mind, a sense of distance from the role I performed.

Again, announcing my sociological goals during the overt period did not relieve me of the need for "getting by" techniques. Because of my status, I could take more time away from the group and from my chosen role performance. On several occasions I isolated myself

---

[15] I quote from my field notes an argument I had with Sunflower about leadership while we were out litnessing:

> [S]he said that I had to obey her because she was an older sister. I pointed out that I was at least six years older. She said "older in the Lord." I said that I did obey my leaders, Shalom and Artemas [the colony leaders]. She said that I had to obey her too because she was leading our team [of two]. I said that I thought it was a mutual effort. She had started the argument by asking why I always contradicted her—I said because I thought she was wrong. She ended up crying and trying to patch up our relationship on the way home on the bus.

Although this incident was extreme, it does reflect one method, perhaps suicidal, of coping with the role stress.

in the colony or went to the local library to read and look over my notes. Occasionally, I would discuss my research project with non-Family members I met in bars and cafés the Family frequented. Although most of my time was spent in routine Family interactions, the time I spent with leaders engaged in less Family-like discussions about the group permitted me to express my nonattachment to my role and provided a haven from the daily role-stress of my research.

"Going Native," Almost

Using these discussions with leaders in this fashion, however, over-emphasized the supposed authenticity and reality of those relationships when compared with others—I was dependent on them to re-affirm my sense of self. This fact caused me on occasion to want to be a more integral part of the leaders' projects. I sometimes forgot that I was a sociologist, and I yearned to be accepted by leaders as a partner in their enterprise. This manifested itself most clearly while I was visiting a colony in Amsterdam during July of 1977. At the time, I thought I had had a brush with conversion.

A leader with whom I had a special relationship had been with me all day. We had discussed a variety of organizational matters in detail. At some point, we were discussing the Family's concern with secrecy and security, and I was complaining about the fact that I was refused information on the current activities of some of the upper leaders. The member turned to me and said I was a "sheep," a potential convert. I quote my field notes:

I felt a rush to just emotionally fall on him—not Jesus—or not physically—I wanted to rest emotionally on him; things clouded up—and I was unclear about my exact relation—researcher/member—[it] came after [he] listened and understood my problem about security and answered some questions forthrightly—also after I mentioned some things Roy [Wallis] said [to me about the Family] then I realized I was trapped . . . I thought maybe the Lord was moving me.

I tried not to let him see the emotional reaction I was experiencing and began to ask some "sociological" questions. That night while lying in bed, I began to think about what I would do when I returned to university in London; I had no definite plans concerning where I would live or with whom. I thought that if I joined the Family, I might be able to litness and witness. I woke up early and thought the same things again, but I became more against the idea at breakfast.

This experience, I believe, was in part a product of the cooperative, dependent relationships I developed with several leaders. In using the relationships to express some role distance from my performance of membership, I attached more reality to the relationships. I had an inchoate desire to work with the leaders on their project. What kept me from the brink was the fact that when I sat back and thought about the actual purpose of their project—witnessing to the world Moses David's message—it seemed absurd: the project was completely unacceptable to me.

ONE

IDEOLOGY AND PROSELYTIZATION

TO THE outsider, the religious beliefs of Family members are extreme. Ideas such as the imminent onset of the millennium, the necessity for total commitment to a proselytizing life-style, and the irredeemably evil nature of the secular world are not widely shared in our society. From the perspective of this study, however, what is important is the role these beliefs, eccentric as they are, play in the everyday life of COG members; that is, how do members comprehend and use the COG ideology in daily life? (I define "ideology" as the set of beliefs members have at their disposal to interpret and to act in the world [Van Zandt 1987:915].) For each member, these beliefs arise from the flow of social interaction. In this chapter, I distinguish between different manifestations of the ideology and the basic imperatives that the ideology provides for activities in the Family.

Manifestations of Ideology

Ideology is not a unified and abstract social phenomenon existing apart from everyday life; instead, it exists only in specific social contexts. Within the Family, there are three specific types or manifestations of ideology that appear in different social interactions: the formal ideology, the practical ideology, and the kerygma. The formal ideology is the more or less systematic collection of beliefs and propositions presented by people trained or specialized in interpreting them.[1] It is the "official" version or rendition of a social group's view of itself, its place in the world, and the appropriate moral order. In the case of the COG, the Mo letters and the bible, along with interpretations of them by a few Family ideologists, constitute the formal ideology (Neitz 1987:7). Members acknowledge its authority and rely on it as a resource in their daily lives. As an "official" version, how-

[1] Such persons—ideologists—are "experts" in analyzing and elucidating the group's beliefs. In some religions, they occupy a special social role. The Family has had several ideologists who worked closely with Moses David and in the early days taught bible or prophecy classes to all new members. Because the ideologists' interests and activities differ from those of most members, the descriptions of beliefs they provide observers are unlikely to represent the beliefs of more typical members or, more important, the saliency of belief in those members' everyday lives (Gellner 1970:46).

ever, it is perspectival: it is not the overarching sacred canopy (Berger 1967), but only one of many discrete manifestations.

A COG member's practical ideology is his or her actual understanding of the formal ideology. The product of the member's practical activity, including reading of the formal ideology and discussions with other members, it is the understanding that the member finds adequate in most circumstances for accomplishing any task that the member is called upon to perform. Members of religious groups, as do members of society in general, routinely attempt to understand their behavior by formulating accounts of it from the information—including here the formal ideology—available to them in the social context (Garfinkel and Sacks 1970). These accounts form part of the member's "stock of knowledge" of the world (Schutz 1972:81); together with more commonsense beliefs or ideas—which members share with members of society in general—the practical ideologies enable members to recognize and interpret new experiences (Schutz 1972:81–83). As I found in interviewing members, their practical ideologies were often a mere shadow of the more systematic and articulated formal ideology presented in COG publications and by group ideologists.

COG members also operate with a second understanding of the formal ideology, the version employed in proselytization efforts. This version is intended to interest the potential convert and to draw him or her toward deeper investigation of and possible commitment to the movement. It is both derivative from the practical and formal ideologies and a product of the practical activity of proselytization. I borrow the technical theological term "kerygma" (Bultmann 1958:36; Dodd 1936:3–11; Green 1973:48–77) to refer to this manifestation of ideology.

Members are conscious of the difference between the kerygma and their practical ideology. They recognize the distinction verbally by stating that prospects should be given only the "milk," or more basic doctrines, until they are ready for the "meat" of the full ideology. Members also consciously manipulate the specific content of the kerygma in order to make it more effective in attracting the world to the COG message. Members recognize that the kerygma has changed over time as the nature of their proselytization efforts have changed.

Creating the COG Formal Ideology

The formal ideology is produced by Moses David and his staff of editors and ideologists, whose life experiences within the COG are significantly different from those of most members. From the beginning of the Family, Moses David has been the principal generator of the formal ideology. Most of what he has spoken and written has been accorded special significance by members. His dreams and prophecies, which he claims come from God, have particular importance, but simple practical advice is always treated as being profound, if not normative.

Moses David was raised, trained, and ordained in the heart of southern Protestantism, and the formal ideology is a development of southern Protestant evangelicalism with important Anabaptist additions. In this tradition, the most important question has always been "What must I do to be saved?" and this concern has permeated most of Moses David's activities. As have others within this tradition, Moses David regards the conversion of people as the sole task of the church (Hill 1967:73, 119–134). Throughout his life he has stuck closely to this theological core, although he has added twists of his own.

In the early years of the movement, Moses David participated in the group prayer meetings and frequently taught bible classes. At the time, the King James version of the bible[2] was the only written text of the formal ideology. Some of the first Mo letters were transcribed recordings of those lessons. The formal ideology was often a group project in which Moses David was only one—although the most important—of a handful of bible-class teachers; it was the product of the social interaction of the leaders.

From 1970 on, however, Moses David isolated himself from group members and began to write frequently to highly placed COG officials with directions, advice, and words of inspiration. Many of these early letters stated his claim to be God's last prophet. Gradually, Moses David recognized the value of the letter-writing motif as a social control device and encouraged the leaders to reprint some of the letters and distribute them to all members. By the summer of 1971, Moses David directed the movement almost solely through the use of Mo letters and had established a fairly secure monopoly on the production of the formal ideology. He lives isolated from most of the Family with Maria, his secretary and consort. (Moses David claims to dictate many of the letters to Maria in the evening, while the couple is in bed after a period of drinking wine.) His only significant source of interaction with other Family members is visits to his home by high-level leaders and those involved in the production of the Mo letters.

The text of each letter is highly repetitive; Moses David states that

---

[2] That version is used because Moses David considers it to be both the most-inspired and the most-used translation (62:9–11).

he must keep hammering home the same points in order to get them across. The letters reporting his prayers, prophecies, dreams, and visions are written in a stylized King James English. In other letters, Moses David speaks in a late 1960s vernacular sprinkled with American southern Protestant terms. The couple decides whether and when to release the letters; they also classify the letters according to their appropriate audience.[3] Those slated for release go to a small group of COG editors and illustrators working in colonies near Moses David's secret location. The manuscripts are edited, illustrated, and sent to a publications unit where they are printed up as Mo letters (Appendix B) and shipped to various distribution points. Distribution techniques have varied throughout COG history.

While some Mo letters are simply Moses David's advice to members on practical matters, most state or imply divine inspiration. Many are reports of Moses David's dreams, or recountings of visions that he has experienced while awake. Often, he claims, the visions occur while he is engaged in sexual intercourse with Maria or other partners. More frequent are prophecies he claims to receive from God. Prophecy—a common phenomenon in the Pentecostal strand of American southern Protestantism—normally occurs while Moses David is in prayer. As described, a prophecy involves him speaking in a slightly different voice in King James's biblical English while in some state of dissociation. Moses David also claims to have a spirit helper named Abrahim, a twelfth-century Christian gypsy-king beheaded by the Turks (Davis 1984:78, 86–93), who first visited Moses David in 1970. According to the Mo letters, Abrahim possesses Moses David's body and speaks through it with a different voice. Maria is able to ask Abrahim questions about the past and future, and she records the answers. Material derived from this source usually relates to the spirit world, a prominent realm in the formal ideology.[4]

---

[3] In the very early years, a small number of photocopies of the letters were read only by the highest leaders of the group (53:13). In 1972, however, as the Family spread into smaller colonies, Moses David established a classification scheme based on who should receive the letters. The scheme initially included five categories of letters: DR— do not reprint; LT—print for and read to leaders and leadership trainees only; LTA— print only for leaders and leadership trainees, but read to all members; DO—print for all disciples or members including neophytes; and GP—print for the general public. By 1975, LTs became LTOs ("leadership trainees only"), and a new category, DFO ("disciples and followers only"), was created for associate members and sympathetic members of the public. Beginning with letter 501 in mid-1976, the use of the LTO and LTA classifications almost disappeared, as Moses David sought to exercise direct control over the movement through the letters. In effect, by 1981 there were only three classifications: DO, DFO, and GP.

[4] The formal ideology asserts that there coexists with the material world an extensive realm of spiritual beings. The ideology speaks little of the spirit world causing material effects, and its relevance seems limited to providing inspiration and information to

The Content of the Formal Ideology

At present, there are over twenty-five hundred Mo letters. Although they cover a wide range of topics[5] and are replete with advice on a variety of practical matters,[6] the letters exhibit some common ideological strands that together form the formal ideology. The first strand provides the foundation for the others. Beginning in 1952, Moses David claims he received a series of prophecies reported in the Mo letters, identifying him as God's "Prophet of the End-Time" and directed to the current generation. Alongside the common evangelical view of the bible as literal and infallible, the Family has added the Mo letters as equally valid sources for determining God's will (329:22). Later statements in the formal ideology suggest that the revelations of the Mo letters may even override biblical rules (592:29; 635:58,67). This belief, of course, has important implications for authority and ethics within the COG movement (O'Dea 1957; Wallis 1982) because it concentrates authority in Moses David.

This power is enhanced by the fact that each revelation issued by Moses David is not necessarily the last word. The revelations are considered to come through the human vessel of Moses David and are subject to later revision by God. In fact, Moses David has rarely claimed that a particular revelation is the direct word of God; most of the time, a particular letter is his inspired report of what he believes God has said to him. Moses David has on several occasions used this fact to revise earlier predictions that were apparently disconfirmed.[7]

Moses David. Members read these letters with a sense of awe, but rarely does the spirit world have concrete significance outside the reading context.

[5] Topics include the spirit world, the events of the end-time, God's love, sex, politics and economics, discussions of particular famous people, descriptions and analyses of current films and songs, predictions of the destruction of America and other countries that have rejected the Family, directives to leaders, reports to all members of Family events, and directives to all members to reorganize the Family authority structures.

[6] These range from proper nutrition, childrearing, and clothing, to how to use video equipment.

[7] The problem of prophecy disconfirmation (Festinger et al. 1964:24–30; Lofland 1966:267–68) is dealt with by a reformulation of the erroneous prediction. Because of his control over the formal ideology—buttressed by his claimed revelatory preeminence—Moses David is well positioned for this type of work. These techniques have been applied on several occasions in COG history. In 1972, Moses David strongly suggested that the comet Kohoutek would cause the physical destruction of the hated United States. In a letter issued after the comet turned out to be a dud, Berg stated that he had never specifically foretold the exact consequences of Kohoutek; instead, he had suggested only that it could portend bad times for the Americans. He went on to state that America was in an extreme state of disrepair and that the comet was one of God's last warnings. After Kohoutek, COG statistics on the amount of literature

This flexibility has meant that the content of the formal ideology has varied to some extent over the past twenty years.

Within this revelatory context, several other themes exist. The first is the traditional concern with personal salvation. God is seen as both a vengeful judge of those who violate His will and as a loving father who cannot bear to see his children go astray. In order to be saved from eternal damnation at the coming Judgment, a person has only to accept God's love, offered through Jesus to all people: salvation depends on personal decision. Once saved, a person is always guaranteed a place in the Kingdom of God; good works, however, determine what position the believer will have in that future kingdom. The formal ideology also refers occasionally to the Pentecostal doctrine of the Baptism in the Holy Spirit, but this is muted.

Another, Anabaptist, strand (Cohn 1970:252–80; Hill 1967:127–32) is strident criticism of society and contemporary social relations—the System. Moses David espouses a form of Christian socialism to criticize capitalist economies. America is the epitome of the degenerate capitalist system and is the prime object of Moses David's excoriations. Socialist social formations are the only proper social organizations, although the present "godless socialism" of communist societies is viewed as just as great a danger as the capitalism of the West. The ideology is not backward-looking to a former, simple, and rustic age, but in many respects embraces modern technological advances.

There is an anti-Semitic element in the economic views of the formal ideology. Although Moses David initially believed that Israel might be the promised land and that the return of the Jews to Israel in 1947 was a significant millennial event, he found on a 1970 trip that the Israelis were quite hostile to Christian proselytization (Davis 1984:94). In later years, Moses David issued letters that claimed that Jews controlled the international monetary system, as well as American and English politics, and were in league with communist sympathizers. Moses David has consistently sided with the Arabs in the Arab-Israeli conflict, and has visited and promoted Colonel Moammar Khadafi of Libya; he believes that Khadafi may be a Third World facilitator of the Antichrist, who until the Tribulation can be used by the Family. More recently, the anti-Semitism has spread to anti-black statements about events in southern Africa.

Because of the corruption of Western society, the formal ideology warns members not to become overly entangled in it. Unlike the uto-

distributed as well as on the number of salvation experiences facilitated rose sharply in January and February of 1974, supporting the hypothesis of increased proselytization after prophecy disconfirmations (Festinger et al. 1964:208–15).

pian separatists who aim to create a new, insulated, perfectionist society (Wilson 1973:23–24), the Family's separatism is in service of its goal of proselytization and is flexibly reinterpreted to achieve that goal. The level of contact desirable has changed over time. Generally, however, while members must rely on secular society for support, no long contractual or other relations should be established. According to the formal ideology, members are not to hold System jobs unless no other means of support are available. Most entertainment—films, music, dance—are corrupted by the System. Members instead should live together communally in small groups modeled after the social organization of the early apostles in the Book of Acts (S:14).

Another strand in the formal ideology is the emphasis on total discipleship or total commitment. While the formal ideology has never made membership a requirement of salvation, it has consistently stated that the only true and complete way to follow God is by a total commitment to His work. All who can make this commitment must; those who do otherwise let God down and will not be looked upon favorably when God judges their works. Total discipleship consists of full-time living within a COG colony; "forsaking all," the surrender of all possessions to the Family and the cutting of all ties with the world if necessary; obedience to COG leaders; and above all else, full-time proselytization. Both the sacrifices and joys of this total commitment are emphasized.

Most striking are the millennial beliefs in the formal ideology. The System and its ungodly structure are soon to be replaced by a new social order during the imminent millennium. The eschatology is premillennial and posttribulationist:[8] Jesus will return prior to the millennium, but after the Great Tribulation. According to the COG formal ideology, the world will be racked by war and economic collapse (initially expected sometime in the early 1980s), and communism will grow in strength.

A great socialist leader will rise from the area of Egypt that was the locus of the old city of Memphis. This person will take over the world, end the wars, stabilize the economy, and establish a benevolent, socialistic dictatorship. For three and one-half years, he will permit religions to flourish and everyone will be satisfied. By the end of

---

[8] It is grounded in Daniel and the Johannine Revelations but mixes in certain Joachimite tendencies. It is premillennial in holding that the messiah will return prior to the millennium on earth. This is the position of most Jewish apocalyptic literature and of the Johannine view in Revelations (Grier 1945:14–15; Talmon 1968:349). Premillennialism reflects a pessimism about the ability of human actors to save the world (Shepperson 1970:44–45). Christ, however, will return after the seven years of the Great Tribulation on earth, the posttribulationist view (Enroth et al. 1972:186).

this period, however—by which time Moses David will have died—
the world dictator will show himself to be the Antichrist. He will demand that all people worship him, and will exterminate those who
refuse—members of the COG, in particular, who by this time will
have gone into hiding. He will destroy all bibles, and Family members will depend on their memory and hidden copies of the Mo letters and bible for ideological sustenance.

Christ will return three and one-half years later (originally thought
to be 1993). He will "lift up" all living believers who have been saved,
and then will defeat the Antichrist, subdue the Devil, and establish a
physical millennium on earth. There will be a general resurrection of
all deceased believers—or rapture—and all Family members will be
given supernatural spirit bodies that will also be physical: members
will enjoy sex in heaven and will be able to materialize and demate-
rialize at will. Family members and other past, martyred saints will
assist Christ in ruling this earthly millennium and help convert the
remaining unsaved souls. A member's position in the divine government will depend on his or her works before Christ's return.

After the expiration of the thousand years, Satan will be freed and
will again try to organize the wicked to dislodge Christ from his divine seat. God will pour fire out of heaven, destroy the rebellion, and
imprison Satan in a lake of fire forever. Then, the Judgment will occur. All people will be judged by their works, and God will mete out
appropriate punishments and rewards. Those who did not accept
Jesus during their lives will be banned from heaven and sent to live
with the Devil in the lake of fire; those who did, even despite their
lack of good works, will become citizens of heaven.

The surface of the earth will be purged clean by atomic fires, and
God will send New Jerusalem—a city one thousand miles high, long,
and wide—down into the new earthly atmosphere. This New Jerusalem will be the perfection of the earth.[9] Sexual freedom will
abound, and there will be no hunger or despair. God will permit
those who are sufficiently purged by a time in the lake of fire to live
outside New Jerusalem's walls. Family members and saints will retain a proselytization mission among these half-citizens of New Jerusalem and to other worlds.

The last major strand in the formal ideology is the emphasis on sex
which, although always present, has evolved over time towards pure
antinomianism. Initially, Mo letters spoke of sexual activity within

[9] This event is similar to the Joachimites' Third Age of the Spirit, an age of perfec-
tionism (Cohn 1970:108–9), in which the Old Testament and New Testament dispen-
sations will be abrogated in favor of the reign of the Holy Spirit.

marriage, offering practical advice for newly married couples and strict rules against nonmarital sexual relations. Over the years, however, the Mo letters increasingly advocated more sexual freedom within the group. They have recounted Moses David's copulation with spirits and with many women members, as well as his early childhood sexual activity, which he regards as normal, healthy, and positive for all children. In the mid-1970s, the formal ideology advocated the use of sex as a proselytization access strategy. By the late 1970s, Moses David approved and encouraged members to engage in free sexual activity.[10]

Proselytization: The Preeminent Ideological Activity

Although most Mo letters are available to members for consultation, the formal ideology as summarized above is not imprinted in toto in members' minds. Rather, it is a resource that members invoke to interpret events or guide actions, and it is employed pragmatically. One belief, however, is incorporated into every member's practical ideology: the imperative to proselytize. Based on the formal ideology's concern with personal salvation and total commitment, the proselytization imperative states: "Our job is to sow the seed (Word) to every creature (Mk. 16:15). Some is bound to fall on good ground, so remember—(2 Cor. 9:6). Mk. 4:14 tells us as sowers, to sow the Word. Gal. 6.7 tells us that what we sow, we'll also reap."[11] Members' incorporation of at least this aspect of the formal ideology into their own practical ideology is complete. To not proselytize is to abdicate responsibility.

Proselytization is an ideological activity because members recognize it as being required and guided by the formal ideology or "God's command." It is an activity not conducted by non-Family members, and marks members as true followers of Jesus. Generally, this ideological imperative requires the presentation of the COG kerygma to the world. The precise goal, however, has always been ambiguous. In one sense, it requires members only to "sow the seeds" or to pro-

[10] The theological justification for this emphasis is found in the Pauline doctrine of grace (called within the Family's leadership the "All-Things" doctrine [Davis 1984:100]), rather than in some perfectionist theory associated with the category of Free Spirit heresies. The Mo letters (648:1) state that as long as sex is used in love and for group purposes, the old law against nonmarital sex is not applicable.

[11] Witnessing, in *The Revolution for Jesus* 76 (Dallas, Tex.: The Children of God, 1972). This booklet is a compilation of bible lessons given by Moses David and Joel Wordsworth, a Family ideologist, between 1968 and 1972.

claim the message. Success at this venture is measured by the number of people who are exposed to the kerygma or "hear the Word." On the other hand, the imperative contains the idea that the conversion of people or the salvation of souls is the goal. In this case, success is measured by the number of people who proclaim Christ for the first time as a result of COG proselytization.

The different access strategies the Family has used through its history have straddled this ambiguity. First, access strategies in and of themselves proclaim the message to all who are exposed; second, they bring COG members into interactions with potential converts and members that might lead to salvation experiences. Simply performing an access strategy achieves the goal of proclaiming the COG kerygma in many cases; members believe that contact between the public and a member engaged in an access strategy transmits the COG message, despite the fact that little of the content of the kerygma is transferred. A Family member, it is stated, "shines with God's love"; in some unarticulated manner, this has an effect on every person who sees or hears a Family member. Similarly, when a member of the public receives a piece of literature, regardless of its topic, the Family member has successfully proclaimed the kerygma to that person.

Access strategies or interactions, however, also function to facilitate the second general goal of proselytization: they bring the member into an interaction that may enable him or her to lead a potential convert to a salvation experience. Conversion or witnessing interactions take over when access strategies have succeeded. While access strategies have varied historically and situationally, and while the kerygma used in them has changed depending on the nature of the potential converts, the witnessing interactions themselves have remained remarkably stable.

Similar to the practice of witnessing in the American southern Protestant tradition, the individual in witnessing interactions is encouraged to ask Jesus into his or her heart as personal Lord and Saviour. This act, which is viewed by members as an act of free will, is considered to solve essentially all the new believer's problems. While the formal ideology stresses that the prayer for salvation is to be a well-considered and moving request, the actual practice of witnessing can be quite formalistic and routine. Moreover, the formal ideology encourages members to follow up by ministering to a saved person; in most cases, however, a saved individual's contact with the Family member terminates with the salvation prayer.

Conversion does not normally mean recruitment and commitment of the individual as a member in the group. Recruitment is normally restricted to those few saved individuals whom members believe can endure the life of total commitment or whose skills and resources will make them particularly valuable. Achieving the salvation experience thus differs from recruitment and membership. While members are always looking for potential new members, recruitment is less prominent than other proselytization activities.

Since 1973, the most pervasive access strategy has been litnessing, the street distribution of literature, which is largely proclamatory.[12] Other access strategies have waxed and waned with the historical and social circumstances of the Family. Some have emphasized proclamation such as mail campaigns, radio programs, sales of products; many others—such as café singing, serving food on beaches and at rock concerts, holding meetings and parties open to the public, and running discotheques—have been designed to encourage witnessing interactions intended to cause a salvation experience (or even recruitment). "Flirty Fishing" falls within this latter category.

Variation in Access Strategies

The ideological imperative does not dictate the specifics of the proselytization activity, and the Family has always been extremely flexible in adopting and discarding access strategies. The test of a strategy is its pragmatic value: anything that works is a possible candidate. There seem to be no rules restricting the universe of possible access strategies, as the phenomenon of Flirty Fishing demonstrates (cf. Beckford 1975:160–63). The choice of an access strategy, however, is not left to individual members. Major shifts have generally been dictated from above by the COG leadership, albeit often in response to changes occurring at the colony level.

Through the history of the COG, two factors have affected the selection of access strategies. First, access strategies were chosen with an eye to the actual or potential social reaction to the group and its message at the time. Thus, litnessing is impossible in many Third World countries, and other forms have displaced it in those areas. Flirty Fishing was adopted in part to reach a new type of person: as

---

[12] I disagree with Professor Wallis's characterization of litnessing as routine proselytization (Wallis 1976a:825; see O'Toole 1975:178). This view misses the proclamatory function of litnessing. For the most part, members viewed litnessing as satisfying the ideological imperative to proselytize; that is, members believed that their litnessing was efficacious as a practical matter in proclaiming God's Word. It may be that this belief is empirically incorrect, but that does not make the activity of litnessing ritualistic or symbolic.

the Family left more affluent parts of the world, its normal recruiting pool of young and unattached people started to dry up. Flirty Fishing brought the Family into contact with people who tended to have more status and responsibility in the local community, an asset the Family wanted to exploit in pursuit of its mission.

The second factor has been the internal organization of the Family itself. In times of financial strain, litnessing became more prominent because of its secondary function of collecting money. When finances were more solid and when the number of experienced members was greater in proportion to total membership, access strategies more likely to achieve a greater number of salvation experiences and new members grew in importance. In other periods, COG central leadership exercised rigid control over colony life. This often meant that predominant access strategies were those that produced good statistics for leaders to evaluate.

The choice of a specific strategy affects life in the Family. When access strategies involve potential converts visiting colonies, great efforts are made to fix up the houses. In contrast, during heavy litnessing periods when outsiders rarely visit colonies, living conditions are more spartan. In the early years members dressed, talked, and for the most part behaved as did those hippies and young dropouts whom the access strategies of the time targeted. Flirty Fishing, in contrast, has dictated better clothing, more concern with cleanliness, and even the use of makeup to facilitate members' participation in the nightclub and discotheque scene.

TWO

A SHORT HISTORY OF THE CHILDREN OF GOD

THE BASIC ideological activities and interactional patterns that make up the everyday life of Family members—the subject matter of this book—have remained relatively stable over the years. Around this core, however, the Family has experienced a series of changes in its access strategies, sources of recruitment, the doctrinal emphases of its kerygma, and its organization and authority structure. As I have already suggested, proselytization has oscillated between proclamatory and more intensive conversion efforts. In fact, most Family members would say that radical or "revolutionary" change has been the constant feature of the COG from its beginning.[1]

Indirect Charismatic Authority

Dominating almost every aspect of the organizational history of the COG, however, is Moses David's charismatic innovation: by virtue of his authority as God's last prophet and the vessel for God's will on earth, he defines the movement's goals and general structures and appoints its leaders. His word is final in all matters; authority does not rest on an interpretable text, but only in his own pronouncements. His decisions are not subject to challenge by reference to any external rule or source. This authority, however, is not the pure type of charismatic authority described by Weber (1947:358–63), in which the leader exercises his authority by virtue of constant interaction with the members of a small group. Moses David has not been in day-to-day personal control of the Family since August 1970. His authority, however, continues to control situations through the flow of Mo letters.

Approximately every one and one-half to two years, Moses David, via Mo letters, has ordered and achieved wholesale and radical changes in Family activity and organization. In between these points,

---

[1] For a more comprehensive history of the Family, see Van Zandt 1985:122–392. I have identified twelve natural periods in COG history following the lead of Professor Wallis (Wallis 1976a:823–25; see Pritchett 1985:ix–xxix).

he says little that affects the practical activities of members. Instead, a type of rational-legal authority has filled these gaps (Weber 1947:330): during such periods, Moses David's utterances provide the abstract, rational-legal rules that guide members' decision making at the colony level. Members follow the letter of the rules strictly. Even when the rules are extremely specific (their specificity has varied over time), however, their actual implementation in a practical context is often problematic, a fact that gives Moses David an opportunity to intervene again with his charismatic authority.

The Charismatic Background: David Berg and His Family

David Berg's (I use his legal name in the following sections) claims to charismatic authority are supported for members by accounts within the group of his quasi-mythological activities and experiences prior to the formation of the Family. The basis of the claims is Berg's assertion that at discrete times during his life, God has spoken directly to him or has caused others to recognize God's influence on his life. Another related theme in the story is that Berg and his family were both well connected and highly talented and could have led successful conventional lives, but were called by God to follow a different path.

According to the Family, Berg's mother (Virginia Brandt Berg, known in the Family as "Grandmother") followed in her father's footsteps, and together with Berg's father spent most of her life on the road as a full-time evangelist. David, their second son, was born on February 18, 1919, in the Melrose section of Oakland, California. After a sickly childhood, Berg claims he was drafted, and while serving as a conscientious objector contracted a severe case of pneumonia and received a disability discharge. He promised to serve God for the rest of his life if healed, and he "was instantly healed in answer to prayer, to the amazement of all my doctors and nurses." He returned to California and immediately launched into full-time evangelic work with his mother. In 1944, he married Jane Miller (known in the Family as "Mother Eve"). They had two children: Linda (known as "Deborah"), born in 1946, and Paul (known as "Aaron"), born in 1948.

By the time of Aaron's birth, Berg had been ordained into his parents' denomination, the Christian and Missionary Alliance, and requested a missionary position in Vietnam. The denomination's hierarchy instead placed him in the tiny desert town of Valley Farms, Arizona, where the members of the congregation, a mixture of Mexicans, Indians, and whites, were at each others' throats. According to Berg, the whites aligned with the denominational hierarchy did not like his "integration policies and radical preaching that they should share more of their wealth with the poor." The denomination removed him, and he, Jane, and their three children—Jonathan (known as "Hosea") was born in 1950—returned to road evangelism. After a short period of traveling, Berg took a job as a junior-high-school teacher at his children's Christian school to support his family, which had grown with the birth of Faith in 1951.

Berg's sense of mission remained unfulfilled, and he pleaded with God for guidance. God, he claims, answered his pleas in a prophecy, called the *Key of David* (78) by the Family, which was Revelation 3:7–13, that led Berg to quit his teaching job in early 1954. He attended classes at Fred Jordan's Soul Clinic in Huntington Park, Los Angeles. Jordan's approach de-emphasized buildings and ceremony, and at the time encouraged graduates of his program to become missionaries in the new land of Israel. Berg, however, received another prophecy, the *Call of David* (79:2–3), which he interpreted to mean that he was to be a missionary in his own land among his own people, to direct them to give up their evil ways.

Berg and his family moved to Miami and set up a small Soul Clinic missionary-training school named the Florida Soul Clinic. He trained missionaries on his own and acted as a way station for those sent by Fred Jordan to South America. During this period Berg developed a new tactic of spreading his message: he organized his children and a few of his Soul Clinic students into religious "commando groups" for "raids" on the churches every Sunday morning. While parishioners were worshipping, the commandos bombarded the buildings and parked cars with literature. When this activity attracted police attention in 1957, Berg once again packed up his family and left town.

After several short stints at Jordan's Soul Clinic Ranch in Mingus, Texas, the Berg family returned to Miami. During the Christmas holidays of 1961, a bedridden Berg received a new message from God, the "Message of Jeremiah" (77:6): no longer was he to deal with Christians who had rejected his message; instead, he was to announce that the established churches were doomed for forsaking God and rejecting His message. As might be expected, his second effort was no more successful than his first, and Berg and family again, according to Berg, were run out of town. Traveling in their mobile home, they visited almost every state, along with Canada and Mexico. During this period, John Treadwell (known as "Jethro"), a "young witnessing Christian from Florida Bible College," accompanied them, and sometime prior to 1964 married Deborah. The family eventually returned to Texas for another stay with Jordan.

While at the ranch, Berg was visited several times by his mother, who in late 1965 received the "Warning Prophecy." This prophecy (the "warning tract"), which foretold the coming of the Antichrist out of Memphis in Egypt (201:33–34), was widely distributed by COG during its early periods and serves as the basis for its millennial beliefs. On another visit in 1966, Grandmother received the "Understanding of David," which was later seen as an early sign of Berg's ability to foretell millennial events. At the time, Berg read the prophecy as a sign that he should leave Jordan's ranch again and set out on the road. Throughout the fall of 1966, the extended Berg family traveled. They were joined by Arnold Dietrich (known as "Joshua"), who married Faith; Arnold's brother, Arthur Dietrich (known as "Caleb"); and Arthur's wife, Lydia. By Christmas 1967, they wound up in Grandmother's small cottage in Huntington Beach, penniless and not wanted by local churches.

Huntington Beach: February 1968 through April 1969

Virginia Brandt Berg died in early 1968, and her son made a new commitment: "I openly declared war on the hypocritical old bottles of the religious system who were lined up on the back seat, and I cast in my lot with outlaws, drug addicts, maniacs, and the younger generation" (M:31). He quickly put this commitment into action. Berg and his family affiliated themselves with an evangelical coffeehouse in Huntington Beach called the Light Club run by the national Teen Challenge organization. Teen Challenge's churchlike rallies were not attracting many youths, and at Berg's request the local members of Teen Challenge agreed to share the Light Club with Berg's small group.

The coffeehouse was the primary access strategy for initiating witnessing interactions: the Family attracted visitors with food and music. From the beginning, Berg and his family had good rapport with the dropouts and hangers-on of the contemporary California culture, who were attracted to the family's music and nonchurch orientation. Berg himself conducted bible lessons with those visitors who became more interested in the faith. The witnessing kerygma focused on the corruption of the System that would soon bring its destruction and the necessity for total commitment to the true faith. All potential converts were encouraged to become full-time modern disciples for Christ. Those who were willing to make a total commitment and to forsake all—that is, give up all ties to the secular world such as jobs and school—were asked to move into the Bergs' home. The group also conducted more "church visitations," which, reminiscent of Berg's Miami activities, involved going *en masse* to local churches during Sunday services and sitting together in the front, usually vacant pews. This activity was essentially proclamatory and attracted substantial local press attention.

By the summer of 1969, the size of the live-in group, now called "Uncle Dave's Teens for Christ," had grown to fifty. Their only sources of financial support were the savings that new members gave to the group and donations from sympathetic outsiders. Berg claims that the hippies taught him about "scrounging & procuring & provisioning, & they established the sandwich routes & food shops where we had regular pickups" (897:191).

Berg maintained control over the ideological aspects of daily life and concentrated on the religious development of the new members. He was at last in a position to achieve his long-sought goal: he could apply Jordan's techniques to train people to evangelize in their own country. The group engaged in intensive bible study and reading, guided by Berg's interpretations. In addition, there were frequent group meetings at which speaking in tongues and prophecies abounded. A common activity involved members standing in a large circle and holding hands silently to wait for some prophecy.

Because of their total commitment life-style and aggressive proselytization activities, Family members received substantial local press and public attention and even some abuse, which they typically viewed as "persecution." Several members were arrested while demonstrating outside local schools. Near the end of the period, a number of members received prophecies that California was going to sink into the Pacific on April 15, 1969. These prophecies led to what members refer to as the Exodus, their departure from "Egypt" for the "promised land."

Road Travel: April 1969 through February 1970

The fifty COG members left Huntington Beach in small groups under cover of night. After a short stay in Tucson during which they doubled their membership, the Family traveled extensively through the United States and into Canada. This period was the Family's most formative: many of the social practices that mark the everyday life of COG members were developed, and members' identities as part of a revolutionary group were solidified.

In August 1969, Berg and a team of about seventy members settled in a campground in the Laurentian mountains of Quebec. There,

Berg announced the first of many organizational structures for the COG. Some fifty leaders—"bishops, elders, and deacons"—were ordained. Shortly thereafter, Berg called all the bands of the Family together at Vienna, Virginia, where he announced that while in Quebec he had received a new prophecy entitled *A Prophecy of God on the Old Church and the New Church* (A). Although it literally compared the COG with the established churches, describing the latter as prideful and rejecting God, the prophecy also marked a personal change for Berg: the day after the group left Huntington Beach, Berg began a sexual relationship with a young member known as "Maria." Berg announced the new relationship to only his extended family in a private meeting in Vienna, stating that although he had been faithful to Eve for twenty-five years, his relationship with her stood in God's way and had to be replaced by one with Maria. Although Berg has had other liaisons, including an incestuous one with Faith (Davis 1984:12, 193), the relationship with Maria has been the most important and constant.

The first public act of the new organization was to conduct a sackcloth vigil at the funeral of Illinois Senator Everett Dirksen, the defender of school prayer. About eighty members stood around Dirksen's coffin in the rotunda of the Capitol, mourning the "death of America" and attracting their first national press attention. From Washington, D.C., the members headed south. They met with unfriendly receptions in Alabama and Louisiana, due in large part to their hippie appearance; as a result, the COG leaders decided that it would be best if the males cut their hair. The group continued west, setting up various campsites around Houston for the several months spanning Christmas 1969.

Except during the stay in Tucson and after the group arrived in Houston, proselytization was largely proclamatory. The COG used demonstrations and spectacles to present its message to the public and to initiate some witnessing interactions. During the vigil—a primary access strategy—members dressed in red sackcloths and wore large wooden yokes around their necks. They carried long staffs in one hand and bibles or scrolls in the other, and they smeared ash on their foreheads. The scrolls contained portions of the Warning Prophecy and other statements in large letters. The members formed a line and began to move, taking a step and pounding their staffs on the ground as their right feet hit. At signaled times, they turned toward the object of protest, lifted the staffs, and yelled "Woe" or "Abomination." For such events, members cultivated the look of wild-eyed prophets—long hair, beards, and fierce expressions—in part to gain attention.

During this period, actual face-to-face witnessing interactions were less prevalent, due in part to the group's transience. When access strategies did result in face-to-face encounters, the members stressed the impending doom of the world at God's hands and the corruption of the System. The interactions were stern and designed to impress upon the prospect the imminent danger of not heeding God's word. Nonmembers were urged to forsake all their worldly possessions and connections and to work with the COG. These interactions were rarely followed up, and as a consequence few new members were recruited. The targets remained the young dropouts of the hippy drug subculture.

The difficult road conditions were seen by members as a test of their faith, and the period is now looked back on as the group's mythical "forty days in the wilderness" or "long march." The group traveled in a caravan of twenty-nine campers organized into twelve sex-segregated "tribes," which Berg consciously patterned on the twelve tribes of Israel. Each tribe was responsible for a specific function, such as truck maintenance, food preparation, child care, or food gathering. Berg laid down strict rules and regulations for just about every activity. The COG lived off surrounding society by "spoiling Egypt": collecting discarded material, "procuring," and relying on members' forsake-alls and their family's resources. If a joining member had a credit card, the group would use it until the credit was canceled. Members were encouraged to ask for aid from their families: any gift or inheritance that came to a member was considered group property. "Procuring"—later called "provisioning"—was the source of most food and other daily supplies.

Aside from chores, members participated in several ideological activities. While breakfast was being prepared, most members attended a bible class led by high leaders. The basic class for newcomers taught that God has always chosen one through whom to work his will, such as Moses or Joshua, and that leadership and obedience are ordained by God. All members also spent part of the day memorizing a standard set of bible verses, and leaders quizzed members throughout the day.

Berg and his family continued to be the central leaders, with each member of the extended family responsible for one of the tribes. Berg himself, however, withdrew from his role of constant supervision: he rarely emerged from his camper and never participated in public demonstrations. The average members had little idea of the activities of Berg's extended family or of Berg's sexual eccentricities. At this point, his direct charismatic authority had reached its zenith.

TSC and Skid Row: February 1970 through October 1971

By February 1970, the total number of members approached 200. Concerned with the size of the group, Berg contacted his old mentor Fred Jordan and secured the use of the then abandoned Texas Soul Clinic (TSC) Ranch near Thurber, Texas, and the old Soul Clinic mission building on Skid Row in Los Angeles. There, the COG consolidated its gains; it gave up road travel and settled into a more sedentary life-style. Although the Family sought more accommodation with the outside world, it came under increasing public criticism, in part because it was no longer a moving target. From early February, Berg urged members to form socialistic colonies that would not simply proclaim the group's message, but would give the world an example by which to live. Berg and others saw the arrival at TSC and the Soul Clinic mission as the end of the group's wandering and its finding of the promised land in which it would establish a new nation.

In January 1971, NBC's "First Tuesday" ran a not unfavorable story on the Family, causing many inquiries from youth wishing to discover more about the group. The COG's practice of demanding new members to forsake all possessions and worldly ties, however, quickly subjected it to blistering attacks from the religious press. In August 1971, a group of parents whose children had joined the movement formed FREECOG and accused the Family of kidnapping, drugging, hypnotizing, and brainwashing its members. Many distressed parents attempted to kidnap and "deprogram" their children.

In reaction, the Family grew extremely protective of members whose parents disapproved of their membership. First, Berg stressed that underage young people could not join the group without legal authorization from their parents or legal guardians. Both TSC and Los Angeles maintained a security watch—called "greeters"—at the front gate and doors to keep out potential troublemakers. When antagonistic parents (known as "10:36ers" after the verse in Matthew) or other disgruntled family members came to visit a COG member, the leaders frequently insisted, with the member's apparent consent, that another COG member be present. In addition, certain colonies—those housing leaders and new members (known as "babes")—were designated "selah" colonies: their locations were known only by leaders on a need-to-know basis. All this contributed to a siege mentality that emphasized the difference between the group and the surrounding society.

The Family's growing public-relations sophistication was a more lasting, if not immediate, effect of increased publicity. During this period, public relations was an important function of all leaders, and Berg specifically instructed them to put the COG's best face forward: controversial practices were to be described in conventional terms. A public persona was developed that hid the more strenuous aspects of the group's existence.

Berg continued to leave the day-to-day supervision of the COG to members of his extended family. In August 1970, he and Maria left TSC for Europe to see the original promised land, Israel, as well as to scout potential locations for new colonies. Berg had hoped that the Israeli kibbutzim would provide a model for future COG organization, but he was disappointed by Israeli society, particularly its laws against proselytization, and developed a strong antipathy toward the Israeli state. On the trip back to England, Berg and Maria ran into some groups of traveling gypsies in Cyprus and other places, and in the gypsies Berg found a social model to replace the Israelis. In April 1971, Berg and Maria settled in London, and Berg, through letters to COG leaders in the United States, began to insist that the group develop satellite colonies in other parts of the United States; these letters started the tradition of Mo letters. Despite resistance by some members, by the end of the period the Family had established forty colonies that tended to follow the TSC and Los Angeles models, but on a smaller scale.

The period was one of intense witnessing. The shift away from mere proclamation to strong efforts at recruitment and conversion meant that demonstrations and spectacles such as the sackcloth vigil virtually disappeared. Access strategies were employed more to initiate witnessing interactions than to spread the message. Although the COG experimented with several new access strategies—the first COG musical groups were formed and members often put together open-air skits to attract attention—the most prevalent strategy was simply to walk into a public area where young people lingered and approach them. The targets during this period remained young adults and the unsettled. Members paired up and engaged in conversation those who appeared approachable.

The content of the witnessing interaction was often a challenge to the potential convert's stated beliefs: the point was to show him or her that Jesus and the member were more radical than the potential convert. Unlike during the previous period, the damnation of the System was now broader: the attack was directed at all forms of secular activity, education, jobs, sports, and recreation, as well as to church activity. Members frequently "blasted away" the potential converts, using both harsh language and personal criticism, and consequently the witnessing interactions often terminated before reaching a successful conclusion. A second strong element in the witnessing kerygma was the necessity of removing oneself from the System by making a total commitment to Jesus and the COG. This involved a plea for the convert to forsake all, including family and other ties. These techniques were quite successful: by the end of October 1971, the COG had grown to 1,475 full-time members.[2]

The exigencies of supporting life in large communes often dominated members' experience, particularly at TSC, which provided both training and support functions to the colonies more actively involved in witnessing. Members at TSC felt they were participating in the physical building of God's new nation and, being more removed from fertile witnessing areas, spent more time on projects directed at self-sufficiency and repairing Jordan's ranch. Los Angeles, in contrast, was viewed as the frontline outpost in the battle against the System. Conditions in Los Angeles were less relaxed and the colonies there had the harsher atmosphere of a military camp.

The daily schedule for all members remained strict and left little free time: the number of bible classes increased dramatically, and members rarely read magazines or newspapers, believing it a waste of time. Members also believed that education was useless, and even damaging. Free time was applied to personal study of the bible or work on songs and letters. The tribe structure employed during the road travel period continued at the larger colonies. Strict regulation of sex and marriage accompanied this spartan life-style. COG members were predominately male, thus creating a scarcity that had to be rationed: no dating was permitted for members until their sixth month in the Family and until they had received a message from God to approach a possible mate. At least among members, no sexual activity occurred until after marriage. Because the Family does not believe in the use of birth control methods, however, the birth rate began to rise, and the group began to provide systematically for the care and education of its new child-members.

The influx of new members increased the internal resources upon which the group could draw, in addition to the financial support Jordan and sympathetic outsiders provided. The COG also continued to spoil Egypt by using credit cards and requesting money from mem-

---

[2] Some of the growth—about 175 new members—occurred by "conquest": in 1971, the COG annexed two large groups of radical Christians, David Hoyt's Atlanta-based "Atlanta Discipleship Training Center and the House of Judah" and Linda Meissner and Russell Griggs's Seattle- and Vancouver-based "Jesus People Army." Meissner also brought with her the publication *Truth*.

bers' families. Procuring, however, remained the primary means of meeting daily needs, and its importance grew when the COG realized that TSC could not be self-sufficient through farming. Almost every colony had members specifically assigned to procuring; the more successful procurers went out in coats and ties to persuade possible benefactors to help.

As the number of COG members grew, and as the press paid more attention to the group, the leadership became more authoritarian. Members considered themselves to be soldiers in a hierarchical army, and they were conscious of the need for obedience and security. Leaders frequently opened members' mail in order to check on their commitment and to look for contraband. They also maintained tight control over transfers between colonies, shifting members between locations on short notice. Also reflecting the hierarchical structure, Berg created different levels of leaders: the chief leaders, now called "Directors," remained Berg's extended family; below them were "Regional Shepherds," who supervised all colonies in their geographical regions; and "Shepherds" were the leaders of individual colonies.

Worldwide Expansion: October 1971 through February 1973

In September 1971, after a dispute with Jordan, the COG abandoned the properties on Skid Row and at TSC. This gave more urgency to Berg's call for the group to expand into other countries and reduce colony size: the number of COG members increased dramatically in the early part of the period, the size of each colony shrunk, and colonies sprang up around the world. While personal witnessing remained the major activity, both the approach and the message were altered to be more effective in the new environment. Moreover, members now lived closer to witnessing areas, and the reduced size of colonies freed them from many of the survival related tasks that dominated the TSC days.

In the face of a rising tide of negative press and public reaction, Berg directed members to go underground and keep low-key. Although dissembling for the public has always been a COG skill, it reached sophisticated levels at this time. The COG continued to view itself as a group of revolutionaries—"the storm troopers of the Jesus Revolution"—completely committed to winning the evil world for Jesus. They realized, however, that explicit statements and some of their past practices were counterproductive. Thus, the COG began to present to the world a softer face. In furtherance of this policy, Berg directed that all members return home to their parents and family for the Thanksgiving and Christmas holidays of 1971. A second initiative was the publication and wide distribution of *Survival* (172) in June 1972, which gave a capsule history of the group and explained some of its beliefs.

By the beginning of 1972, the COG had a foothold in Britain and on the Continent. Berg wrote a steady stream of letters urging members to form teams to come to Europe and open and populate new colonies. In the spring of 1972, several Mo letters triggered the first of a number of mass exoduses from America. However, the rapid movement of Family members in the last months of 1972 slowed down the rate at which new members were being recruited. As of October 1972, Berg claimed 2,348 "disciples" (as members were now called) in 134 colonies in 41 countries: of these, 1,399 disciples and 81 colonies were outside the United States.

Proselytization during this period emphasized witnessing almost exclusively and was directed at attracting as many new members as possible. Although COG access strategies changed little, the move out of the United States caused significant changes in those approached and in the content of the kerygma. While members in America continued to proselytize among young, radical dropouts from society, their European counterparts focused more on dissatisfied Christian youth. The American kerygma stressed the COG's anti-System and total discipleship message; the European kerygma, in contrast, emphasized God's love for the potential convert—only if the initial interaction showed some signs of success did the European witnesser "hit" the prospect with the COG "forsake all and drop out" message. Family members also used more COG literature in witnessing interactions during this period.

Part of the reason for this change in kerygma was that the strong anti-System message used in America held less attraction for European youth: it was no great relevation to them that American society was far from perfect. A second, and probably more important, factor was the effect of the change of situation: the initial public reaction in Europe was more open and trustful than the reaction the Family had received in America. Moreover, Family members realized that they had to adjust their behavior to a much greater extent simply to make witnessing possible. Finally, the prolonged public relations problems taught Family members that a more sophisticated approach was necessary for witnessing success.

Despite the softening of worldview brought by Europe, joining the Family remained a severe test. The *Revolutionary Rules*, which each potential member was required to read, described COG members as "rebels against the rotten, decadent, decrepit, hypocritical, self-righteous, inflexible, affluent, self-satisfied, proud, stubborn, disobedient, blind, bloodthirsty, Godless, dead, selfish, churchy, unchangeable older generation of their day!" (S:1), emphasized total discipleship, and stressed the rigid qualifications and sacrifices that membership required. Obedience was essential, dating was banned, absence without leave was to be considered desertion, late hours were required, and arguing with leaders prohibited. Colonies were smaller, more dispersed, and isolated from one another; COG members viewed themselves as persecuted revolutionaries in a hostile environment. Members referred to the Family as the "team" and would ask each other, "When did you join the team?" Another factor contributing to this sense of isolation was the constant discussion within the group of the "end-time": in *The 70 Years Prophecy of the End* (156), Berg brought together his view of the final days of the world. Many bible classes emphasized the coming of the end, and babes were given lengthy and detailed lessons on the books of Daniel and Revelations. The spartan daily routine in most colonies served to underscore that members were living in the days close to the end.

As the preceding paragraph suggests, the use and status of the Mo letters changed dramatically, and COG publications began to play a more central role: they provided the organizational link between the increasingly small and decentralized colonies. In a February 1972 Mo letter, *The Laws of Moses* (155), Berg announced for the first time that his letters were the very "Voice of God Himself" through his prophet Moses David. In response to this, reading and studying Mo letters as well as the bible became a routine part of the members' day. During this period, the Mo letters were for the first time distributed directly to all members rather than through leaders. COG also published a movement newsletter, first called *New Improved Truth* then *New Nation News*, that reported on COG activities throughout the world and included statistics on number of members and colonies.

As COG expanded, the structure of leadership became more complex. Members of Berg's extended family remained in the highest positions of authority, and Rachel, one of Berg's early consorts, was his official roving representative. Berg constantly revised the assignments of the highest leaders, and during this period the administrative office was moved from Dallas to Bromley, England. Berg used these changes among the top leaders to enforce their loyalty and to impose his will. Although the lower levels of organization remained fairly stable throughout the period, reductions in colony size and geographic dispersal were financially disruptive, causing most colonies to live close to the edge of economic survival. Provisioning and forsake-alls continued to be the main means of material support, and members became more willing to dress up and play the role of the "Systemite" to elicit donations. In some places, members found it profitable to sell *New Improved Truth*, instead of giving it away while witnessing.

Litnessing: February 1973 through February 1975

By January 1973, intensive witnessing increased the size of the Family to 2,400 full-time members in 140 colonies in 40 countries, and COG suffered from a lack of experienced leaders. In response, Berg adopted a new access strategy that slowed the growth appreciably. In a series of letters in early 1973, he directed COG's proselytization activities away from intensive witnessing and toward more proclamatory activity: COG members were to eschew one-on-one personal witnessing in favor of massive distribution of Mo letters, thereby spreading the group's message to as many people as possible. To provide COG members with literature to distribute, Berg went on a letter writing tear in which he issued almost forty-five new letters on a wide variety of current political and social themes. Litnessing continues to this day as a major access strategy and as a primary source of financial support.

Initially, however, rank-and-file members were slow to adopt the new proselytization method. In *Shiners!—Or Shamers?* (241), Berg ordered members to be simply "God's Newsboys!" and to sell the literature; there was no need to stop with each person and explain its significance. Moreover, to ensure that the literature was not given away, Berg directed that each member keep a distribution record and that leaders set distribution quotas and impose sanctions and rewards for performance. The effect of *Shiners!—Or Shamers?* was immediate. Leaders set fairly drastic quotas for members: around one hundred pieces of literature per day, priced from FF0.40 to FF0.50 or £0.05 to £0.10 per piece. Members turned in literature reports and the funds collected each day. Punishments meted out for "shamers" included special kitchen duty, no food, and banishment from the colony for weekends during which the member was to make up the shortfall. Despite the 1974 introduction of Poorboy Clubs—COG discotheques designed to draw in young people for more intensive proselytization—one-on-one witnessing and recruitment occurred infrequently.

Litnessing helped the COG regroup organizationally by significantly reducing the rate at which new members were recruited and providing a stable and increased source of income for the group. Less direct, but perhaps more profound, litnessing increased the COG's sophistication with respect to the System. No longer did members insulate themselves completely from the System, and no longer did they approach only society's young and lost. It was easier to meet litnessing quotas in the shopping malls and train stations that dot western Europe: the large flow of people passing through these types of areas increased the number of possible litnessing interactions. This change, in turn, brought COG members into contact with a wider cross-section of the populace than before. It also forced them to tone down both their approach to people and their appearance; members spoke of "becoming one" with their targets.

Litnessing also altered the daily routines of the group substantially. Regular field colonies were dedicated to this strategy and were located in cities to provide access to good litnessing areas. If members, who spent eight to ten hours a day litnessing, met their quotas, which was the usual case, a colony in western countries would have a comfortable cushion to pay rent, to buy cheap but healthful meals, and to take care of other needs. This offset the reduction in income from new members. Provisioning for food and for places to sleep also became less frequent. In fact, provisioning was done more as a socialization method and test of faith than out of any acute need. To support the upper leaders, Berg directed that local colonies pay a tithe—10 percent of their total income—to the central offices to support publications and other activities.

Despite these and other changes in daily activity, leaders within the colonies remained authoritarian. Although some leaders, following Berg's example, experimented with taking on new or multiple partners, sexual mores among the members at the colony level remained strict.

The New Revolution: February 1975 through May 1976

Berg used his birthday in 1975 to once more impose radical changes on the Family. To respond to the falloff in new members—by 1975, only 18 percent of the members were neophytes—Berg's "New Revolution" placed renewed emphasis on recruitment and personal proselytization and sought to reorganize and democratize local colony life. In a series of New Revolution letters, Berg set a maximum limit on the size of a colony at twelve and demanded that each colony add one new member per month. By the end of 1975, Berg reported that the COG consisted of 725 colonies in 70 countries with 4,215 full-time members. At the same time, Berg also concluded that the English had begun to reject God's word: the remaining large London colonies were shut down; members relocated to Paris, and, throughout the spring and into July of 1976, members streamed into Paris and other parts of France.

Litnessing continued to be the major access strategy during this period. However, in order to achieve the quotas on new members set by Berg, the focus of litnessing was changed slightly: it was used to engage prospects in witnessing interactions. Other access strategies more suited to recruitment, such as café singing and the Poorboy Clubs, were also employed. To attract potential converts, the discos were upgraded and the members more well-dressed. Those visitors who were "saved" were encouraged to go to the colony or to return to the club on some later date.

Instead of society's dropouts and young radicals, the COG pursued those who were employed or in school. The COG found that such people were more receptive to the message, made better long-term members, and required less time to be spent dealing with their problems. Potential members also tended to be somewhat younger than before, a fact which led to the creation of a new status, "catacomb member," to account for members who, for reasons of age or legal condition, were unable to live in colonies as full-time members. This innovation, of course, reflected the COG's growing flexibility in dealing with the System. These revived aggressive recruiting efforts once again brought vocal opposition from parents and press in Germany and England, and Berg suggested that every member keep a "flee bag" of essential supplies close at hand in the event a colony was forced to decamp.

In fomenting his New Revolution, Berg also believed that older COG leaders, especially the members of his extended family (then known as the "Royal Family"), were overly authoritarian and unresponsive to the needs of members. His solution was to revamp and multiply the leadership positions and to require that leaders be elected by the members. The New Revolution established a series of leaders above the colony level—district shepherds, regional shepherds, bishops, archbishops, and, later, ministers and prime ministers—forming a chain of command all the way up to Berg. At the same time, Berg pushed his extended family into special ministries. Except for Jethro, who continued to serve as the chief administrator, this effectively shut out the Royal Family from control of the movement.

These latter changes led to substantial disaffection among some members of the Royal Family and other old COG leaders, and much of Berg's time in 1975 was spent resolving leadership disputes. In

GOSHEN COLLEGE LIBRARY
GOSHEN, INDIANA

addition, marital and sexual problems continued to plague COG leadership throughout the period. Despite Berg's insistence that leaders keep their families intact, mate swapping and the use of surrogate mates were widespread. All these problems started a run of defections by older leaders. In October 1975, Berg lost his chief ideologist, Joel Wordsworth, as well as several other longtime COG bible teachers. Berg took advantage of these losses to consolidate his control through the Mo letters. He directly reviewed the content of all COG publications, whose production he centralized in the World Services office in Geneva. Financially, World Services (and Berg) were supported by the "gift" of 10 percent of every local colony's revenue from litnessing.

Flirty Fishing: May 1976 through December 1977

In May 1976, Berg began to distribute to all COG members accounts of his experimentation in England and the Canary Islands with the new access strategy of Flirty Fishing. A series of Mo letters entitled "King Arthur's Nights" recounted Maria's pursuit and seduction into the COG of Arthur, an unmarried businessman in his thirties, and his marriage to Rebecca Newlove, one of Berg's female companions, in 1974. While living in suburban London in 1973 and early 1974, Berg and Maria attended a dance class for diversion and relaxation. Forever on the lookout for proselytization opportunities, they perceived that such classes were filled with lonely young people in their late twenties and early thirties who held respectable, but unfulfilling, System jobs. Berg encouraged Maria to dance with the lonely men, and he danced with similarly unhappy women. While doing so, they developed friendships that they then exploited to witness. In Arthur's case, Berg encouraged Maria to pursue a sexual relationship as a way to bring him into the Family.

Berg and Maria left England on March 13, 1974, to travel to the Family colony in Tenerife, Canary Islands, to try out Flirty Fishing in an isolated area. They surrounded themselves with some of the most trusted women members and referred to themselves as the "Family of Love," a name soon adopted by the entire movement. The women frequented discotheques and bars and slept with a significant number of men in Flirty Fishing attempts. This colony was "selah" or secret: most COG members had no idea of its existence or activities until the formal introduction of Flirty Fishing in 1976.

Berg and Maria continued the Flirty Fishing operation in Tenerife into early 1977, reporting their activities in frequent Mo letters. While most encounters did not result in sexual relations, the frequency of

David Berg (Moses David) and Maria (on Berg's right) with other members of Flirty Fishing selah colony in Tenerife on the Canary Islands in 1977. Taken from *The Children of God* by Deborah Davis with Bill Davis, used by permission of Zondervan Publishing House.

interaction, the predominantly American makeup of the group, and the possibility of sexual relations attracted considerable, and initially favorable, local attention. The run of good publicity did not last long. On February 28, 1977, Berg received a summons to appear before a local magistrate investigating the group at the request of local Catholic authorities. Although no charges were pressed, Berg and Maria and most of the other Americans fled Tenerife, fearing deportation.

Members in other colonies followed the new series of Mo letters with excitement, awe, and in some cases grave reservations. The original King Arthur's Nights Mo letters were immediately followed by letters describing Maria's and other COG women's exploits in Flirty Fishing with hotel and nightclub guests and staff on the Canary Islands. Berg provided explicit descriptions of these encounters to explain the dangers involved and the techniques employed. Maria was described as the prospects' "loveslave": she demonstrated God's love by satisfying their physical needs.

These activities provided the model for Flirty Fishing throughout the movement. As practiced, a group of COG members—typically, four or five women (the "bait") and one or two trusted males (the "Flirty Fishermen")—entered a bar or discotheque. The women searched out unaccompanied males, approached them, and asked them to dance. While dancing, the women held the prospects or "fish" close and normally did not fight off physical advances or groping. After several close dances, the women asked the prospects to sit with them at their table with other members; conversation was low-key, but always came around to God's love. Any prospect that appeared receptive was asked to visit the Family colonies or to return to the discotheque on a later evening. During this period, only the wives of top leaders and several women personally selected by Berg actually became involved in sexual relations with potential converts. For the average member, the new access strategy took a milder form of simple dancing and witnessing.

Despite the excitement generated among members by Flirty Fishing, litnessing remained the primary access strategy and its practice differed little from the prior period. The Family also continued to run discotheques to initiate witnessing encounters. Consistent with Flirty Fishing, these clubs changed from a youth oriented, pop music format to a more mature, seductive adult environment, and the Poorboy name was dropped. Finally, the colony on Tenerife experimented with a new access strategy called the "Church of Love," an "open house" or "Sunday School" at the colony directed at children and prospects who might not be able to join immediately.

The real impacts of Flirty Fishing were a softening of the kerygma and a change in the type of prospects approached through the access strategies: God's love for the potential recruit became the overriding message in all access interactions (not just Flirty Fishing), and witnessing was directed at professional young adults. Even to a person considering membership in COG, the message was softer. Although little changed in terms of organization and financial support, colony life became more comfortable and the leadership style relaxed.

The Reorganisation Nationalisation Revolution: January 1978 through January 1979

Flirty Fishing refocused attention on Berg's personal activities and reenhanced his charismatic authority. In late 1977, Berg announced that he would reassume more direct control of all aspects of the movement, stating that many leaders had corrupted the Mo letters and his teachings. Berg forbade alteration of the letters and, in what he dubbed the "Reorganisation Nationalisation Revolution" (the "RNR"), dissolved the chain of command installed during the New

Revolution by removing all leaders between his immediate advisors and local colonies. Local colonies were renamed Homes and were to be led by Home Servants elected by adult members. In addition, the RNR required that at least 50 percent of members of all Homes be nationals (citizens of the host country).

The RNR disappointed some of the top COG leaders. Over three hundred Americans were removed from long-held positions of authority, including members of Berg's extended family. For all practical purposes, Caleb, Joshua, and Lydia dropped out of the mainstream of the movement. Jethro and Deborah Berg, now in South America, were also demoted for bucking Berg's authority. The discontent spread even into Berg's personal household. Timothy Concerned (Michael Sweeny), who had been Berg's executive assistant since his days in Tenerife and had been converted through the Flirty Fishing efforts of Rachel, began to have doubts about Berg's authority. In the last months of 1978, Rachel and Emmanuel, Deborah and Jethro, and Timothy Concerned all left the movement. Although each had his or her own reasons for leaving, a consistent theme was their growing discomfort with Berg's divine claims and the radicalization of sexual activities, as well as their disaffection with Berg's volatile style of authority.

The organizational disruption caused by the RNR also upset normal proselytization activities. Berg expressly wanted local Homes to practice Flirty Fishing and chastised old leaders for discouraging regular members from the practice. While prior to the RNR Flirty Fishing was largely carried out by upper leaders, after the RNR just about everyone got into the act. A second effect of the RNR was that litnessing dropped off dramatically, witnessing declined, few new members were recruited, and actual membership declined drastically. In December 1977, the Family had 5,191 members: 3,650 full-time members and 1,541 children; adult members dropped to 3,259 by May 1979, and, with 1,699 children, the Family had a total of 4,958 members. The removal of the leadership and the subsequent turmoil caused most local Homes to spend more time in reorganizing, moving, and Flirty Fishing than in the more traditional, revenue producing activities of litnessing and provisioning. As a consequence, local Homes suffered a radical decrease in income that threatened their survival.

Along with the RNR came several new access strategies. At Berg's urging, many parents began to place their children in public and private schools and used school events as an opportunity to witness to local families. Other emerging techniques included the "mail ministry," in which members wrote to potential converts, which brought in sizable donations, and the "Music with Meaning" ("MWM") tapes, produced by World Services and broadcast over local radio stations on purchased time.

For the first time since the COG's road travels in 1969–1970, the RNR brought individual members directly under the authority of Berg and Maria. These members looked to the Mo letters directly for guidance, rather than to a fixed leadership hierarchy. Each Family Home was required to post Berg's address in a conspicuous place so that any member could write directly to him about problems. Every full-time member was required to fill out a confidential, detailed questionnaire and mail it directly to Berg. In addition, new Mo letters, at least at the beginning of the RNR, were sent directly to every member; formerly, only one or two copies were sent to the colony shepherd. Each Home was self-governed by its Home Council, whose members were residents over twelve years of age.

Berg's removal of almost all rules granted members the utmost liberty in many areas. A Home or any member within it was free to move anywhere without permission; members could set out to "pioneer" new areas without authorization. Within the Homes, Flirty Fishing was not limited to leaders, and women did not need to have men as fishermen. Marriages did not need consent, and no permission was needed for sexual relations between members. Berg stated that he had gone sour on the idea of formal, legal marriages. In fact, members were encouraged to share sexually with other members even on a casual basis. Children, whether from informal liaisons, Flirty Fishing, or marriage, were called "Jesus babies" and were the responsibility of the entire Family. It appears that members enthusiastically embraced these new freedoms.

After the RNR, only three organizational units remained: the local Home, the Service Centers, and World Services. Berg and Maria directly oversaw World Services, which was responsible for disseminating the Mo letters and for special projects. Between World Services and local Homes were the Service Centers, located in different language areas. Each Service Center housed a "sprint" shop or publications operation that translated and printed general public literature for distribution in the local language and provided it to local Homes at cost.

The Nationalise Re-organise Security-wise Revolution: January 1979 through April 1980

The RNR started the breakdown of the communal organization of the Family that had existed from Huntington Beach. With the tragedy of

Jonestown in late 1978, the press, looking for the next People's Temple, began to reexamine the practices of many religious groups. Berg sensed that this would bring on a period of increased scrutiny and persecution, and the defection of many older leaders at the same time accentuated this fear. In a series of Mo letters, labeled the "Nationalise Re-organise Security-wise Revolution" (the "NRS") letters, Berg called on members to scatter and go underground; large Homes, he believed, were an attractive target for anticult animus. And, for both public relations and economic reasons, he also urged members to go back to their national homes for a time. Called "furloughing," members were to spend time with their parents if possible and take System jobs if necessary.

With the NRS, the number of members, the number of Homes, and the size of each Home decreased. In many cases, a Home was identical to a nuclear-family unit, in that over one-third of all members were children. Each Home was financially self-supporting, and members often had little contact with Family members outside of living units. In some cases, members returned to their native homes, took jobs, and began to live like Systemites again. Beginning in July 1979, Berg issued a series of letters that encouraged members to live in campers and mobile trailers and travel around witnessing. Part of the motivation for this was the belief that after the crash or world war, members would have to survive in the wild.

A second feature of the NRS Revolution was Berg's attempt to reach lapsed members and the public directly. In a January 1979 Mo letter, *Dear Friend or Foe* (754), Berg invited the public and former members to subscribe to Family publications. He acknowledged that some mistakes were made in the past, but stated that there had been a major reorganization and that many of the former leaders had been removed or had left the group. The letter asked for a donation or tithe and for the names of other ex-members or friends. To bring back those who had dropped out of the Family, Berg set up the "IRF" program. Anyone could receive most of the Family literature by sending in an Individual Report Form on a monthly basis and contributing at least $10. In August 1979, Berg announced a distinction between IRFers and TRFers (Tithing Report Forms) or regular members. Berg abolished all other distinctions between full-time and part-time members. A Home could continue to receive all Family literature by filing a brief TRF report and by tithing (contributing 10 percent of its income). To handle these functions, Berg created the World Wide Mail Ministry (the "WWMM"), a World Services unit based in Zurich, Switzerland.

These changes and those of the RNR broke down the social support system that had maintained strong group ties over the first ten years of the Family's life. The constant contact with and supervision of local members by the higher levels of the organization were replaced by the *Family News Magazine* (the *FNM*), a successor to the *New Nation News*. The *FNM* reported testimonies from members, reactions of outsiders to Family activities, and some new Mo letters; an expanded version, sent only to TRF Homes, included all new Mo letters. The magazine quickly became the movement's organizational lifeline, the only source of contact with the Family hierarchy for most members. As a consequence, the distinction between TRF and IRF became extremely important: members worked to achieve TRF status and therefore receive all the literature. Through the *FNM*, Berg created a tenuous form of group solidarity based on his indirect charismatic authority.

With the scattering of Family members and the return home of many, organized litnessing and other proselytization efforts again declined. Members feared adverse public reaction and even physical persecution as a result of the expected Jonestown backlash. Berg tried to stem the decline by emphasizing the proclamatory function of litnessing and accommodating this to the new organization of the Family. Encouraged by Berg, Family members were now living in small groups in travel trailers or campers, and children were used extensively to draw attention and increase donations. A family might distribute literature and collect money in a town near their campsite, litnessing in any one area for only a few days before moving on. Under these conditions, follow-up witnessing interactions were more difficult and less frequent.

The new conditions also spawned several new access strategies. In some areas, particularly in Thailand and Australia, women members signed up and worked for escort agencies. These jobs provided a steady stream of witnessing targets as well as substantial financial support. One *FNM* report estimated that 75 percent of the targets were led to a salvation experience. Members also began to litness by going door-to-door with their children in the local community. This access strategy proved more effective than street litnessing: people were more receptive to the message in their own homes. In addition, residents were much more likely to give donations or to provide members with tea and a snack. Another new access strategy was called "churchgoing." Reminiscent of the early church visitations and the later Churches of Love, Berg suggested that members living at home infiltrate local churches and preach the true message. He also expressly called on members to take advantage of churches' Christian charity as a means of support in some cases. The most prominent new access strategy, however, was the centralized WWMM, which compiled large mailing lists and sent out material to potential converts. In addition, the donations received from the mailings became a major source of support for World Services operations.

Sexual practices took another step in the antinomian direction during the NRS. In February 1979, Berg issued a letter that discussed in some detail his own childhood sex experiences, including the first with his baby-sitter when he was three (779). He called on members to encourage children to express themselves sexually at an early age. Apparently parents, childcare workers, and other adults were to facilitate this expression. By April 1980, Berg stated that children should be encouraged to marry when they become physically able to bear children: he thought it cruel to deny them the satisfaction of their normal desire to procreate (904). Although it is extremely difficult to determine how much sexual activity between children and adults did occur, it was not an uncommon event.

Consolidation and Migration: May 1980 through April 1981

The impact of the RNR and the NRS on the organization of the Family and its activities continued into this period. From the beginning of 1980, Berg had been warning that the end was near, and he feared a nuclear war that would destroy much of the northern hemisphere. In May 1980, he issued the letter *Americans Abroad!*, which stated that only Latin America would be safe from the coming holocaust and that the fifteen hundred members then in North America should leave for the south. Berg apparently believed that the Middle and Far East and Latin America would be relatively untouched by a nuclear war. The impetus to migrate was bolstered by some negative societal reactions in Europe. Berg encouraged members to get benefactors in their home countries to make pledges to support the members' work in the south. Actual compliance with this directive to move south was uneven and slow.

During this period, Berg also grew disenchanted with the IRF program. He believed that the program, intended to reclaim backslidden members, had run its course and had claimed all those who were recoverable. The FNM was to be henceforward available only to full tithers: Berg now wanted only "110% members"—members working full-time for the Lord and giving 10% of their income (928). For members who did not tithe, WWMM published *Love is News*, a thin pamphlet with photographs and testimonies about Family activities. The FNM also reported in some detail Berg's problems with the remaining upper level leaders—in particular, the travails of Berg's son Hosea and his wife Esther in Hong Kong. Each incident formed a discrete morality play that recapitulated the parable of the Prodigal Son.

Proclamation continued to be the emphasis of proselytization. By summer 1980, Berg was pushing the Music with Meaning program as an access strategy. He called on musicians to send their songs to the MWM for possible use on MWM radio shows. He also wanted all Family members to act as agents for the shows in their areas and to sell the tapes to local radio stations for broadcast. Because more and more members were traveling in southern countries and living in tents or campers, litnessing and witnessing had to adjust to the more mobile life and changed political situations in the new environment. In Third World countries, Berg advised that members use "milky" literature, only using political literature where the Family's viewpoint was popular. To help members with this problem, the Family began to print "True Komix" literature: Mo letters rewritten in comic strip form.

Although the Family underwent no major organizational changes during this period, members were more isolated from other members than at any time in the Family's history. The sole organizational link between Homes was the FNM. The sexual norms remained the same: Berg opined that neither incest nor sex with capable children was prohibited by God and that there should be no age or relationship limitations on sexual activity (999). Only sodomy remained banned (1110). Berg recommended that every Home have a little orgy now and then as an expression of the Family's sexual freedom (919:5, 29–30). He acknowledged, however, that many Homes suffered from venereal disease, and he suggested that when the ailment was going around, members choose regular sexual partners and stick with them until the disease was gone.

The Fellowship Revolution: April 1981 through April 1982

At the beginning of April 1981, the Family claimed 2,188 Homes in 76 countries, with a total of 8,715 members. The lack of some overarching organizational structure, Berg felt, was becoming a problem. In Fellowship Revolution! (1,001), he commanded that all Homes within reasonable proximity meet together on the first Sunday of every month, and members periodically gather in fellowship meetings that included a wider geographic range. Berg also created a more hierarchical structure; at these local fellowship meetings, the Homes elected a local government, called the Local Area Action Committee, and a Local Area Shepherd. All members over the age of twelve had a vote. Family videotapes prepared by MWM were presented at meetings (including striptease and nude dance videos, for which Berg provided express instructions [1026]).

The push to leave the northern hemisphere continued during this period. By July 1981, Berg and Maria had moved out of Europe, first to Puerto Rico, then to the Mediterranean and Hong Kong. By that time, Berg had called on all members to be out of the north by December 1981. He announced in January 1982 that South America was saturated with Family members and that those remaining in the north should migrate to the Far East. The movement south resulted in a 26 percent drop in World Service income from April 1981 through February 1982. In response, Berg increased World Service gifts to Homes in the Far East and drastically reduced such gifts to European Homes.

With the move, Berg suggested more organizational changes for World Services in January and February 1982. First, he wanted to create Publication and Distribution Centers for each hemisphere, believing that the impending war would halt the mails and other forms of communication. (In the likely event that Berg died or was cut off from the Publication and Distribution Center in South America, he hypothesized that Faith might become God's vessel in that region.) The second change was the creation of "COMBOS" in each country. A COMBO—a hotel or campground near the capital city of each National Area—would provide a national headquarters including a national video library and meeting place.

Conclusion

Although my detailed sources of information on the Family end in April 1982, the Family lived on in Third World countries. I have no reason to believe that the consistent pattern of indirect charismatic authority with its alterations between direct charismatic guidance and legal-rational authority has not continued. That pattern provides the Family with a highly effective and flexible organizational form to react to new conditions. In the early eighties, for example, Berg was already manipulating that pattern to avoid a major prophecy-disconfirming event: he was laying the groundwork for revisions to his predictions of the exact dates of the end-time events. On the other hand, the rapid organizational changes that have given members a conception of a common purpose may not be a sustainable social pattern over a longer period. A group that so firmly and selfconsciously eschews routinization may fall prey to the lack of stability that routinization provides.

THREE

THE ORGANIZATIONAL SETTING OF

EVERYDAY LIFE

BEFORE analyzing specific everyday activities in subsequent chapters, I here describe some of the organizational features of everyday life in the Family.[1] The social organization of the Family is not dictated in toto by the formal ideology (cf. Durkheim and Mauss 1963:62–66): specific organizational forms are judged within the Family by their instrumentality in achieving ideological goals, not by their consistency with some ideological picture of the perfect society. Of course, the social organization must satisfy the demands of the formal ideology—in particular, the ideological imperative to proselytize. But more secular factors also affect the actual organization of COG activities. The group's cultural history, a convergence of American southern Protestantism with the sixties' youth culture, is reflected in the COG argot—a mixture of evangelical and drug-culture terms—prayer and devotional activity, food, clothing, and personal behavior. Similarly, COG music is folk and soft rock—guitars are the preeminent instrument—adapted to evangelical lyrics. Moreover, much of the social organization is also a practical adaption to surrounding environment.

Despite the diversity of such pragmatic factors that affect individual colonies, the COG social organization is remarkably uniform from colony to colony. Practices that developed in earlier periods continue to be accepted in every colony. New members are faced with an ongoing, established, and legitimate body of social patterns to follow. A type of inertia freezes many practices into the COG social organization; this inertia is partly attributable to the legal-rational aspect of Moses David's pronouncements, but even when no such authoritative statements buttress a practice, it tends to be identical throughout colonies. Deviations in long-standing practices either come from the highest levels of the authority structure or develop from slow and extremely cautious experimentation by local leaders.

[1] This chapter examines such features as they existed during my period of participant observation; history has passed by many of the phenomena I describe. (See Postscript.)

The Organization of Local Colonies

The primary social unit, the small colony, has been a persistent and resilient organizational form. Beginning in the TSC period, the Family allocated organizational functions to individual residential units. Although the division of labor has grown less strict in later years, specialized colonies continue to provide services for regular "field" or "frontline" colonies engaged in the bulk of the proselytization activities.

The vast majority of Family members live in field colonies of between ten and fifteen members. While most members are nationals, this is less often true in large urban areas such as Paris, Rome, and Amsterdam. The ratio of male to female members usually exceeds two-to-one, and most members are unmarried, caucasian, and in their late teens or early twenties. Colony shepherds or leaders, however, tend to be married, older, and, in almost every case, male. Members' socioeconomic classes vary geographically: North Americans come from middle- or upper middle-class backgrounds and have some university training, while Europeans tend to come from the lower middle-class and are rarely university educated.

Field colonies are typically located in lower middle-class urban areas close to preferred proselytization locations, such as market places, transportation centers, and congested public streets, with good access to public transportation. Detached houses with some sort of enclosed yard and a second, back entrance are preferred to permit members some degree of privacy from neighbors. In almost every case, housing is obtained in the month-to-month rental market. The Family prefers to inform the landlord of the number of people to be living in the house and to stay in the landlord's good graces by keeping the house and yards scrupulously clean and inviting the landlord in on a regular basis for tea and cookies.

Colony houses are divided into functional areas. Several rooms are designated for sleeping: one for "boys" or single male members, another for "girls" or single female members, and one room for each married couple. The shepherd's bedroom is used as a colony office, where files, money, and sensitive Mo letters are kept. Any small children sleep with their parents until the age of two or three, when they are moved into the appropriate room for single members. Of the nonsleeping areas, one room is set aside as a "visitor's room," used to greet outsiders who are generally potential converts or relatives of members. It is kept meticulously clean and may be decorated more invitingly than the other rooms; members are careful to keep it free

The COG colony house in Arnhem, the Netherlands, showing the back entrance and small play area.

of Family literature and other signs of Family activity. In many colonies, however, different areas must serve several functions.[2]

The specialized colonies include publications colonies in each language-area that translate and print Mo letters and other Family literature. Staffed by up to twenty members, they use their own printing equipment, but on occasion contract out large jobs to System printers. The location of such colonies is secret, and often higher level leaders reside there. Music colonies house the better Family musicians. From the beginning, the Family has encouraged them to write and record as much music as possible. Most of the music generated has been distributed in cassette form to members, who listen to it for inspiration or to learn new songs for proselytization. On several occasions, Family musicians have recorded songs commercially and distributed them through industry outlets, which is viewed as proclamatory proselytization.

World Services, the umbrella administrative office of the Family,

[2] In some colonies, a basement or outside shed is used to store supplies. Because of the Family's apocalyptic beliefs, colonies often keep a wide variety of emergency items that they believe will be needed in the coming days, including candles, propane gas, kerosene lamps and heaters, and dried and canned food. Bibles and extra Mo letters are secreted against the coming persecution by the Antichrist.

operates several small colonies. Those in Geneva edit, illustrate, and compose the Mo letters and write the *New Nation News*, producing negatives for posting to the local publications centers. World Services' "Wild Wind" unit contracts for the manufacture of cassettes, COG yokes, and other specialty items sold to members and occasionally to the public. Gold Lion Publishing in Hong Kong prints the bound Mo letter volumes and special Mo letter books for distribution. Finally, a small computerized office in Geneva collects statistics on proselytization and membership for publication in the *New Nation News*.

Another set of specialized colonies provides for the needs of the growing number of children in the Family. In childcare colonies, the younger children of traveling leaders are cared for by unmarried female members. Although children tend to be educated by their parents in the local colonies, specialized school colonies are necessary for older children—mostly preteens—whose parents are in other areas or are unable to educate them on a day-to-day basis. Whether in local or school colonies, children are taught reading, writing, and simple arithmetic through a modified form of the Montessori method in which ideological elements predominate. Children learn verses from Mo letters through COG educational publications, and incidents from Mo's or the Family's history are used to illustrate new words and ideas.

A small number of colonies (selah colonies) are supervised directly by Moses David and the highest leaders. Selah colonies are often engaged in sensitive proselytization efforts as was the Tenerife colony or a small colony in Holland Park, London, that attempted to recruit wealthy Arabs. Their existence is generally unknown even to members in the immediate area. These colonies rarely litness or witness overtly for fear of compromising their security, and they attempt to cultivate the image of young, upper middle-class, professional families.

Routines of Everyday Life

The most significant feature of the daily experience in every colony is relentless, socially organized activity. Members do have time to themselves, but even those periods are delineated by the group as "free time," when members are expected to engage in ideologically productive activities. Between seven and eight each morning, members are awakened by a guitar player singing a COG song. In the next hour members take turns washing up and reading quietly in their

Childcare worker teaching children in publications colony in countryside near Amsterdam.

rooms. Although there is some conversation, it is normally kept to a minimum. This period of quiet reading of religious texts and prayer is referred to as "temple time," a time members spend "hearing God's voice." Neophytes use this early morning time to continue to memorize bible verses from their "set cards," a standard set of verses memorized by all new members.

After temple time, the colony shepherd calls members into the visitor's room for morning devotions. Members sit in a circle on the floor or on chairs for a group prayer followed by a group reading of a Mo letter or biblical passage. Another group prayer ends the devotions. At this point, several members are assigned by the shepherd to prepare breakfast. This task is spread among members, but everyone quickly becomes aware of who has a "gift" or knack for such work, and those people do proportionally more of the food preparation. Before starting to prepare food, members often gather for a short prayer. Other members are assigned to clean different portions of the residence: every day the bathrooms are cleaned and the house swept.

Breakfast begins with a short prayer by the shepherd or another older member. The meal is usually light but wholesome.[3] Breakfast

[3] In Bradford, members were served cereal, toast and jam or honey, and coffee. The

conversation is often led by the shepherd, who asks members what verses they are memorizing for the day and tests them on verses from previous days. He may also ask members about litnessing or other proselytization activities, or for a report on the progress of potential converts or recruitment targets. At other times the conversation is more spontaneous and marked by joking and other types of chatter.

After breakfast members prepare for their day's litnessing. Although on some days musician members may stay in to practice, by ten or eleven the colony is empty except for the shepherd and any small children and mothers. While proselytizing, members buy or provision a small meal from a local merchant. During breaks, members take "Word Time": they sit down, eat a snack, and read a Mo letter or bible passage together. At seven, members return to the colony for the evening. If a member is assigned to help prepare dinner, he or she usually returns an hour earlier.

Dinner is the major meal of the day. As with breakfast, the dinner

Two members of the Arnhem colony taking Word Time reading the bible while on the road.

Arnhem diet was more extensive. It often included scrambled or soft-boiled eggs, yogurt, and tea. Bradford members also prepared something called a "Mo Drink" for breakfast: a banana, a pint of milk, a package of Angel Delight, two eggs, and honey were mixed in a blender.

menu reflects both local preferences and COG ideas about what constitutes a healthy diet. Dinners are balanced and almost always include some sort of meat and vegetable; the type of each depends on what is available locally and cheap.[4] The use of whole grains, such as brown rice and wheat germ, brown sugar, yogurt, bean sprouts, and honey is common to all colonies and reflects the natural food bias in the Family. Although coffee is an important part of breakfast, it is rarely served at dinner, as members, citing Moses David, state that coffee in the evening interferes with their sleep.

Dinner conversation tends to revolve around members' experiences during the day. The colony shepherd again takes the lead in initiating topics. Members are encouraged to give "testimonies"; that is, to describe encounters with the public. Members frequently discuss major current events, interpreting such events in terms of COG beliefs about the end-time or world political disputes. The shepherd may give members news of COG activities in other parts of the world, announce that COG visitors are arriving, or report that changes within the colony are on the way. Finally, as at breakfast, there is always some bantering and joking.

After dinner, while two or three members wash the dishes, everyone else begins an hour of free time. Members may use this period for any one of several activities. They visit or "share" with other members in groups of two or three, practice their guitar playing, write letters to parents, write letters and send literature to potential converts, or take temple time. In some colonies, members try to catch a television news program if possible. If the shepherd has a need to speak individually to members, he often uses this evening free time for a private conversation.

Once the kitchen is cleaned, the evening devotions begin in the visitor's room. Devotions in the evening are more lively and often begin with the singing of COG songs and "gypsy" dancing, the latter a liberal borrowing from traditional Israeli dances. The more gregarious members ask the shier ones to dance, and the women make an effort to be sure that all the men get to dance. At some point the shepherd indicates that it is time for more serious devotions, and the singing and dancing stop. The pattern followed is similar to that of the morning devotions: a prayer followed by a group reading of a Mo

[4] The Bradford colony served chicken and liver frequently; in the Netherlands, horse meat and sausage were common. In England, the vegetables were typically tubers, carrots, or beets; the Dutch colony served more potatoes, onions, and celery.

letter or biblical passage and concluded with another prayer. A colony meeting, when necessary, may occur after the last prayer. Sometime near the end of the evening, one or two assigned members prepare and serve a light snack of hot chocolate and cookies, and members spend a short period talking quietly among themselves. The shepherd announces that lights-out will be in fifteen or twenty minutes, and everyone gives each other a good night "love hug," accompanied by statements such as "Jesus loves you" and "Lord, let [member's name] get a good night's sleep." Members then wash up and retire. The shepherd checks that everyone is in bed and the lights are out. Although members occasionally talk among themselves for a short period in each bedroom, it quickly becomes quiet in the house. The shepherd almost without fail sets reveille time so that members get eight hours of sleep.

The foregoing pattern is typical of weekdays and Saturdays. Absent special circumstances, Sundays are designated "free days" or "visitors' days." On such days, the normal routine is relaxed: members do not litness and have more time to themselves. Most members use the day to catch up on letter writing or to read more Mo letters; others take walks in the neighborhood. If there is a movie playing that has some ideological significance, the colony shepherd may take a group to see it. Sunday is also the day that members entertain visitors at the colony or conduct a Church of Love. Potential converts or relatives are invited to visit late in the afternoon and to eat dinner with the colony members. Part of Sunday morning is used to spruce up the house and to plan dinner. When visitors arrive, members mingle with them and take them for walks to witness to them individually. Later everyone is gathered together for singing and the reading of a mild Mo letter followed by dinner. Generally, visitors leave around eight, but those close to a decision concerning their relationship with the COG may stay later.

Full-fledged colony meetings dedicated to administrative matters occur infrequently because such matters are usually decided by the shepherd. When colony meetings do occur, it is because the shepherd wants some contribution from members about a proselytization project or seeks to use group pressure and commitment to enhance members' dedication to a specific project. The shepherd sets the agenda by presenting a particular course of action or several limited alternatives. On most subjects, the discussion can involve disagreements about the proper course, but in the end a consensus is formed—at least overtly. Instances in which a particular member is

Dancing with prospects on a Sunday visitors' day in the woods near the Arnhem colony.

outspoken or insistent about an issue are handled as a personal problem of the member and not a matter for group discussion.

Prayer and Other Ideological Activities

Prayer is a ubiquitous activity: although members differ in the frequency with which they pray during the day, prayer is invoked in almost every possible circumstance including the most mundane, such as washing dishes. Prayer is most observable in group meetings, where it is probably in its most elaborate and structured form. The pattern of group prayer is fairly consistent regardless of the particular occasion. Members hold hands, close their eyes, and bow their heads. The shepherd begins the prayer by repeating "Thank you, Jesus." Other members join in with this phrase for a short period. The frequency of these invocations gradually decreases, leading to a period of silence. The shepherd then begins a substantive prayer or asks another member to do so. The content of the prayer varies with the occasion: it can concern litnessing and a plea for God to bring more sheep into contact with proselytizing members, or be a request for inspiration and understanding during the following devotional reading of religious texts. It may simply be a prayer of thanksgiving or for a good night's rest.[5] The prayer itself is in short sentences, with a rise and fall in intonation during each. After each sentence, members individually utter expressions such as "Praise the Lord" and "Thank you, Jesus." The end of the substantive prayer is marked by the speaker's stating "in Jesus' precious name." Another period of individual expression follows, with some members speaking in tongues,[6] prophesying,[7] or shouting out routine expressions as

[5] For example, the following is a reconstruction of a prayer from my fieldnotes:

Help us Lord to be united. We aren't islands, Lord. We work together, Lord, to be a sample of heaven here on earth. All the miracles, you do Lord. Lord, help us win souls to your kingdom, and never be divided. Lord, help us to work and play together. You took those twelve, Lord; it must have been a big problem. That sample, Lord, inspired them. Lord, help us to teach others what we've heard from leaders, and not teach ourselves, but others. Lord, help us yield ourselves. In Jesus' precious name.

[6] Unlike among the Neo-Pentecostals (Goodman 1969; Samarin 1972), glossolalia is rare and less developed in the Family. New members rarely speak in tongues, and those that do manifest a simple and repetitive phoneme structure.

[7] In COG, prophecies in prayer are statements made in the first person that members attribute to God or the Holy Spirit. Such statements are inspirational rather than predictive and are composed of an amalgam of bible verses, Mo letter quotations, and connecting sentences, and are relevant to a current concern in the group. For example, the following prophecy was delivered by the shepherd during a period when the colony was attempting a new proselytization push in a local town. The shepherd had been encouraging the musicians in the group, who were sometimes reluctant, to be aggressive in their singing.

Oh my children, I do love thee . . . and I hope in thee for thy childlike faith to go into these battles . . . and everyplace you tread I will give you—none that stumble will be weary if you trust in me and I will be a shining light and bring forth great fruit—I do delight in happy praises and through me may . . . find what they sought after, for ye are a chosen generation, a holy nation royal priesthood, a peculiar people, let your light shine before—so you can glorify your father which is in heaven, go in love for ye cannot help but win them for I am love.

About the same time, the shepherd also prophesied the following:

Is this too much, far beyond the limits that you and them have said? I said them and not I for have I not said: For if a brother or sister be naked . . . what does it profit? And which of you that is a father and has a son, the son said: give me a piece of bread, will he give him a serpent? Nay, but He will give unto him that what he seeketh an . . . that his joy might be full. For all things are lawful unto you. Did I not give all my life, will ye be willing to do less? Will ye . . . ? Will ye hide yourself in a [unintelligible] for fear for being sold, as do the church people? Will ye hide your talent for fearing the so-called church or will he ride the wave of my ever new ever revoluting revolution? And if the good man has tired you, What will ye do if the horseman comes. Above all remember: love is of God and

before. Again, the individual expressions die down after several minutes, and the shepherd squeezes the hands of those next to him and lets go. Other members do likewise and open their eyes.

Another prominent ideological activity is the "faith trip," in which a team of two members is sent out for a period of two days to up to two weeks. While on the road, members must "live by their faith in God." The shepherd gives them a city or area to go to and provides a small amount of bus money to get them out of town. Once that money runs out, the team must live off what it collects from litnessing. More experienced members often stop off in known productive litnessing spots on their way to the designated area. While on the road, the team spends nights camping, sleeping in other COG colonies, or provisioning a sleeping place from members of the public. The team calls their colony on a daily basis. Members explain this practice as a way to relieve temporary overcrowding in the local colony or simply as a method to break up the routine of colony living. In some cases, the shepherd may use the faith trip to test a wavering member or to remove members from the colony who are having trouble living communally.

As with most COG activities, members are outwardly happy when informed that they are being sent on a faith trip. Other members congratulate the team, saying "Praise the Lord! I bet you're happy." A faith trip is seen as a time of getting closer to God and letting Him guide members more directly. Some members, however, despite formal expressions of pleasure, are not so enthusiastic. They procrastinate, complain about details, and ask the shepherd to shorten the length of the trip.

In addition to litnessing, several other access strategies are used in field colonies. While most colonies engaged in some Flirty Fishing during my observation, it was infrequent and did not involve actual sex. Another access strategy, "café singing," is far more salient in everyday life. In this strategy, COG musicians and singers entertain—with the management's approval—the patrons of a café. Other members take seats among the patrons and order wine, beer, or soft drinks. As the musicians play, members lend support through cheers, applause, and occasionally singing along. After the musicians finish a set,[8] they pass around a hat for donations, which can total

---

born of God. And everyone that loveth is born of God and knoweth God. "The earth shall be filled with the glory of the Lord as the great waters cover the seas." [Hab. 2:14.]

[8] In a set, musicians mix fast and slow songs, which get "heavier" later in the set.

$40 to $60 a night, and all members attempt to witness to those at their tables.

Other access strategies used in COG colonies include the mail ministry and the related Catacomb Kids Clubs. In the former, members write to past friends and people they have met on the street, talk about their experiences in the Family and how it has changed their lives, include a Mo letter or two, and request a donation. The Catacomb Kids Club is a mail ministry for local children who are too young to join the Family. The member in charge of each colony's Club sends issues of Kidz Comics and other COG literature, along with a membership form for the Club, to children in the area.

Café singing on a street in Nijmegan, the Netherlands: the colony shepherd and other members are interspersed in the crowd listening to the COG musicians.

The performers adjust the song list to respond to the audience. A commonly used "heavier" song, during my research, was "The Fisherman":

"Throwing out the line for you now; Gonna catch you somehow
Gonna try to reel you round; So I may be small in giving all
That I might fall in love with you; I'll give you my life, my mind, my body, my soul;
    I'll give you my time, all the love I know; I'll give you my days, my mornings,
    and my nights; I'll go all of the way to bring to you my love; I know a friendly
    fisherman; and he is making me his hand; Reaching out to you,
Reaching out to you."

Colonies' and Members' Financial Support

Colonies are independent economic units expected to provide for themselves through litnessing. In North America, western Europe, and the developed urban economies of the Far East, this expectation is not unreasonable. Litnessing in these areas is extremely lucrative: estimates range from $1,000 to $5,000 per week per colony.[9] Colonies maintain accounts with local banks, under the System name of the shepherd, in order to deposit these often large sums. Additional sources of income include donations from such activities as café singing and a small number of gifts from parents of members and other supporters. Many colonies continue to provision or to solicit basic and perishable food supplies: they request donations of leftover vegetables and meat from local green grocers and butchers. A dwindling source of income is forsake-alls, the personal property surrendered to the colony upon joining.

Colonies must forward 35 percent of all cash proceeds to the administrative level at which the publications colony is maintained. An additional 10 percent is sent to World Services to support its staff and Moses David and Maria's household. To enforce these obligations, the COG organization must rely on local shepherds' honesty. The frugal and simple life-style of the colonies, however, reduces the impact of this 45 percent tax, and many colonies run surpluses,[10] which are often donated to colonies in more difficult locations or to the Moses David household.

Although the Family was more communistic in earlier days, it now operates a form of distributive socialism with retained individual rights in minor personal property. Despite the fact that forsaking all is no longer literally enforced, members, upon joining, are encouraged to donate their free cash and valuable items of property to the colony—and most do. Most colonies maintain a "forsake-all closet" in which new members place unwanted clothing and from which other members may take needed items. Members keep and control other items of personal property; even if a member urgently needs to use another member's possession, the member-in-need must ask the possessing member and may be refused.

[9] For example, I conservatively estimate the income of the Bradford colony at £720 per week (cf. *Wash. Post*, Apr. 13, 1975, pp. 18, 19, col. 3 [$500 to $1,000 per week in Arlington, Virginia, in 1975]; and Hopkins 1977:19 [$2,500 to $5,000 per week in American colony in 1977]; see also Wallis 1976a:823 [close to $500 per week]).

[10] I estimate that the living expenses of the Bradford colony did not exceed £300 per week. Thus, after the 45 percent administrative fee and colony expenses were paid, the colony ran a surplus of close to £100 per week.

Most members maintain small accumulations of cash to pay for incidental expenses such as toiletries or snacks. These funds come from gifts from parents and friends, amounts retained on joining, financial awards for reaching litnessing goals, and even a little unauthorized skimming from litnessing collections. Should a member have a pressing personal need, he or she may request the shepherd to provide colony funds to make up the difference in a purchase price. In some cases members attempt to accumulate cash in order to pay for tickets to new areas. The colony frequently subsidizes this effort by permitting litnessers to keep up to half of their daily intake.

External Organizational Features Impinging on Colony Life

Several features of the COG organization external to local colonies also affect quotidian experiences. Movement from colony to colony and from area to area is an expected feature of life in the Family. Although lengths of stays in particular colonies vary, six months is typical. The higher leaders keep track of the location and distribution of all members, and in almost every case initiate a member's transfer. Should a member wish to move, he or she can make that wish known, but must wait for the leaders' approval. Frequently a member is informed by a leader of a transfer on the day before or even the morning of the move. Caught unaware, the member must pack quickly and say good-byes within a short period of time. This feature of transfers produces a sense of urgency that members cite as evidence of the importance of the Family and their role in it.

The main reason for transfers is to provide personnel for attempts by the Family to "pioneer"—establish a presence in—new areas and new activities. Leaders frequently decide to establish colonies in new cities or countries; in other cases, they want to try out a new access strategy or some other organizationally desirable activity. A second reason for transfer is to correct what leaders view as unproductive situations. If a colony is having trouble in meeting its financial needs, or if its proselytization statistics are dropping off, members may be transferred in order to shake up the colony and add new blood. Finally, transfers are also employed to address specific personnel problems: they are used to break up undesirable romantic relationships or to eliminate personality conflicts in a particular colony.

As with faith trips, members are expected to welcome transfers as a new opportunity to serve the Lord within the Family. Typically, members do react favorably upon being informed of a future transfer: they state in the abstract that movement to a "new field" is invigorating. At the actual time of transfer, members are more reluctant, but it is rare for a member to refuse a move that leaders desire. A member may share reservations about a particular transfer with the colony shepherd in private, and they will attempt to work out the problem—that is, the shepherd listens to the member's concerns and tries to persuade him or her that the transfer is desirable both organizationally and personally. Out-and-out refusal to accept a transfer is normally respected, but it may signify to leaders that the member is suffering from "deeper" problems.

Statistics impinge on the everyday life of members. From daily reports of members, the shepherd summarizes the colony's proselytization activities on a biweekly or monthly basis and transmits the findings to World Services[11]; these statistics permit leaders to check on the performance of colonies and members in ideological activities. Because of this, members may be more concerned with generating statistics than accomplishing the ideological task well. When proselytization is more proclamatory, this is a less significant problem; when, however, it is more conversionistic, statistics may be deleterious. In the latter case, members have an incentive to cause a potential convert to utter a quick salvation prayer rather than to ensure a real, heartfelt conversion.

Despite this problem, leaders rely on statistics to both monitor and motivate the performances of members in field colonies. Higher leaders with less direct knowledge of particular colonies use statistics to evaluate the state of the organization; leaders then urge colonies to improve their statistics in any area found lagging. In a similar way, local shepherds use statistics to goad their colonies into greater ideological activity.

Colony shepherds also use statistics to monitor individual members' problems. If a member's numbers begin to slacken, it is a sign that the member is having problems either with proselytization specifically or, more generally, with commitment to the Family. The statistics of new members are watched to see if they improve on a normal course. Colony shepherds realize that some members are better proselytizers than others: what they look for are aberrations in an individual's pattern.

In the same way, most members develop a sense of their normal statistical level and use it to judge their own performance over time. Falling below this level is a sign of trouble, and a member in this

[11] The statistics collected include estimates of the number of persons who saw COG members in proselytization activities, the number of pieces of literature distributed, funds collected, the number of persons brought to a salvation experience, and the number of new members.

situation often tells others that he or she is experiencing difficulty in litnessing. Members recognize that a fall in statistics is a public signal that something is wrong: formerly private problems are now likely to become public ones, or at least are available as such to the colony shepherd.

A final external feature of colony life is the Family publications, such as the New Nation News, which distribute information about both organizational activities and individuals in the Family. The New Nation News provides a sense of the extent of the organization to which members have committed themselves, and they read each issue with great interest. Members with any length of tenure in the movement pore over the faces and names reported in the newsletter for information about members they have met or worked with in the past. Moreover, the New Nation News uniformly reports successes of the Family in both pioneering and proselytization efforts. Members reading these accounts are provided with additional evidence of the efficacy and power of the movement as a whole.

FOUR

SOCIAL RELATIONS IN EVERYDAY LIFE

THE TOTAL commitment feature of life in COG colonies has spawned a specific type of interaction within the group between super- and subordinates. In addition, even interactions between Family members are starkly different from those between members and nonmembers; while the former are generally relaxed interactions between people sharing common ground, the latter are intense and involve more stylized behavior on the part of members.

Authority Interactions

In earlier days, authority in the Family was quasi-military: members were blindly obedient to their leaders, and orders were often shouted. This style contributed to the group's self-perception as a revolutionary army for Jesus, challenging the prevailing society and Satan himself. The advent of litnessing, the migration out of North America, and the New Revolution changed this self-perception and altered the authority style. Authority relations are now marked by benevolent paternalism. Not coincidentally, the practice of referring to the group as the Family rather than the COG has also spread.

Despite this change of face, however, authority within the COG remains hierarchical. Although the authority of leaders over members is formally based on the "democratic" rules of the New Revolution, in practice higher leaders send shepherds to colonies with a strong recommendation that they be accepted, and colonies ratify such appointments without dissent. Shepherds are the organization's representatives in colonies and answer to higher leaders. Moreover, shepherds' authority within the colony is based on their perceived experience: most shepherds have more tenure than other colony members and have lived in other Family colonies.

Leaders employ both sources of authority to establish paternalistic relationships with members under their supervision. They take the initiative to investigate members' problems and concerns, while remaining solicitous of their feelings and physical well-being. They consult with members individually whenever they believe a certain action may cause a member displeasure. Preferential treatment of individual members is avoided unless there is some articulable institutional justification. Leaders are quick to praise and slow to criticize; criticism, when it occurs, is almost never delivered publicly. The effect of this authority style is a relationship of paternal inequality in which shepherds, much like fathers or significantly older siblings, incur and act on a responsibility to members for both their growth within the COG and their relations with the outside world. Perforce, leaders rarely grow extremely close to members.

Shepherds take a strong lead in managing colony activities. Direct imperatives, however, are not frequent; instead, such orders are more likely to be delivered in the garb of a request or question. The leader's tone of voice, however, supersedes the form of the order, and members apparently recognize such utterances as more than mere questions of preference and respond affirmatively. Consequently, a negative response may be taken as an expression of a problem—one that the shepherd treats seriously and investigates. When direct commands do occur, they usually are in situations in which the shepherd is frustrated by members' failure to respond to more subtle suggestions.

Challenges to commands in either form are rare. When one does occur, however, the leader may simply ignore it and tacitly permit the speaker to withdraw the challenge. Alternatively, he may try to persuade the member of the necessity of doing the activity in the way the command specified. In extreme circumstances—due either to the member's recalcitrance or to the need for quick action—he may address the challenge directly by the invocation of formal authority: "Do what I say, because I am in charge here," or "Because that is the way it is done in the Family."

The shepherd's paternalistic authority extends deeply into even the most mundane of matters. He frequently utters statements about improving a member's appearance and even table manners. For example, a shepherd told a member holding his dinner plate in his lap that it was "better" if he kept his plate on the table. The member began a long explanation to justify his practice, but put the plate on the table. At the end of the "defense," the shepherd simply uttered "hmm." The shepherd chose to exercise his authority by invoking the pragmatic justification that one practice is "better" than another. If pressed to substantiate the claim in such instances, a shepherd may cite the organizational concern of fostering good manners and presenting a good face to the public and potential converts.

When a member is misbehaving willfully in the eyes of the shepherd, he may "rebuke" the member. Rebuking involves stopping the activity and telling the offending member that he or she is not behaving correctly. The chastisement may or may not have a religious content, but when it does it usually is a statement that the member is letting God and His work down by misbehaving. Members generally respond to such direct correction with displays of contrition, often hugging the rebuker and thanking him for his guidance. In one instance during my period of observation, two musicians were late in meeting the shepherd for an appointment. Being late for a playing date, stated the shepherd, risked the loss of potential converts: "We lost souls—time is souls." In addition, being on time, he said, is "part of being a good witness. . . . We must gain the respect of the System. . . . We are reaching for a new class [of potential converts]." Finally, the rebuke included the statement that being on time helped to prepare members to be officials in the coming millennial government. After a little antagonism, one member hugged the shepherd and thanked him; the other said a short prayer, asking God to help her not to be late in the future.

Secretiveness plays an important role in the benevolent paternalism of COG authority relationships. The general rule is that members have access to information about COG organizational activities only on a need-to-know basis. Information about the location and identity of top leaders is kept from members, problems of individual members are rarely imparted to other members, and the organizational activities of one member are not always revealed to others in the same colony. An expressed justification is that members have so much to occupy them day-to-day that it makes no sense to burden them with information not essential to their activities in the group. A less frequent justification is that it is better to keep such information in a small number of hands to avoid inadvertent disclosure that might risk the enterprise.

Generally, members appear to accept these justifications and often state that they have little interest in a broader picture of the movement's activities. Occasionally, however, members do seek information that leaders feel they should not have. Questions about the movement of leaders and about the affairs of other members are the most frequent, and some members are simply more inquisitive than others. In such cases, the leader deflects the inquiry by being evasive or, if pressed, by asserting that the member should not bother himor herself with such matters.

This incomplete flow of information is an organizational attribute of the authority relationship common to many large organizations, rather than an insidious practice of a self-aggrandizing COG leadership. Although there may be arguments for a different and more general distribution of information in a communal religious group, the existing practice is not unusual from an organizational view. Of course, when members suspect "foul play" they may try to obtain information that they would not normally receive. Members of the Family do not presume, however, that their lack of access to certain information is sinister.

Interactions between Family Members

Between members of the Family, social relations are a type of institutionalized gesellschaften relation: members interact according to organizational rules that assume they are committed to a common ideological goal (Parsons 1968:688). Members are constantly moving, leaving familiar members, and meeting new ones, and the rules of interaction function to smooth these frequent changes and to provide a universal group of acquaintances for any member of the Family. Of course, closer and more individualized relationships do develop, but these are less frequent.

A member assumes certain traits about, and has certain expectations for, interactions with another member. One assumption is that the other means no harm, and that information transmitted in the interaction will not be used against the Family. This permits the member to relax and to let down his or her guard. A second expectation for the interaction is that the other member holds COG beliefs and embraces the COG ideological purpose of proselytization. Finally, the member assumes that the other is fully committed to the COG beliefs and purpose and that he or she is not simply "acting as" a member. This latter presupposition exists even if the member is not so committed and is questioning COG beliefs and activities.

Members routinely greet other members in a warm and physical fashion with a "love hug": both persons engage in a full embrace while standing with their heads on each others' shoulders. While in the embrace, each says "God bless you, [name]!," "God loves you, [name]!," or "We love you, [name]!" The latter phrase is used most often with persons on the verge of joining or with neophytes. The embrace lasts several seconds, and then the partners disengage and smile at each other. Although the love hug almost always occurs when a member greets another member arriving in the colony after an extended absence and when a member meets another for the first time, it also is frequent between members in the same colony. The love hug also acts as a sign of forgiveness and resolution of disputes between members in conflict.

Conversations between members have similar formal characteristics: the implicit rule is that appropriate or interesting interactions between members involve information flows about COG activities. Topics include discussion of experiences in proselytizing, colony efforts to reach new potential converts, news from other colonies, or simply events within the colony. Although conversations do drift to more secular topics, for the most part they remain related in one way or another to COG activities. For example, participants may relate a movie they have seen to COG beliefs about the end-time; or, they may discuss current events and trends in order to learn what is happening to today's young people so that members are better able to speak with them and witness to them. On the rare occasions when a member introduces a non-COG related topic, the other members often seem bored. In one such case, I observed two members discussing System music without any attempt to link the discussion to COG activities. The reactions of listening members varied from inattention, to attempting to change the topic, to outright statements that the speaking member should "not get tripped off" on that type of subject.

This conversational focus is not as strange as it may initially seem. Members in colonies often share nothing in common other than their commitment to the Family. While they are generally of the same age, they frequently come from different cultural and even national backgrounds, so it is not surprising that conversation centers around their mutual activities in the Family. Moreover, the reality of colony life is that a member's waking hours are virtually monopolized by COG activities. Therefore, a member's current experience, the source of most conversational material, is dominated by COG activities and information.

There is, however, also a strong normative element in the selection of conversational topics. Because members assume that their conversational partners are committed to the Family's goals and beliefs, lengthy discussions of topics that bear little connection to COG goals are relatively frivolous and to be avoided. In some cases, preoccupation with non-COG topics is a sign of "spiritual" problems and even of the "Devil's influence." The normative element even rules out certain COG-related topics: members do not discuss problems they are experiencing or reservations about their commitment to the group. Topics are to be "upbeat" and to reaffirm the value and benefits of commitment.

Connected with this latter feature is the implicit requirement that members be overtly enthusiastic about descriptions of COG activities and events. A member's recounting, for example, of a successful witnessing encounter is punctuated by affirmative expressions from listeners such as "Wow!," "Praise the Lord!," "What a blessing!," and "Thank God." Members display interest and "genuine" enthusiasm in conversations, and open disagreement with COG methods or with a member's description of an event is rare. Smiles, though not always present, predominate in interactions, while frowns or looks of sadness rarely occur. Generally, members express happiness and enthusiasm about their commitment to the group and life in it.

Despite the transitoriness and instrumental character of most relationships in the Family, members do from time to time develop closer personal bonds. When members reside in the same colony or work together on a COG project for a lengthy period, they have an opportunity to get a better sense of the personality of their partner than is normally possible. The same factors that determine selection of friends in society-at-large function in these situations: friendships display more traits of gemeinschaft relations, in that members share a variety of interests and confidences that often extend beyond their common membership in the Family.[1] Even when separated for organizational reasons, friends within the Family tend to keep in touch through letters and remain interested in one another's activities.

The organizational features of Family life, however, make such relationships infrequent. In secular society, people populate their personal world with a network of friends independent of their more gesellschaft-type relationships with business and other associates; in this way, a person can make contact with others to suit his or her desires. In the Family, the organizational setting makes such control impossible; a member is forced to associate on a pervasive and fairly intimate level with persons who are not necessarily close personal friends. He or she has little control over the nature and length of such contacts, as organizational imperatives require almost constant interaction.

Members do pair off into romantic relationships somewhat spontaneously within a colony, but such relationships between a member

[1] The confidences friends share may include their problems and reservations about participation in the Family. This is more certainly true with married couples, who in most cases share a more gemeinschaft-type relationship. Historically, close romances or friendships acted as a breeding ground for dissent from Moses David's and the Family's activities (e.g., Davis 1984). On the other hand, the majority of these relationships are not catalysts. It may be that even in such relationships, truly heretical or dissenting ideas are not discussed. Moreover, it is probable that such relationships provide the best plausibility structures to support the secondary socialization that members undergo (Berger and Luckmann 1966:154–55). If one's spouse or closest friend remains fully committed to the group, dissenting ideas receive little social support.

and a nonmember do not exist,[2] except in Flirty Fishing situations. Although the development of relationships is often actively encouraged by the shepherd, his gentle prompting is initiated by his observation that some attraction exists between the two members, and he may suggest to the male that the female would make a great mate. In the rare cases in which the leaders disapprove strongly, they may transmit their displeasure directly, suggesting that the members look elsewhere for mates. In extreme cases, leaders attempt to end relationships by transferring one partner to a new colony.

Such relationships are developed within the structure of the colony life. The partners begin to spend more time together during the day: they litness, read literature, prepare meals, pray, and spend their free time together. Occasionally, they go for walks alone, and sometimes the colony shepherd sends them to a movie or out for an inexpensive dinner. Partners in a relationship receive the support of colony members, but are subject from time to time to some good-natured kidding. They do not sleep together within the colony; otherwise, there is little chaperoning of their behavior, and it is not unlikely that many unmarried couples are sexually active to some extent.

The notion of marriage at the local colony level is fairly conventional. Although the formal ideology expresses a somewhat different perspective on marriage,[3] most members enter into it as a permanent relationship marked by exclusivity in sexual activity and by the expectation that they will remain together physically in the future; in short, members adopt a commonsensical romantic notion of what it means to be married. At some point in the relationship, the couple

---

[2] Marriages between people outside the Family are recognized when the couple joins the group. If only one partner joins, however, the marriage is treated as if it were ended, and the new member is free to find a new spouse within the Family. Likewise, if one member of a couple leaves the Family, efforts are made to find the remaining member a new spouse.

[3] Marriage in the formal ideology is a more or less permanent sexual relationship whose permanency is subject to organizational requirements:

> As in marriage and all other social relationships with each other, God's laws of love are still the same: 1. Is it good for God's work? 2. Is it good for His Body? 3. Is it good for you? Does it glorify God, His Body and edify your own soul? . . .
>
> Any variation from the norm of personal relationships, any substantial change in marital relationships, any projected sexual associations should have the willing consent of all parties concerned or affected, including the approval of leadership and permission of the Body. If this is lacking in any quarter and anyone is going to be harmed or unduly offended, then your action is not in love nor according to God's law of love!

(302C:13–14).

decides—or the shepherd suggests—that it is time to be married. The marriage ceremony consists of an evening devotion session led by higher leaders in which all colony members participate. After group readings of Mo letters on sex and marriage, the couple is congratulated and sent off to their own room in the colony for their wedding night.

Separation and divorce, although disapproved of, are not uncommon. As in the wider society, serial monogamy is a pattern in the Family (Wallis 1979:80–81). Marriages formed in the early 1970s seem to be particularly fragile. This may be somewhat due to more direct matchmaking tactics on the part of leaders during that period. When a separation does occur, members rationalize it by saying that it is sometimes necessary for the work, and they point to the fact that biblical prophets took many wives. Members having marital difficulties are counseled, but when differences are believed to be irreconcilable, the couple separates. Leaders may facilitate this separation by transferring one partner to another location.

While the life of nonmarried members in the colonies is sexually ascetic, sex between mates is strongly encouraged as a healthy activity. Moreover, variety in sexual practice is viewed as important to the sexual relationship. Only anal intercourse and intercourse during menstruation are forbidden by the formal ideology. Although members are not forbidden to practice birth control, to do so is considered a sign of a lack of faith: God will not permit conception if a couple is unable to handle the burden. The effects of this belief are soaring birthrates and no open acknowledgment of what little birth control is practiced (namely, limited methods such as rhythm, particularly after childbirth).

Interactions between Members and Nonmembers

Members' interaction with nonmembers is limited. Membership in the Family, with its concomitant time requirements, leaves little chance for the maintenance of preexisting friendships and relationships. Most members approach the world as if it were divided into two camps: members of the Family and outsiders. Although in particular situations members recognize and act on differences between outsiders, they automatically attribute to them several propensities that affect members' interactions with them. Members presuppose that outsiders potentially pose some danger either to a member or to the group as a whole; they may be enemies of the Family, such as antagonistic officials, snooping journalists, unsympathetic members of traditional churches, or deprogrammers. Although in most cases the danger never materializes, members are oriented to any interaction with a nonmember in such a way as to protect the Family. Members also presume that outsiders have little understanding of either the Family or of the "true" construction of the world, that they are lost in the System, experience little love, and are bound up in secular ways of thinking.

The vast majority of interactions between members and nonmembers takes place in the context of proselytization attempts, whether in litnessing, witnessing, or some other access strategy. Thus, members enter interactions with nonmembers with the specific goal of proclamation or persuasion, and this mode carries over into situations that are not strictly ones of proselytization. A member, in dealing with any outsider, attempts to persuade the outsider that the member's activities are harmless, good for the members, and even good for the interactional other. This is done through a presentation that expresses the member's happiness with his or her life and that demonstrates the member's loving concern for the outsider. Even when the member's organizational affiliation is unknown to the outsider, this presentation always affects the interaction. The result is often a highly formalized interaction in which the member controls the nature and quantity of information flowing to the nonmember and attempts to elicit from that person information necessary to the member's purposes.

Membership in the Family naturally strains prior relationships with family and friends. The member's desire to commit him- or herself totally to the Family and its communal life-style can be incomprehensible to relatives. Moreover, the intensity and time commitment required by membership normally reduce the contact a member has with those who formerly could demand more of his or her time. These nonmembers react in diverse ways to the member's withdrawal of intimacy, and the particular reaction affects the member's future interaction with those people. In most cases, the member also wants to share his or her newfound happiness with his or her family and friends.

The result is that at first members adopt a proselytization stance toward these intimates. By demonstrating their happiness and energetic commitment, members strive to persuade their parents that the Family is the way to live as well as justify their choice of life-style. In some cases, the proselytization stance may be employed protectively: it shuts down the two-way flow of information, thus routinizing what otherwise might be an unpleasant encounter for the member. As time goes by, the member's attempts to proselytize to these people grow less intense, and the interactions fall into lower pitched and stable encounters. Because of the member's organizational commitment, the interactions also decrease in frequency. Face-to-face encounters that do occur typically entail both the parents and the member attempting to avoid arguments about the member's affiliation. Instead, encounters are simple exchanges of information; the member tells his or her parents what has been happening, and the parents, in return, transmit information about family and other events that the member has not been in a position to know.

When parents, however, do not accept their child's decision and remain hostile to the group, the interactions between the member and these outsiders continue to be carried on in the proselytization mode, which is a defensive shield. It provides a response to parental attacks on the member's beliefs and practices. Often, other members accompany the member in interactions with hostile parents to provide both moral support and occasional arguments for the member, as well as protection against a kidnapping attempt. In extreme cases of parental hostility, the member is moved away so that the possibility of interaction with the parents is decreased.

A third instance of interactions with outsiders is that of the chance or nonpurposive encounter. This includes interactions with shopkeepers, bus drivers, landlords, and others necessary to accomplish mundane tasks essential to survival. Members' interactions with such people vary with personal style. Some members view every interaction as a proselytization possibility that they are obliged to exploit: any opening that a bus driver or shopkeeper provides is taken up. Others, however, are more circumspect. Although they certainly will proselytize if the nonmember shows any interest, they do not actively seek to turn the situation into a proselytization interaction. Instead, they follow commonsense rules of civility that govern such interactions in society-at-large. This latter orientation seems to prevail among COG leaders, who realize that excessive proselytizing can interfere with the more secular, but still necessary, tasks members must perform.

Because members presume that outsiders pose some danger, they are constantly on guard. Although practices vary with the reception the Family has received in a locale, a number of them limit the types of information that outsiders receive. The general rule is that an outsider should receive no more information about the Family than is necessary for the purposes of the interaction. Thus, in proselytization encounters, a litnesser or witnesser never reveals the address of the colony, just the telephone number. Only when the prospect telephones and the shepherd is informed of the situation is the actual address revealed. In some questionable cases, the shepherd may suggest that the member arrange to meet the prospect at some other location.

Answering the telephone itself involves security considerations. When answering, a member simply gives a conventional greeting in the native language such as "Hello, can I help you?" If the caller asks for someone or requests information, the member asks "Who is this, please?" If the caller asks for an unfamiliar name, the member says something to the effect of "just a minute, I will see," and then seeks guidance. In contrast, if the caller identifies him- or herself as a COG member, the answering member immediately says warmly, "[name], God Bless You," and begins a conversation.

When nonmembers are to visit the colony, members conduct a "security sweep" to be sure that sensitive Mo letters or other material are not lying about (this includes closing the door to the literature closet). In some cases, a few members may leave the colony for a period to prevent the appearance of a large communal cell. Another security practice, used to avoid undue attention, is for members to enter the colony either singly or in small groups. Whenever a large group is returning to the Home, members split up and take turns going in the front and back doors. Finally, any major outdoor activity around the colony, such as moving or transferring supplies, is often done at night to avoid attention.

FIVE

LITNESSING: STREET PROSELYTIZATION AS AN
ACCESS STRATEGY

P
UBLIC streets have always been the marketplace of ideas as
well as wares, and the sale of both has been vigorous. The
COG in the early 1970s recognized this timeworn feature of the
public street and set out to exploit it with litnessing, a form of street
proselytization.[1] Litnessing, as I have discussed, is an access strategy
in which a member stops a passerby on a public street by offering
him or her a piece of COG literature, or "lit," and asking the recipient
for a donation. The encounter introduces the passerby to the Family
and opens up the possibility of further proselytization. In addition,
the encounter generates donations used to support the group. Litnessing relies on the establishment of a relationship between a member and a potential convert in which both verbal and nonverbal information is communicated by the manipulation of the rules
generally governing public places.

The Purpose and the Kerygma in Litnessing

In number of hours spent, litnessing takes up more time than any
other COG activity, and while members' attitudes toward litnessing
do vary, most state that they enjoy it. Moreover, since 1974 litnessing
has been the primary source of financing for the Family (Davis and

---

[1] Despite the centrality of street proselytization to many religious groups, it has received little detailed analysis (but see Beckford 1975; Lofland 1966). The following account by a disgruntled ex-Jehovah's Witness illustrates the pervasiveness of street
proselytization in the life of a member of one of these groups.

I would spend all day Saturday travelling on the *Ring-Bahn*, a railway around the
outer periphery of Berlin, standing in the third-class compartments witnessing
loudly about *Millions Now Living Shall Never Die*, and selling the booklet for 25
pfennigs. Some Saturdays, huckster-like, I would dispose of three hundred copies
getting about 75 Reichsmark for the Watch Tower. . . .

(Schnell 1959:22).

Richardson 1976:334–36; Richardson 1982:257–58; Wallis 1976a:820–23; see Bromley and Shupe 1980), and members have been required to meet quotas for literature distribution and donations collected.

The stated ideological purpose of litnessing is largely proclamatory: it is to spread the kerygma as far and as wide as possible.[2] The litnessing kerygma emphasizes personal salvation, and God's love in particular. "God loves you" and "we love you" are frequent phrases used by litnessers. The other strands of the formal ideology, such as the utopian criticism of society, the Family's communal living arrangements, and millennialism, are proffered only when the prospect appears to share similar feelings and thus to be open to a witnessing interaction. Consistent with this, members in litnessing attempt to present and demonstrate God's love for the prospect. Depending on the particular interaction, other factors can be brought forward, but the pervading tone is always love. Moreover, the kerygma is presented nonverbally as well as verbally. In COG terminology, the member is to "luv 'em up": "Your greatest witness . . . is the love they can see in you" (344:58).

Litnessing Preparation and the Public Street

In learning how to litness, a member is given little formal instruction. The day after I moved into a COG colony, I was out on the streets, "getting out the lit." Much of litnessing, however, depends on a general and usually unarticulated commonsense understanding of the social rules that govern all interactions in public areas. Specific and special knowledge of litnessing is picked up in practice and fortified by helpful hints and comments from other members (cf. Goffman 1959:79).

There are, however, several explicit rules that are made clear to new members before they begin to litness. These rules are as follows:

1. Never lose sight of your litnessing partner: "[Y]ou can't ever tell what might happen with the 'Romans' [police] and everything."

2. If you are stopped by police, do not argue: simply listen, be polite, and obey them.

3. Try not to give away the lit. Get at least a few pence for each piece. (The rationale behind this third rule is that unless the person pays for it,

[2] "It's not the kid's responsibility to preach a sermon and persuade them. Our main job is not soul winning, but witnessing. . . . "They're not the ones now preaching the sermons. It's God who is preaching the sermon through the Letter itself, and they are only delivery boys and paper boys!" (241:6–7).

he or she will not read it. Moses David is greviously hurt if he sees a single one of his letters lying in the street or in a waste bin.)

4. Never carry sensitive literature with you on the street. Leave all DO and DFO material in the colony to keep it from falling into the hands of—unspecified—enemies.

In preparing each day to go out and litness, members pay close attention to personal appearance. Clothing must be clean and in good condition before members are allowed out of the colony; a bath must be taken every two or three days; and males are not allowed out unless they are properly shaven or their beards trimmed. Beside displaying a good appearance, members must also be properly dressed for the weather. After breakfast, the shepherd reads off a list of teams for the day's litnessing: most teams are paired, although occasionally trios go out. A member "older in the Lord"—that is, a member in the movement longer—is always paired with one younger. The shepherd usually takes into account personal preferences when he knows they exist.

The next step in preparing to litness is to organize a "lit bag." A lit bag normally is a shoulder bag in which a member carries the literature to be distributed. It is either open or has a top zipper that may be pulled back for easy access while on the street. Lit bags also have small side pockets in which litnessers deposit money collected. In most colonies, a room or closet is set aside in which literature for the general public is kept in large quantities. In filling the lit bag (about 300 pieces), each member selects literature on his or her own, relying on a set of rules of thumb about lit selection. Often, these rules take into account local considerations such as sensitivity to sexual matters or specific political issues.[3] One constantly articulated if not always obeyed rule is that members should only distribute letters they have read. These theories about the efficacy and appropriateness of specific Mo letters cause members repeatedly to choose literature for distribution from a narrow list.[4] However, despite this selection process,

[3] One of my first partners gave me some hints about selection. He warned against taking out *The Money Explodes* (294). The letter refers to Jews as manipulators of the international financial system, and there had been some trouble in Liverpool over this depiction. He also suggested that some of the sex letters, such as *Mountin' Maid* (240) and *Revolutionary Women* (250), might be too "heavy" even though they have a GP rating. *Flatlanders* (57), he said, was really good for "sheepy" or receptive people, and *Mountain Man* (B) should be saved for those who are really interested in the Family.

[4] At the time of my covert litnessing, most members chose to distribute the basic letters on faith, such as *Diamonds of Dust* (3) (see Appendix B), or letters on prophecies of coming events, such as *The Deluge* (339), which describes the destruction of England by a flood. A letter depicting the late Jimi Hendrix as a revolutionary hero was carried

all members state that every Mo letter is "a pearl of great price." No matter what its specific content, members believe that each letter is effective for the proclamatory function of spreading the COG kerygma. The most important concern is always to get a Mo letter, any letter, into every receptive person's hands.

Once the literature is selected, the member counts it and checks to be sure that the COG postal box address on the back of each is correct. At some point, the shepherd gives money (about $4) to the senior member of the litnessing team to cover each member's bus fares and any other expenses. What the members do not spend of this initial outlay, they keep. Before leaving the colony house, each team holds hands and prays. During my stay, two prayer themes were always present. First, God was asked to send plenty of hungry "sheep" or receptive prospects to the team, and second, He was asked to send guardian angels to surround the team and to protect it from Romans and "goats" (antagonistic passersby).

Each team selects a town and travels to it by bus. The colony shepherd keeps track of the towns chosen to guarantee that no area is hit too often. The area selected for litnessing in each town, such as a shopping precinct or tourist region, is one that supplies a steady flow of pedestrian traffic. Not only does this ensure a large number of possible access encounters, but a certain amount of commercial activity is usually conducted and accepted in these places so members are able to litness without overly disrupting the life of the area.[5]

Rules of Behavior in Public Places

Public spaces are generally governed by implicit rules or norms of behavior that affect and facilitate litnessing. In public streets, people are generally unrelated to and uninvolved in each other's activities. The situation can be described as atomistic: individuals are discrete units moving around with no fixed relation to others in the same situation. Each person is instrumentally oriented toward a goal or goals of individual importance. Of the many implicit social rules that govern interpersonal interactions in this situation, those affecting "acces-

by many for distribution to young people. Some members preferred to carry mini-lit, which is smaller and has more pictures than regular Mo letters.

[5] In Yorkshire, England, where my covert participant observation was conducted, the new postwar concrete shopping precincts were always used. In Paris, members tended to move through tourist areas and around train stations. Dutch members in Arnhem also concentrated on shopping precincts that were filled with both Dutch and German shoppers.

sibility"—the openness of the individual to an approach—are key to litnessing. Usually, on the public street, pedestrians simply accord each other "civil inattention": one person should give another enough visual notice to acknowledge the other's presence. Then, the first should withdraw the notice to indicate that the other is not a special target (Goffman 1963:84). The social propriety of street life assumes that everyone will mind his or her own business.

People on the street, however, maintain themselves in a state of controlled alertness (Goffman 1963:104). Although they are prepared to accept approaches, they do not generally expect them to occur; a person on a public street must have good reason for initiating an encounter with an unacquainted person (Goffman 1963:124). A person must only initiate an interaction with a stranger in order to offer help, as to a person who has, for instance, dropped some money, or to request help, as when asking for a light or for the time (Goffman 1963:130). A person must have a "ready instrumental rationale" for initiating a street interaction (Goffman 1963:89). Of course, in walking through a public street, a person is partially open to approach. Certain solicitations are expected from shopkeepers or printed advertisements.

A final rule of the public streets relevant to this analysis is that if an individual is approached, more latitude must be given to the approacher's definition of the situation so that a working consensus of the interaction can develop. The initiator broke through the barrier of civil inattention for some reason; the passive subject should be receptive to the initiator's explanation for altering the situation. In street life, a person must recognize the heterogeneity of viewpoints and practice a tolerance that may not be required in other more controllable situations, as in his or her home or place of work.

The Litnessing Interaction

In litnessing, Family members exploit these situational rules to break through and establish a transitory interaction in which a complex of information, both verbal and nonverbal, is communicated. This relationship is asymmetrical in that litnessing keeps information flowing largely in one direction: from the member to the prospect. Only certain types of information or cues are allowed to flow in the opposite direction. When the flow in the opposite direction becomes too great, implicit rules are invoked that change the character of the interaction or break it off.

Members initiate an interaction by behaving in a way that suggests that they are engaged in a commercial solicitation. Once they have broken through, they slowly reveal the true purpose of their intrusion: proselytization activity. The assumed "covertness" of the litnesser's approach is often cited by critics of the Family as a morally reprehensible "deception." This, however, is only a half-truth: almost every approach to the unacquainted must be covert for structural reasons for a short period (Goffman 1959:71): the target of the approach initially assumes that the initiator is appealing for free help. As the interaction proceeds, the purpose of the access attempt is gradually revealed.

The first step in initiating a litnessing encounter is to select a prospect. While COG members speak of relying on the "Spirit" to lead them to receptive people, two empirical considerations play a part. First, age and sex are relevant: female litnessers tend to approach more young males, while male litnessers interact with a higher number of female prospects. The sexual situation is often consciously exploited (cf. Lofland 1966:115). The second factor is whether a person is in an "open" position. In contrast to the majority of people in the public who are rushing to accomplish some task, the open person is typically looking around with no obvious purpose and is standing or strolling against the prevailing traffic flow. For example, the woman carrying three bags of groceries and walking briskly is an unlikely candidate for selection. On the other hand, the person who looks at the litnesser with interest is always approached. Generally, however, the person approached is one who, while not necessarily fascinated by the litnesser's activity, is not pursuing a goal with obvious ardor.

Once a candidate has been spied, the member must put him- or herself in a proper "opening" position. In order to break through the street-life rules against approaches to the unacquainted, the litnesser employs a series of techniques. First, on the public street, his or her presence in the middle flitting about from person to person with a lit bag gives the member the status of being "out of role" for persons on the street: the member is not just another person going about his or her business. Since the litnesser is apparently out of role the litnesser is granted the "license associated with anonymity" because it is assumed that the litnesser is not fully responsible for his or her conduct (Goffman 1963:130). In other words, the approached prospect is willing to stretch his or her definition of the situation in order to accommodate this strange approach.

Second, in a particular encounter, the litnesser offers the prospect a piece of literature, thus ostensibly establishing an instrumental rationale for the approach. One of several verbal overtures is employed: "Hi, have you seen this?" "Hello luv! Would you like one?"

COG litnesser with lit-bag on street in Nijmegen, the Netherlands, approaching prospect.

and "This is for you!" are examples. Each member generally finds one introductory phrase that suits him or her and uses it regularly, making necessary adjustments for the age and sex of the prospect. Coupled with this verbal approach, the litnesser also employs physical tactics. He or she may walk alongside the prospect and lean into the prospect's space; approach the prospect from the opposite direction and partially cut off the prospect's path; or remain in one spot and lean into the paths of prospects as they pass by. One rule common to all these moves is to simultaneously put the piece of literature into the prospect's body space and visual field and to establish eye contact with the prospect. Regardless of the method employed, however, members agree that a good litnesser is someone who moves around a lot and who makes a large number of approaches.

Through these moves, the litnesser implicitly suggests a sales relationship with the prospect, a not unexpected event on the public street. This is the instrumental rationale that justifies the breach of the normal requirement of civil inattention. On this ground, an initial "working consensus" between the litnesser and the prospect is formed in the prospect's mind. The litnesser is controlling the definition of the situation from the first. By the use of these opening maneuvers, the breakthrough is seen by the prospect as novel, yet not utterly inexcusable. The prospect does not know exactly how to act and strives to come to some definition of the situation.

Normally, the prospect attempts some type of acknowledgment of this overture. The type of acknowledgment determines whether the litnessing interaction continues. Many people attempt to act as if they never received the unavoidable message of the overture. They keep their gaze focused straight ahead, alter their course to avoid physical contact with the litnesser, and continue walking. Other people offer a more decorous negative acknowledgment. They keep walking, but turn their head and say, "No, thank you" or "Not today." A more ambiguous acknowledgment is offered by those who keep walking, but turn their heads and say, "Yes?" The interaction is then continued with the litnesser walking alongside the prospect. A few people indicate a willingness to enter the encounter by stopping and turning their bodies toward the litnesser. One of these last two types of acknowledgment is necessary for the litnessing interaction to continue.[6]

Once the prospect positively responds to the litnesser's overture, a more substantive interaction can begin (Goffman 1963:89). What becomes important is the mutual working consensus achieved and the prospect's attempt to define the situation or make sense of it. The litnesser seeks to feed the prospect information that will help him or her to construct that definition in a certain way. It is at this point that the kerygma is put forward, performed, or proclaimed.

The interaction phase of the litnessing encounter is initially a sales relationship. The litnesser is offering a product to the prospect, and the prospect is soon made aware that some monetary compensation is expected. The general rule is that before the encounter ends, the litnesser must ask for a donation: "Could you spare ten pence to help us with our work?" In most cases, the litnesser keeps a hand on the literature throughout the interaction. If at any point the prospect gives signs that he or she is about to depart, the litnesser must ask for a donation. Some prospects take the literature, say thank you, and walk off, as if the member were merely distributing handbills for

---

[6] The rate at which approached members of the public respond positively to litnessing overtures is low. I conducted no systematic survey of this phenomenon, but did occasionally keep a running count. On one occasion, during a ten-minute period, an experienced Family litnesser approached twenty-nine people. Of these, five, or 17.2 percent, accepted a piece of literature; two, or 6.8 percent, were engaged in at least a short witnessing interaction; and two, or 6.8 percent, gave a donation. The same day, in the same place, a catacomb or part-time member approached thirty-five people in a subsequent ten-minute period, of whom eight, or 22.8 percent, accepted the literature; none, or 0.0 percent, were witnessed to; and one, or 2.8 percent, contributed. Relatively less competent litnessers give away more literature.

a local merchant. When this occurs, the litnesser walks alongside the prospect and requests a donation. If the answer is no, most litnessers try to withdraw the literature, often with success. Very often, people hand over a few coins without question. Occasionally, a prospect offers a bill or large denomination coin and requests change. The litnesser typically states (often falsely) that he or she cannot provide change; asking for change in this situation is viewed by members as bad form, just as is taking change out of a collection plate or box in a religious service. Often enough, the prospect simply gives the litnesser the bill or coin.

Prospects may purchase the literature out of some general sense of duty to support charities; they may simply lack the motivation (see Beckford 1975:44) or competence to refuse such an aggressive approach; or they may believe that if he or she unilaterally and abruptly leaves the interaction it may express a lack of respect to another human being (Goffman 1963:116). Another motivation to give may simply be that by purchasing the literature, the bothersome encroachment is brought to a quick close.

When the prospect is interested less in the kerygma than in discovering why the litnesser is trying to sell the literature, a fairly routinized exchange takes place. In response to "What is it?" the litnesser explains that it is for youth work. If the prospect presses with the obvious question, a succession of answers is used: "We help young people with drug problems and loneliness"; "We are a group of young Christians"; "We live together and work full-time for the Lord"; and "We live in [name of town]." Members are wary of announcing their organizational affiliation at the outset of the interaction, but, if pressed, will respond, "We are the Children of God."

This evasiveness, while perhaps excessive, is often justified. Members not infrequently are subjected to abuse and threats due to their affiliation. For example, I was once accused of being a devil by an overwrought young man. In the middle of a shopping mall, he screamed at me for several minutes about my hating his people, and then he ran off. More pragmatically from the viewpoint of members, salvation of individuals and preaching the kerygma are more important than organizational affiliation. Moreover, premature revelation of affiliation may terminate an interaction with a very receptive prospect before it can catch hold (see Lofland 1966:79–80).

A small number of people do ask, "What is it?" in a way that demonstrates some interest. The novelty of the overture gives the approached person the right to inquire into the nature of the litnesser's intention. At this point, the sales relationship begins to change into a presentation of the kerygma. The commitment of the prospect to the interaction has grown deeper. This can be seen when the prospect changes his or her bodily attitude to be open to the litnesser. It is at this point that the kerygma is overtly presented. The kerygma, while achieving some verbal expression, is more thoroughly given in nonverbal expressions and in the comportment of the litnesser's body. The litnesser is to be "a sample, not a sermon." The emphasis in the kerygma on personal salvation through God's love is presented by members, not through words, but through expressions of love the litnesser gives off to the prospect: the litnesser is the medium for God's love.

Structurally, there is an attempt to establish a quasi-gemeinschaft relation (Goffman 1959:58) between the litnesser and the prospect in the litnessing interaction. This new relation is a shift from the *zweckrational* orientation of the initial sales relation to an affectual orientation (Weber 1947:115). The litnesser stresses those things he or she has in common with the prospect. Dwelling on differences only prevents a working consensus from developing. This, of course, involves the member's using different approaches with different types of prospects; young dropouts from society are receptive to some ideas to which older, more established people might object. By altering the approach to fit the prospect, the quasi-gemeinschaft relation has more chance to develop. The litnesser's interest in the prospect is emphasized by his or her responding to questions with great personal concern for the individual and listening to personal questions and problems.

A number of nonverbal techniques are used to establish this friendly relationship. The litnesser tries to be spontaneous (Goffman 1959:58) by appearing informal. His or her body movement seems unrestricted while moving around during the interaction. A smile is always on the litnesser's face, and he or she is quick to laugh. The tone of the voice is always warm and affectionate. Closely related to this is the presentation of "happiness." Along with the verbal professions of joy, nonverbal signals are given off. The prospect is presented with a clean and radiant face with lively eyes and hears a voice that is bright and cheerful. The litnesser faces the prospect and focuses all his or her body attention on the prospect. The interpersonal space is closed to the optimal distance, close but not too confining, to demonstrate the litnesser's total commitment to the interaction.

A major nonverbal tactic is the use of the eyes (see Goffman 1963:93). Members state that the love of God expressed in the kerygma is transmitted through the member's eyes to the prospect. Members establish and maintain almost constant eye contact with prospects, closing out most other stimuli from the interactional space between them. While the gemeinschaft-type relation is being established on the nonverbal level, the litnesser begins to witness directly to the prospect (see Chapter 6). The important point here is that verbal interactions are always reinforced by nonverbal expressions. In this way, the litnesser establishes the asymmetric relation of the interaction, and a full witnessing interaction can occur.

The intensity experienced by outsiders in encountering COG members on the street, often attributed to the "zombie-like," "hypnotized," or "drugged" nature of members, is a product of the verbal-nonverbal technique, and of litnessing and witnessing interactions in general. Few outsiders see the broad range of comportment of Family members in everyday life. Members are usually observed in the highly structured context of litnessing and witnessing, and thus outsiders only see the intensive interactive posture Family members employ during these activities. Far too often, members' postures in this specialized context are taken to be their normal comportment, an assumption which must then be explained by some brainwashing theory. In actual fact, the posture is an artifact of the litnessing or witnessing interaction that is situationally specific and quite temporary.

The use of nonverbal expression is also stressed to help members bridge language gaps; while COG literature is always distributed in the prospect's language, the group's rapid geographical expansion often leaves members litnessing in situations in which they themselves do not speak the language. Nonetheless, members arriving in an unfamiliar language-area jump right into litnessing after learning just two or three phrases. Of course, the possibility of a subsequent, significant witnessing interaction is reduced, but the proclamatory as well as the financial functions of litnessing are not unduly impaired in such situations.

Typification: Categorizing Prospects

All through the litnessing interaction, the litnesser attempts to typify or categorize the prospect (Schutz 1972:186–94) according to one of four types. The process is based on the prospect's reaction to the litnesser's initial approach. All people by definition fall into one of these categories because they are "others," not members of the Family. The categories used on the street, while sometimes mentioned in the formal ideology, are not explicitly presented as a formal classificatory set. They are part of members' practical ideology developed both from the formal ideology and from daily practice and use.

Through these typifications, the litnesser differentiates types within the "they" category and determines how to proceed (or to rationalize an unsuccessful litnessing interaction after the fact: "Oh, he was a goat [unreceptive] anyway!"). Dealing with the prospect by means of specific responses prescribed by the typification allows the litnesser to maintain control over the interaction. He or she controls the flow of information in order to achieve the goals of presenting the kerygma, collecting funds, and initiating potential witnessing interactions.

"Goats" are those who reject the message outright. This includes many different responses. The person who walks by pretending not to notice the approach, the person who responds with "No, thank you," and the person who reacts with a great deal of verbal violence could all be goats. "Sheep" are the opposite. By signs of interest, they show themselves to be receptive to the kerygma. Such signs can be overt interest expressed by questions and discussion of personal problems. A sheep can also be discovered by "discernment": a Pentecostal spiritual gift, believed to be possessed by members, that entails the ability to discover the true nature of someone's spirit (cf. Lofland 1966:97, 118). The practice of discernment relies on both verbal and nonverbal cues given off by the prospect. A person placing him- or herself in an open position to the litnesser is usually typified as a sheep. However, even when a person is hostile to the kerygma, members might claim that he or she is actually a sheep: "sheep often wear goat's clothing."

Two other less frequently occurring typifications are "devoids" and "Romans." Devoids want simply to talk with someone or they have their own ideology to present. Of the latter type are members of the National Front and Jehovah's Witnesses frequently encountered on British streets. Romans include police and other officials who control public areas. These people are presumed to be persecutors by the nature of their status in the System. After some interaction, however, the presumption can be rebutted and certain police officers can show themselves to be sheep.[7]

For each of these types, there is a specific set of responses that the litnesser employs to handle the encounter. While the prospect is groping for some definition of the emerging interaction, the litnesser

[7] Members occasionally encounter persons who state that they have had a salvation experience similar to that COG members are trying to elicit. Typification becomes a problem. The prospect may be placed in either the sheep or the goat category. If they appear receptive to the more complete COG message, they are viewed as being sheepy; if they do not want to hear more and are satisfied with their current religious state, they are goats.

uses the responses of the prospect to define the interaction quickly and to plan his or her action. With goats, members generally terminate the interaction as quickly as possible; a litnesser is not to argue, but to move on to others who are more open to the message. Devoids are considered to be wastes of the litnesser's time; a member tries to break off an interaction with a devoid, but this is often difficult because this type of person frequently ignores commonly accepted "breaking off" cues and continues to talk. In such a case, the litnesser's partner comes over, stands quietly for a moment or two, and then says, "We have to move on." Often, the cutoff must be quite sharp.

An encounter with a Roman is considered to be a "real test of faith." When a Roman is in the area, members quickly put all the literature back into their lit-bags and stop litnessing until the Roman leaves. Members take on the "normal appearance" for the area, pretending to pursue some task relevant to the context (Goffman 1971:238–333). Sometimes, however, the member is unable to assume the normal appearance quickly enough to avoid detection, or he or she is unaware of a plainclothes police officer in the area; if the member is approached, he or she is to listen, be obedient, and never argue; the member is to attempt to perform some of the same techniques used with sheep in order to "luv 'em up." If the official so requests, the member is to give his or her System name. After finishing an encounter with a Roman, litnessers generally move on to another location, pray, and begin to litness again.

If the prospect is a sheep, a member tries to move into a witnessing interaction. When such an engagement lasts for a while, the partner comes over, checks to be sure everything is all right, and prays silently while the litnesser begins to witness.

Accounting for Litnessing

At the end of the day, the litnessing partners return to the colony and account for their day's activities both statistically and narratively. Each member turns in a litnessing report[8] together with all funds col-

---

[8] The report form covers the following areas: "mass witness"—an estimate of the number of people who saw the member litnessing; "date"; "individual witness"—the number of people with whom the access interaction led to a witnessing interaction; "hours litnessed"; "hours of Word Time"—the time taken during the day to read the bible or Mo letters; "hours witnessed"; "salvations"—the number of people who by means of witnessing accepted Jesus; "Holy Spirits"—the number of people who were baptized in the Holy Spirit; "money spent"—money spent by the member during the

lected to the shepherd before doing anything else. If a member of the colony is on the road, he or she calls in the statistics everyday. Members routinely meet their quotas—100 pieces of lit and £10 per day in Bradford, for example—for both literature distributed and for funds collected. (In the Bradford colony, each member distributed from two hundred to three hundred pieces of lit and collected between £10 and £20 per day.[9]) Each month or biweekly, colony shepherds give a small award—usually money or a COG publication—to the best litnessers.[10]

At dinner, members are asked to give a testimony of their litnessing experiences from that day. The colony shepherd often goes around the table to every member, whose accounts generally describe particularly sheepy prospects the member encountered. However, testimonies also include descriptions of large donations or of encounters with persons who had prior contacts with the Family. Members describe any unpleasant incidents they had with Romans or goats, and the colony shepherd offers advice for the future. Members, when asked the general question whether they had a good day litnessing, almost uniformly answer yes; problems come out later in more specific discussion.

Limitations on Litnessing

Geographic expansion into third-world countries that do not have public spaces similar to those of western countries poses more serious problems. In some countries, public religious solicitation is legally banned. Members have either adopted less overt forms of litnessing (carrying literature printed on very small paper and covertly offering it to people to whom they believe God directs them, or en-

---

day out of the money collected; "funds"—money collected minus money spent; "place"—location of the day's litnessing; and "lit distributed"—the number of pieces of literature distributed during the day. Partners generally confer to determine the mass witness, hours litnessed, and hours of Word Time figures.

[9] My own litnessing statistics were less impressive. My lit distributed figure was generally good. I averaged distributions of 194 pieces of literature per day for the seven days I kept records. My funds figure, however, was poor: it ranged from a low of £1.36 to a high of £5.13 per day, sums far below the general colony quota of £10.00. For the most part, I was giving the literature away in order to appear active to other members.

[10] In the Bradford colony, for example, the top "lit shiner" for the two-week period—the member who distributed the most literature and collected the most money—distributed five thousand pieces of literature and received the COG publications *Free Sex* and *Letters for Leaders* as a reward. The member who had "saved the most souls" was awarded £5.00 for her efforts.

gaging in door-to-door litnessing) or have applied other access strategies. In Turkey and other Islamic countries, for example, members rely more heavily on Flirty Fishing and the mail ministry.

The centrality of litnessing to the Family, however, is demonstrated by the fact that the Family's expansion has tended to reach only those areas where some form of litnessing is possible. Many countries, while occasionally visited by a Family team or even pioneered by a selah colony, have remained virtually closed to Family members because more-or-less open litnessing is impossible. Litnessing thrives where commercial and ideological traffic, legally at least, can flow freely. Away from Western street life, its fate is less promising.

SIX

WITNESSING: TECHNIQUES FOR CONVERSION

ONCE A prospect has been engaged through an access strategy such as litnessing, the member often attempts to convert the prospect. In sociological studies of religious behavior, conversion is frequently the paramount problem. To the outsider or observer, the question "why would anyone do such a thing?" immediately presents itself, particularly in the study of sects. However, for understanding the believer's everyday life, far more salient from this perspective is the activity that is the obverse of the conversion event: witnessing, or the role played by the committed believer in trying to convert others. While conversion usually occurs only once in a member's life, witnessing is a recurrent experience for the believer. Although the characteristics of the prospects do have some effect on the activity of witnessing, it is a mode of interaction that is applicable to any possible convert.

In addition to being prescribed by the formal ideology, witnessing is a frequent topic of conversation within the colony. Numerous normative references are made to "fishing for men," "winning souls," "spreading God's love," and "bringing in the harvest." In conversation, members constantly discuss techniques that they find effective in "reaching people." In actual practice, however, witnessing interactions occur with varying frequency for different members. A member may go through several days without witnessing, while during another period he or she may witness to five or six people daily. A member's witnessing frequency is closely related to the type of access strategy used: litnessing leads to fewer true witnessing interactions than does Flirty Fishing or café singing.

Witnessing is a specific way of interacting by which members attempt to alter the religious orientations of people outside the group by implementing a set of socially provided techniques. Despite situational particularities, all witnessing interactions have similar formal properties. Competent witnessers are able to use and manipulate the societywide rules of everyday conversations to further COG ideological ends. Witnessing, however, is not a form of ritual action or routinized proselytization in which all steps are prescribed and followed inflexibly regardless of the context (cf. Beckford 1975:89; O'Toole 1975:175–78). Although in COG history and in certain deviant forms today witnessing has approached this, it normally is quite responsive to the particular circumstances of the prospect. But, unlike an ordinary conversation between acquaintances, the witnessing member carefully structures the possible directions the conversation can take in a characteristic way through a selective feedback mechanism (Schegloff and Sacks 1973:324). The witnessing interaction will terminate or deviate unless the witnesser is able to alter the prospect's responses in a particular fashion.

As with litnessing, the specific structure of the witnessing interaction is not dictated or described in the formal ideology or expressly taught to neophytes.[1] In-group conversations about witnessing are no more explicit. Members speak of "being in the Spirit" or of "being in the vision" when witnessing. This state of being is believed to guarantee that the witnesser will be both competent and effective. Members learn how to witness by accompanying more experienced witnessers during actual interactions and by attempting to witness themselves.

The Kerygma: The Content of Witnessing

In describing witnessing interactions, members constantly speak of "giving them [the prospect] the Message" or "hitting them with the Word." By this, members mean passing onto the prospect the possibility of salvation through the love of Jesus. Beyond this, however, members are rarely more explicit in describing the witnessing kerygma. Part of the reason for this is that members adjust the content of the witnessing interaction in reaction to the responses of the prospect. Unlike litnessing, in which the kerygma is fairly constant, witnessing involves more flexibility in selecting elements of the formal ideology to present to prospects. During the period I observed the Family, the kerygma rarely included criticisms of Western society and references to COG millennial doctrines as it had in earlier periods.

---

[1] Several written expositions on "how-to" witness contained in the formal ideology include only general guidelines or normative suggestions (344; Witnessing; *Witnessing Tips*). Specific isolated suggestions, such as "you have to hit them with it," "don't be afraid to talk about Jesus," "those closest to Salvation often rebel," "give the Glory to God," or "love them up" serve as folk-recipes to be called upon at particular points of the interaction, but they do not provide details of the process. They are like the manager's admonition to the pitcher to " 'throw strikes and keep 'em off the bases' " (Fish 1987:1773).

Instead, the witnessing kerygma consistently contained two core concepts: the love of Jesus for the prospect and the possibility of personal salvation through Him. Although other ideological elements are used, the kerygma in witnessing centers around these two concepts, which members refer to as the "basics" or the "milk" of the ideology.

Behaviorally, some of the same techniques employed in the litnessing interaction—behavioral posturing and signals—are used to "get the message across" in the witnessing interaction as well. The member attempts to create some sort of interpersonal relationship, no matter how new and short, with the prospect. Through behavioral signals, the member demonstrates "love" for the prospect and attempts to make him or her both comfortable and attracted to the member. Family members speak of "becoming one": adjusting the member's behavior in order to gain the trust of the prospect. The kerygma's mode of presentation is constantly modified to be more presentable to the prospect.

Situations for Witnessing

Witnessing, in theory and in the formal ideology, is possible anyplace, anytime; in practice, however, members witness only in certain situations. Members tend to witness only when they are in a one-on-one situation with a nonbeliever with whom they have been brought into contact by one of the Family's access strategies. Thus, if litnessing is the access strategy, its accompanying witnessing interaction will occur on the public street. If café singing is the access strategy, witnessing will occur after the singers have finished. Regardless of the particular access strategy, the key feature is the initiation of an interaction that can be converted into a witnessing opportunity.

There are occasions when witnessing occurs independently of access strategies. If the prospect is an acquaintance who is visiting a member, the member may try to witness. When traveling, members may witness to fellow passengers; persons picking up hitchhiking members are particularly subject to witnessing. Relaxed rules of accessibility operate between acquaintances and between fellow travelers. The extent to which witnessing occurs outside the access strategies also depends largely upon the individual member's commitment and desire to proselytize. When, however, a member is engaged in a business or instrumental interaction, witnessing usually does not occur. Thus, bus conductors are allowed to sell tickets to

members without becoming witnessing targets. As soon as the interaction moves away from the actual instrumental transaction, however, a witnessing interaction is a possibility. For example, the con-
ductor could say, "A miserable day, isn't it?" or "Where are you off
to today?" Such expressions act to broaden the interaction and raise
the possibility of a witnessing attempt.

The Structure of the Witnessing Interaction

Members carry into witnessing interactions two distinct sets of assumptions. The first includes those pertinent to general conversation
in modern society. COG witnessers presume that their prospects are
competent "conversers." In particular, this means that the prospect
is able to exchange standpoints with the witnesser, and he or she
comprehends objects of the world in the same way as the first
speaker (Schutz 1953:8); it is also assumed that the prospect is capable of following general conversational rules (Cicourel 1973:40), and
that speakers will not have to articulate all the possible meanings of
their words and references (Cicourel 1973:35).

Along with these general or commonsense conversational assumptions, Family members also make several assumptions specific to the
Family witnessing interaction. The first assumption is that all people
who are "unsaved" are lacking something in their lives that can only
be supplied by the salvation experience. A corollary to this is that
some people try to deny the fact by deceiving themselves into believing that they lack nothing and are happy. The first assumption is
usually expressed by COG members with respect to specific situations or people. One member referring to a male nurse he had just
met on the street stated that, "He likes the Family, he is really searching." Another member, in trying to witness to me, said, "you must
be very lonely!" Finally, near the end of a night of witnessing and
singing at a café, a COG leader pointed out a young couple, with two
small children, drunkenly hugging each other in the corner. He said
that he "could really feel the love between them, but that was all they
had." "Really searching" is the most frequent expression used to
summarize this assumed condition of all human beings.

Members in witnessing try to identify "facts" to prove this basic
interpretation in individual situations. In cases in which such facts
are not readily apparent, the corollary permits the interpretation to
remain unchallenged. Even in those rare situations in which prospects claim to be completely happy, the first assumption remains true
for members. In the following, a member reports a meeting she had

with the guitarist playing in a club in which the colony had been Flirty Fishing:

> I ran into him at the Nijmegen festival. He was busking on the street. He said he lost his job at the Kiss [a local nightclub] because he was sick and didn't show up on time. He told me that he had been married, but was now divorced. He said he was very happy now he is free. His story rang hollow.

The member attempts to support her presupposition about the prospect's condition by referring to his divorce to indicate "Well, he says one thing, but we know better." She relies on the commonsense idea, not particular to Family members, that the state of being divorced is not compatible with the state of being happy.

The second assumption is that the religious vocabulary used in witnessing, given proper explanation, is apodictically clear and personally significant to all people. Moreover, this presupposition posits that the existence and nature of "God," "Jesus," "sin," "hell," "love," and concepts expressed by other general religious terms are transparent and important to prospects. The witnesser will use a term and if required will explain it, but he or she will expect the prospect to grasp it immediately. For example, the term "sin" was explained to a prospect as follows: "you know, when you do something wrong?" Although this formulation of "sin" is considered sufficient for the purposes of the witnessing interaction, it nonetheless relies on an implicit conception of wrongdoing as an offense against some distinct moral-religious authority.[2]

These assumptions are consistent with the theory of conversion held by COG members. If a member is asked why a particular person "got saved," the standard answer is "he finally realized he needed the Lord." Members of the Family typically adhere to a type of deprivation theory: people convert because they suffer from some deprivation. According to members, people who are near the "breaking point" are those most likely to be affected by witnessing. Throughout COG history, witnessing has been practiced primarily on those pros-

---

[2] If this transparency does not exist for a particular subject, the subject is unlikely to be a successful witnessing subject. A nonreligious person or one from another culture is unable to satisfactorily, for witnessing purposes, relate to this concept. My impressionistic conclusions about those most likely to join the Family or at least likely to experience conversion from COG witnessing efforts is that they must have at least some undefined agnostic belief in the reality of a divine being (cf. Lofland & Stark 1965; Stark & Bainbridge 1980). Those who are effective atheists—those with no concern for divine realms—are unlikely to be affected by witnessing. Bluntly, such talk is, for them, senseless.

pects whom the COG feels to be deprived either spiritually or materially. In the earlier periods, the dropouts from society were specific targets of COG witnessing. Today, it is the lonely young professionals, the frequenters of nightclubs and bars. The corollary to the first presupposition adds a notion of relative deprivation to the COG theory of deprivation (Aberle 1972:528; Merton 1938): those who are more aware of their lack are easier to convert than those who deny their deprivation.

The parallel between these ethnotheories and the sociological theory of relative deprivation is obvious. Sociologists' explanations of conversion seem to repeat believers' accounts. The fact that sociologists rely on descriptions given by believers of their previous condition at least calls into question assertions of "real" relative deprivation existing among preconverts. Sociological theories of relative deprivation may simply be reformulations of ethnotheories of relative deprivation. Two possible alternative interpretations may be made of this correspondence.

The more radical interpretation states that sociological theories of relative deprivation, with their reliance on postconversion accounts of "what happened to me," merely repeat the stereotyped biography revisions of the believer describing him- or herself as "the type of person who would typically have that experience" (Taylor 1976:18). COG members' testimonies—accounts of conversion—all have the stereotyped form of "I was unhappy/dissatisfied before, even if I didn't realize it then." This interpretation makes the phenomenon of relative deprivation the product of the postconversion reconstruction of biography. Believers do this in order to be able to present themselves as a "converted" person (Blum and McHugh 1971:106). To the extent a sociological theory relies on these "facts," its validity is suspect (cf. Kituse and Cicourel 1963; Cicourel 1964).

A second interpretation, and one relevant to this chapter, would be to see relative deprivation as an artifact of the witnessing situation. Witnessing is the attempt by the witnesser to make the prospect aware of an important deprivation he is presupposed to have. A prospect's sense of being relatively deprived would then be an intentional result or product of the witnessing interaction. It could be based on what a sociologist might call a "real" deprivation, that is, one actually preexisting the conversion experience, or it could be a creation of the witnessing interaction itself (cf. Beckford 1975:157). The important point here is that some feature of the preconvert's life must be transformed and seen as a "relative deprivation" via the use of the witnessing procedures. As my analysis suggests, biography revision would then be an integral part of the witnessing-conversion process itself.

Initiating the Witnessing Interaction

In the witnessing interaction, the COG member attempts to create a sense of relative deprivation in the prospect in order to resolve it in an ideologically acceptable fashion. Once the prospect has been attracted by an access strategy and has begun some form of interaction with a member, the witnesser's goal is to establish a rapport with him or her. In most Family witnessing situations, the witnesser's intentions are usually unclear to the prospect. The prospect treats the encounter as similar to other encounters with strangers in similar contexts, such as on public streets, in cafés, bars, and so forth. The prospect assumes that the witnesser is an individual who is interested in conversation for its intrinsic merit—stimulation, information, or passing time. The witnesser tries to establish a working consensus (Goffman 1959:231) with the prospect that corresponds to this initial definition of the situation.

In order to establish this rapport, the witnesser starts a discussion on a topic that he or she thinks will interest the prospect (cf. Beckford 1975:162). Sometimes, the member uses an aspect of the access strategy to initiate the conversation. For example, if the access strategy is café singing, the witnesser often asks, "Did you like the music?" In other cases, the opening gambit is based on "normal" topics such as the prospect's job, recent news items, or current social problems.

This topic, however, is chosen so that it will be amenable to later ideological development. Certain topics are better in this regard than others. Preferred topics include those that get the prospect talking about him- or herself such as job, personal health, or family background. Likewise, topics that deal with matters of special concern to the Family are auspicious. Some of these are the oil crisis, the Arab-Israeli conflict, or the declining American economy. Of course, topics dealing with subjects on which the formal ideology dwells are easier than those not mentioned in the formal ideology, but this is not a necessary trait of opening gambits.

More important, however, than the content of the initial topic is the witnesser's assertion of dominance in the interaction. By manipulating basic conversational rules operative in all interactions within European-type cultures, the witnesser can control the content of the interaction. First, the witnesser controls the "organization of topic talk" (Schegloff and Sacks 1973:300–303): the rules and procedures by which conversants agree upon the topic to be discussed and how to move from one topic to another. A first topic is given a special status in a conversation by providing the participants with "the reason for" the conversation. It also gives the initiator the right to have that topic discussed to his or her satisfaction before moving onto another topic. Second, the COG witnesser exploits the rules for turn taking in conversations. "A person who has asked a question . . . has 'a reserved right to talk again,' . . . [a]nd, in using the reserved right he can ask a question" (Sacks 1972:343). By asking another question, the initiator can dominate the flow of conversation indefinitely.

This assertion of dominance is illustrated in the following short witnessing interaction reconstructed from field notes:

> [We were hitchhiking and received a ride from a young man. I sat in the backseat while my partner sat in the front.]
>
> WITNESSER: Hi, have a good day?
>
> PROSPECT: Oh, I suppose so.
>
> WITNESSER: What do you do?
>
> PROSPECT: I work in a bank. In the loan department.
>
> WITNESSER: Are you happy with your job?
>
> PROSPECT: I guess so. It depends, you know, from day to day.
>
> WITNESSER: Are you happy, you know, in general?
>
> PROSPECT: Sometimes, yeah, sometimes, no. You can't be happy all the time. You just gotta roll with the punches sometimes.
>
> WITNESSER: Do you believe in God?
>
> PROSPECT: [startled, looks in rearview mirror at me; I shrug] Well not in, you know, the traditional sense . . . [the prospect then gave a long explanation of his agnostic ideas].
>
> WITNESSER: Would you like to ask Jesus into your heart?

Here, the member opens the interaction with questions about the prospect's well-being and follows each answer with another question, thus enabling her to dictate the flow of the interaction. Her first question, inquiring into his well-being, sets the tenor for the interaction. The topic allows her to delve deeper and deeper into his personal status: his job, his job satisfaction, and his happiness in general. The next three questions follow from the first, and the prospect answers accordingly. At the fifth question, the prospect balks for a minute because of the obvious change, in his view, in the topic. But, then he decides to answer; she did have the right to ask a question even if it was a non sequitur.

From the opening gambit, the conversation continues along everyday lines about the chosen topic. The witnesser allows the working consensus reached earlier to continue in operation and within that

consensus steers the conversation in a direction that causes the prospect to reveal him- or herself (Turner 1970:182). The member asks
questions about the prospect's job, his or her views on current
events, tastes in music, and so on. In return, the witnesser might
mention that he or she is a youth worker or lives with a group of
young people. The informational flow is asymmetrical (Goffman
1963:15); the witnesser does not want to "blow his (or her) cover" too
soon, as a point-blank admission of being a Christian, or worse a
Child of God, might irreparably harm the witnessing interaction.

From this asymmetrical information flow, the COG witnesser, as is
done in litnessing, attempts to form a moral picture of the prospect,
which is used to adjust the witnessing approach. Although this activity goes on through the entire interaction, it is most prevalent during
the conversation after the opening gambit has succeeded. The witnesser looks for behavioral and verbal indicators to determine the
prospect's moral type or "personal ideal type" (Schutz 1972:188) and
to predict what the prospect intends (Goffman 1963:16). The set of
types, which varies from that used in litnessing, consists of two continua: "sheepy" to "goat," and "radical" to "churchy." The first pair
refers to the prospect's openness to the salvation message: "sheepy"
types are open to and ready to accept the kerygma; "goat" types are
not willing or ready to accept the message. The second continuum
refers to the prospect's orientation to "conventional" society, or the
System: the "radical" type is already disenchanted with and rebelling
against the System; the "churchy" type accepts conventional values;
and the "churchiest" type is fully committed to one of the conventional religious bodies.

Witnessers try to place prospects on each of these continua
through specific behavioral and verbal indicators (cf. Bittner 1967; Piliavin and Briar 1969). One is the simple willingness of the prospect
to talk: a prospect who becomes actively involved in a serious discussion with the member on any topic is considered a sheepy person.
Eye contact and facial expressions are also a factor: a sheepy person
looks directly into the witnesser's eyes and does not try to avoid such
eye contact, and the frequency of smiles is a gauge of the prospect's
openness to the message. Another test is political orientation: if the
prospect seems to hold or to agree with left-wing political ideas, it is
an indication that he or she is less committed to the System, that is,
less churchy, and therefore more likely to be sheepy. Finally, the
prospect's appearance—in both dress and hygiene—may also indicate his or her commitment to the System.[3]

---

[3] Astrology is often verbalized as an indicator by members themselves. They assert

From the indicators, witnessers arrive at moral evaluations of the prospects that are verbalized through standard expressions: the prospect may be described, for example, as "very sheepy," "sheepy," a "sheep in goat's clothing," a "goat," a "goat in sheep's clothing," and as "radical" or "churchy." Each moral or essential type implies certain guidelines for the rest of the interaction. As examples, I list below several of the members' standard typifications of prospects and then outline the significance of each for the witnessing interaction:

very sheepy:
Press him or her quickly with the kerygma and try to get a salvation decision.

sheepy:
Take it slow: use more nonverbal, supportive measures demonstrating your love for the prospect.

a sheep in goat's clothing:
Use nonverbal demonstrations of love and stay away from verbal expressions of the kerygma.

a goat:
Get out of the interaction—you are wasting God's time. The prospect has heard the message and rejected it.

a goat in sheep's clothing [an enemy or person antagonistic to the Family]:
Avoid any conflict with him or her; get out of the interaction immediately.

radical:
Use the more "heavy" doctrines in witnessing to this prospect. Speak of the anti-System, millennial, and total discipleship beliefs of the Family. Press him or her for a decision to drop out of society.

churchy:
Go slow. Use only the message of personal salvation and nonverbal expressions of love.

Eliciting the Need for Salvation

The preliminary work of finding a hold and moral evaluation orients the witnesser to the prospect so that the witnesser can attempt to

---

that if the witnesser finds out the subject's sun sign, he or she is better able to witness to that person's needs. Very often the question "What is your sign?" occurs in the opening conversation. In my research, however, I never observed astrological information being used in the witnessing interaction itself. Witnessers ask the question and then let it drop.

make the prospect aware of the need for salvation. First, the witnesser attempts to show the prospect a lot of love and concern and to establish some personal relationship based on these affective demonstrations; second, he or she attempts to find a particular shortcoming, dissatisfaction, or lack in the prospect's life and to lead him or her to see that it is a general lack—a lack the witnesser "knows" exists; and finally, the witnesser shows the prospect that this love and concern from the member is really a manifestation of God's love, which can fill the general lack. Members frequently recount these techniques in everyday conversation in general terms: "Show him what he really needs"; "Point out the real reason for his problems"; "Get him to love you and then show him it's only possible because of Jesus."

From the beginning of the interaction, the witnesser establishes the prospect's trust in and even love for the witnesser. Affective ties have often been pointed to as important features of commitment processes (Gerlach and Hine 1970:113–15; Lofland 1977:811–13; Lofland & Stark 1973:41–42). COG witnessing exploits this fact by actively trying to create an affective relation between the witnesser and the prospect. Using various behavioral techniques, members try to establish some ties between participants in the witnessing interaction that encourage the prospect to put his or her trust in the witnesser. Affective ties are not some mysterious causal factor that "explains" conversion; rather, they are an intended artifact of the proselytization activity itself.[4]

The standard technique by which members establish this type of environment is attentional concentration. Many outsiders note the overbearing nature of witnessing encounters with COG members: because of this attentional concentration, the interaction appears to be quite intense. The prospect becomes the center of the witnesser's attention; a closed interactional space envelops the participants. Distractions are purposely ignored by the witnesser in order not to break the contact he or she is trying to establish.[5] Interpersonal distance is

---

[4] The most extreme technique for achieving this rapport with the subject, of course, is the use of physical closeness in Flirty Fishing. Berg states that members using this technique must often make the subject fall in love with the member before that love can be transferred to the group or to Jesus (555:150). In most cases of Flirty Fishing, the love shown the subject is a performance in the artificial sense of the word: the love performed by the member does not necessarily reflect the member's independent feelings about the subject. In some cases, however, the performance becomes authentic: the member conducting Flirty Fishing falls in love with the subject. In such instances, Berg believes that God is calling on the member to marry the subject and bring them into the Family (552:98).

[5] Other members respect the closedness of this space: they refrain from intruding, but if they must say something to the witnesser, they politely interrupt and say,

closed to the point where the witnesser feels him- or herself to be in control of the prospect's attentional field. The witnesser maintains steady eye contact to promote the close relationship and to demonstrate the witnesser's great personal concern for the prospect. Another technique is to listen attentively: the witnesser's postural alignment and facial expressions assure the prospect that the witnesser is listening and is interested in what the prospect is saying. A final aspect of the technique is the attempt by the witnesser to "become one" with the prospect by adopting his or her interests and cultural style as much as possible. The witnesser acts enthusiastic about topics that interest the prospect and adopts speech and behavioral styles that he or she believes will make the prospect comfortable.

If the witnesser succeeds, the prospect may often mention the "friendliness," "love," or "happiness" of the witnesser. Such a statement tells the witnesser that he or she is on the right track and can begin a presentation of the kerygma. The witnesser immediately attributes the noted quality to the love of Jesus, explaining that Jesus' love is more permanent than any human love and that it is the answer to the prospect's own loneliness. Although responses such as, "If God makes you like this, then I'll believe," are sometimes given, prospects in most cases are not likely to be so easily persuaded.

The witnesser must cause the prospect to become conscious of a lack or deprivation in his or her life. In cases in which the prospect does not mention a topic immediately amenable to developing the idea of a deprivation or lack, the witnesser tries to direct the conversation in this direction. As long as the witnesser remains dominant in the conversation, he or she is able to bring in an ideologically relevant aspect of the topic being discussed by fitting the aspect into the prospect's prior utterance (Schegloff and Sacks 1973:301). To do this, the witnesser tries to direct the conversation to a deeper or more personal level. The member asks questions that are designed to reveal the prospect's personal opinion or relation to the chosen topic. In addition, the witnesser tries to show the futility inherent in the prospect's condition or in the object of the chosen topic. The overall pattern is to make whatever is being discussed seem to have fatal internal flaws that normal action is insufficient to correct. The following examples show how COG witnessers try to elicit a sense of lack or deprivation in a prospect:

World Problems. The prospect was discussing the world's problems

---

"Could I have a word with you?" This cues the witnesser either to excuse him- or herself physically from the interactional space, or to prepare to receive a whispered message.

and sharing his belief that he must have a personal commitment to help solve some of them. He expressed the view that, with science and enough effort, man could overcome these problems:

WITNESSER: Then you haven't realized yet how bad you are?

PROSPECT: [He tries to shift the discussion back to world problems.] But you're not doing anything to solve these problems.

WITNESSER: But it must be by a greater power than we—if everyone were like me, the world would be in a terrible mess. To give the love of God will solve the problems—it's a desperate problem right now to get to the source of these problems. The turning point of my life was to realize that I was bad, not just the world: the world's greatest problem is selfishness.

PROSPECT: [He tries to say something, but is cut off.]

WITNESSER: People don't have the power . . . .

Here, the witnesser transforms a particular lack—various world problems—into a general lack—the prospect's "unsaved condition." He succeeds in getting the prospect to speak about a personal matter and then shows the futility in the prospect's present position: he will never succeed in his present course without the love of God to fill that void.

Loveless World. A witnesser met the prospect at a bar and began to converse with him about various topics. The witnesser eventually mentioned God:

[The prospect] said he did not believe in God.

She asked, "Why not?"

He replied, "Because if God existed, why does He let man do all this to himself" [referring to the loneliness of the people at the bar]?

She responded that God did it to provide man with a choice: to follow Him or to live in sin. It is up to you.

The prospect left and came back at the end of the night: You people have really changed my life and shown me the love I really need.

Once again, a specific lack—loneliness—is transformed into a general condition—the choice between God's love and sin.

Job. This incident occurred in a bar after several Family members finished singing to the crowd:

The prospect was asked if she liked the music.

She said she did.

She was asked if she would like to come and visit the colony again.

She said she would like to come by again.

She was asked how her photography was going.

It was fine, she replied, and asked if the witnesser worked.
The witnesser explained that the Family passed out literature and lived
by donations. He asserted that "God takes care of us." He said that it
was the best job he had ever had.

In this example, the witnesser is eliciting personal information.
When the prospect answers the question about her job with a question about what the witnesser does, she has reversed the information flow. The onus is now on the original questioner to answer a question. But it is a situation that he has set up for himself: in our culture, such a question is properly answered by a statement and a reciprocating question. The witnesser uses this reversal to make assertions about his life-style and beliefs. He relinquishes the dominating position in conversation in order to make a presentation of the kerygma.

Evidencing the Lack

Having fitted a presentation of the kerygma into the witnessing interaction and suggested a general lack does not necessarily mean that the witnesser has elicited in the prospect a consciousness of a particular lack being merely a manifestation of the general lack of salvation. The witnesser must still try to prove the veracity of the assertions he or she has made. "Evidencing" is the technique by which members demonstrate the reasonableness and accuracy of their assertions to the prospect (Garfinkel 1967:1–34). All these efforts rely on the (second) presupposition that the witnessing vocabulary is both clear and personally significant to the prospect.

One method frequently used in evidencing is personal testimony. Personal testimonies are multifunctional in everyday life for Family members, but in witnessing interactions they perform the role of "I-was-once-like-you" stories (Lofland 1966:185). Although the witnesser's testimony is tailored to emphasize relevant aspects of the prospect's situation, the structure is always the same—the witnesser shows that he or she was at one time suffering, but that by accepting Jesus his or her life was changed:

> I was in the hippy set, but I never took drugs. Before joining the Family, I never had a girlfriend. I was trying to live a radical life-style in my own way. I was really looking. I used to talk all the time about scientists reporting the exhaustion of world resources, like the Club of Rome . . . . I liked the Family when I met them because they were young and active: it is no good just to believe. My parents would just pray and then hope their prayers would be answered. Now I know in faith that they will be

answered. The world is heading for disaster, but, thank God, I'm going to live with Jesus.

For the witnesser, such a testimony is reasonable evidence that his or her assertion that the prospect needs to be saved is true.

A second method is to quote directly from the bible. Members memorize verses in order to present them to prospects. Such recitations are considered to be proper evidence of the truth of kerygmatic assertions because it is presumed that prospects believe that the bible is a source of truth or at least that it has substantial weight. Probably the most popular and widely used verse in this procedure is John 3:16: "For God so loved the world, that he gave his only begotten Son, that whosoever believeth in him should not perish, but have everlasting life."

A third and more flexible evidencing method uses commonsensical and biblical assertions to demonstrate the truth of the kerygma. The witnesser calls upon the knowledge that any reasonable person would have to demonstrate the truth of his assertions. The following example occurred in a witnessing interaction in which the prospect was having difficulty in accepting the literalism of the biblical account of the creation. The interaction had started with the witnesser pointing out the futility of education, saying that it did not contain the answers the prospect was looking for. As often occurs, the witnesser

COG witnesser sharing Mo letter with prospects at rock festival outside Brussels.

invoked the COG ideas on the falsity of evolution to demonstrate this futility:

WITNESSER: [pointing to the first page of the book of Genesis] Either this page is true or the whole rest of this book is false. If the story is symbolic, why is it so specific in details?

PROSPECT: It could possibly mean six centuries [instead of six days].

WITNESSER: If God made all the grass in six million years and then made the sun in the next day, all the grass would have died. You're saying it's not true. But God said one day.

PROSPECT: But it's a man-made story.

WITNESSER: The principle is God-made.

PROSPECT: How about the half-life estimates of the world's age scientists have made?

WITNESSER: They are not true. They have made a lot of mistakes. God made a tree whole in one day, so you can't count the rings. God made the world already going, including uranium. Adam was probably about seventeen years old. The oldest historical discovery is only from Abraham's time. The bible is the best history book . . . .

In the above discourse, practical reasoning drawing on both biblical accounts and evidence from the modern world is used to prove assertions about evolution theory. An interesting assumption is included in the statement, "[e]ither this page is true or the whole rest of this book is false": if one aspect can be shown to be true, then other aspects of the Family's ideology must be true as well.

One basic problem with these evidencing techniques is that there is often a disjunction between the set of assumptions about the world that members carry into the witnessing interaction and those that the prospect brings. If the prospect is not familiar with or does not accept the significance of the religious vocabulary used by members, the evidencing techniques appear to him or her to be fraught with difficulties (Garfinkel 1964). In witnessing, members depend on a whole set of assumptions, or things taken for granted, that they presume that prospects can articulate for themselves if need be. Evidencing often flounders on this unfulfilled condition.

Salvation Point

In almost all witnessing interactions that reach the evidencing stage, the witnesser will come right out and suggest that the prospect pray and ask for Jesus to give him or her a salvation experience: "Would you like to ask Jesus into your heart?" Sometimes Revelation 3:30 is quoted to encourage the prospect to take the step: "Behold, I stand

COG litnesser reading bible with prospect outside Arnhem colony on a visitors day.

at the door and knock: if any man hear my voice and open the door, I will come in to him and sup with him and he with me." If the prospect consents, the witnesser holds the prospect's hand and closes his or her eyes. The witnesser begins to pray, asking the prospect to repeat the words.[6] The prospect's recital of the prayer marks a successful completion to the witnessing interaction.

Criteria of Success and Accounts

Within the Family, there are several criteria that members use to determine whether a particular witnessing interaction has been successful. The most obvious measure of success is, of course, whether the prospect prays to accept Jesus into his or her heart. But, since wit-

[6] The following is a prayer sample given in the formal ideology:

Dear Jesus, forgive me for all my sins. I believe You died for me, I believe You're the Son of God and I now ask You to come into my life. I open the door and invite You into my heart. Jesus, please come in and help me to confess You before others. Help me to love others and to tell them about You. Help me read Your Word and fill me with Your Spirit that I may understand as I read it, in Jesus's Name I ask. Amen.

I have heard simpler prayers such as "Dear Jesus, please come into my heart. Amen."

nessing very infrequently leads to the salvation experience, a more important criterion of success is whether the message is adequately presented to the prospect. If the interaction reaches the point at which the witnesser can present at least one aspect of the kerygma—even if it is his or her love for the prospect as a veiled expression of the love of God—then the witnessing interaction is not considered to be a failure. If, on the other hand, the interaction breaks off quickly, or if it breaks off with bad feelings on the prospect's part, it has failed. The witnesser must try harder next time.

Members have various linguistic ways of dealing with witnessing interactions that seem on the surface to be inconsequential in that they have little effect on the prospect. In cases in which the prospect politely refuses to pray for his or her salvation, members often later formulate the encounter in the following way: "He was really sheepy." This leaves the interaction formally open for further progress at some unspecified time. By the criterion of the adequate presentation of the kerygma, this linguistic technique converts the interaction into a successful one.

Members also deal with obvious failures in common ways. Prospects who quickly break off the interaction out of disinterest are typed as "goats" even though the witnesser may not have made that evaluation initially. In other situations, when the prospect becomes annoyed with the witnesser, a linguistic usage transforms the situation. The person, like others in similar situations, is simply "rebelling" and will soon get it out of his or her system.[7] Even in interactions which by their own criteria are failures, members try to keep the interaction open, at least formally.

Deviant Witnessing Forms

Deviant witnessing forms are those that do not actually attempt the ideological transformation described above, but are sometimes still

---

[7] The following is a discussion I had with a women to whom members had witnessed extensively about joining, but who had to that point resisted their prompting:

[Subject] came in [to the bar]. I asked her whether she liked the Family and would like to join: she got upset and said that's all anyone wanted to talk about. I said that that wasn't all I ever talked about; she said [a member] always talked about it, and [another member] a lot [too]. She said there are different types of people—she liked having her own room so she could have privacy at times. She said it was dishonest to make friends with people just to convince them of your way of thinking. I asked why, then, she was always where I was at [the bar where Family members witnessed]. She said she liked us and the music; she didn't want to talk about it.

I later told [the colony shepherd], and he said those closest often rebel like this.

referred to as witnessing by members. The most common form is "quickies," or statistical witnessing, in which no effort is made to draw the prospect to a realization of his or her personal lack. Quickies are interactions that are composed of a set of questions the witnesser runs through pro forma with no real attentiveness to the prospect's answers or particular needs. It is a routinized type of proselytization (O'Toole 1975), whose purpose is to pile up the number of "souls saved" in order to enhance the member's statistics. This form of witnessing is most commonly practiced with young children as prospects in the course of litnessing.

The following recounts one incident of this deviant form of witnessing:

> We were walking through the marketplace after having been litnessing in the shopping street that morning. The member saw three children standing on a guardrail by the side of the road. They were between seven and eight years old. The member ran up to them with a big smile and handed each a piece of mini-lit saying, "Have you seen this?" They all smiled, but said nothing. She asked, "Do you know who Jesus is?" They all nodded yes. She continued, "Would you like to pray to ask him into your hearts?" The children giggled and shifted around. "Okay?" She put out her hands and held theirs. "Close your eyes." They complied and she said a salvation prayer for them. When she finished, she opened her eyes and smiled. "There, you all have new lives." We left. She said to me: "They're really sweet—the young aren't really hardened yet."

Later in the day, the member gave a testimony to the other colony members about saving three souls in the marketplace. The significance of the interaction for the witnesser was the statistical fact that three more souls had been saved.

SEVEN

READING RELIGIOUS LITERATURE

RELIGIOUS literature plays an important role in the day-to-day activities of many religious groups. The written word, as the supposed holder of high and sacred truths, has a long history. The control of reading and writing by an elite priesthood is a significant feature of many religious systems. In other traditions, access to such texts has been democratized. Protestantism, in certain lines of its development, has emphasized the necessity of the individual believer referring to the sacred sources in order to understand the truth. In such traditions, the problem of apprehending the "truth" through reading becomes critical.

The importance of religious literature has not escaped the attention of most observers of these types of groups (e.g., Schneider and Dornbusch 1958). Yet, how religious literature actually is read is rarely examined (but see McHoul 1982; Heilman 1983). The distinction between the formal ideology and the practical ideology suggests the importance of reading. Usually, observers assume that the apprehension of the group's formal ideology as expressed in the religious literature by individual members is automatic and unproblematic. Reading religious literature, however, is not a simple matter of incorporating the formal ideology into a receptive or gullible mind. The transformation of the written ideology into a personal articulation of it, the member's practical ideology, is problematic (Fish 1980:184–85) and is an aspect of "socialization" and "ideology maintenance." Through the process of reading, the COG member "becomes" a competent Child of God. Instead of vague references to some connection between ideology and social structure or some unspecified notion of "socialization," this chapter examines the way COG members convert the formal ideology into their individual, practical ideology.

In this social process, COG members approach the religious texts with a specific orientation or stance. From this initial approach, they apply certain interpretive procedures to "grasp" or "make sense of" the written material. There exists among COG members common background assumptions and pragmatic techniques for reading their religious texts; that is, there are habitual and socially structured ways of reading. As with other COG practices, these ways of reading are implicit in that they are not consciously verbalized by members. Although there are in the formal ideology certain general explicit imperatives about reading, none tells the member *how* to read. Moreover, COG members rarely if ever describe or discuss the details of their reading practices. Therefore, I have extrapolated from verbal and other behavioral regularities I observed in instances of public reading activity.

The Salience of Reading

Reading is a pervasive activity in the daily routine of the COG member. In the formal ideology, Moses David continually stresses the need for the daily reading and rereading of the Mo letters and the bible (156A:16).[1] The average member spends at least two hours per day in Word time reading and rereading Mo letters or the bible, although this, of course, varies from person to person. In general, an entire letter is read in one sitting. In addition, members read at least a chapter or two a day from the bible. This reading activity does not include nongroup publications such as newspapers and news magazines, which are read only occasionally. Often, this lack of interest in outside sources is not a correlate of COG membership; rather, it is a continuation of premembership practices. Leaders and older members do read newspapers and newsmagazines (*Time* and *Newsweek*) more frequently to gain an overview on world affairs and, in particular, to see signs of the coming of the millennium.

A folk theory has grown up among Family members, according to which continuous reading is considered to be a necessary condition for success in other daily activities. Members consistently note that unless enough Word time is taken in the morning the day's litnessing will not go well. Unless fortified with the Word, they state, the Devil has an opening to attack the member. Any activity is subject to disruption unless sufficient time is spent "getting into the Word." This folk theory also provides a post hoc account for their failures. One member, for example, who had trouble reaching her litnessing quota the day before, was asked by the shepherd at breakfast how things

---

[1] He suggests that reading prevents organizational troubles (126:18–20); it provides answers to nearly every question (146:10); "[t]o ignore the Word of the Lord through His Prophet is to ignore the Voice of God Himself" (155:30); "Catch up on your Mo letters while you're at it, as you cannot keep on pouring out without also drinking in" (314C:56); and "you'll never have the spiritual strength and stamina nor the spirit that will even sustain your bodily strength and stamina to keep going to get out the Word— unless you yourself are drinking in the Word and being spiritually nourished and strengthened by it yourself first" (320:56).

had gone. She replied that she had had to take "a lot of Word time" while out litnessing; because she had made breakfast that morning, she was unable to "get enough Word time" before going out.

Group Reading: Contextual Characteristics

Reading in the Family occurs in one of three contexts. Members often read the texts privately, a practice more common among older members. Reading also occurs in small groups of two or three members. This is common for newer members and is often preferred over private reading. Finally, as noted earlier, the texts are read in larger groups such as colony devotions. In this form of reading, the colony shepherd guides the reading and provides much of the extratextual discourse and interpretation. It is in these situations that the neophyte acquires the competence to read the texts on his or her own. In the following analysis, I focus on reading taking place in the third context, largely because the techniques and assumptions applied in reading are more often verbalized and therefore observable.

Group readings usually take place in the sitting room of the colony. Members seat themselves in a circle on chairs or on the floor. Although the leader is part of the circle and does not dominate in a physical way, he must be easily visible to the other members. Each member also has visual access to the text that the leader has chosen. If a person does not have a copy of the particular text, someone shares with him or her. When the readings are taken from the bible, each member has a bible in his or her native language. Before starting, the leader checks to be sure that everyone can see a copy of the text.

Reading in this situation as well as in its more private forms has a consistent structure. A prayer is said before starting, in which God is asked to provide help in understanding what is about to be read or is thanked for Moses David who receives these messages and passes them on to the Family. After the prayer, the leader indicates a turn-taking procedure for the oral reading of the text. Generally, members read one or two paragraphs at a time. This pattern continues around the circle until the text is finished. At the completion of the reading another prayer occurs which generally thanks God for the message of the text and asks His help in enabling members to live up to its exhortations.[2]

[2] The following is a transcription of a closing prayer:

Thank you, Lord. Praise God. Thank you, Lord. [A period of glossolalia.] Thank

The actual reading of the text itself is accompanied by certain common paralexical and extratextual features. The paralexical features are the intonational contours and stress patterns given the oral reading. Although readers vary in the complexity of their patterns, most use an expressive intonational contour that includes a build up in intensity climaxing at the end of a phrase and followed by a stop. In the following example, I indicate with stress marks and contour lines how one member read this text:

> I BELIEVE WE SHOULD HAVE MAJOR TEAMS IN EVERY MAJOR CITY IN EVERY MAJOR COUNTRY, but let's not go running off half-cocked before God supplies the necessary personnel! Let's be sure the Lord has added to the Church enough to handle it, lest we be ashamed in finding ourselves unable to finish the job! (23:6)

This intonational pattern, sometimes coupled with a strong stress before a stop, gives oral reading a constant sing-song or "da-da, da-da" effect. As can be seen from the example, this common intonational and stress configuration applies regardless of the content or notational form of the written text, demonstrating that reading is affected by patterns not derivable from the text as well as by textually given patterns.[3]

This feature can be seen further in the case of extratextual expressions. Very often a stress at the end of a phrase or sentence is followed by several types of routine affirmation expressions from other participants in the group reading. Some of these expressions include: "Amen!" "Wow!" "Hallelujah!" "Praise the Lord!" "Thank you!" "Praise God!" and "Yeah!" The occurrence of a stressed word followed by a stop cues this type of expression. Not all members always utter these expressions, but at any such point a number of participants do. A second type of extratextual utterance that can be classed with the above affirmative expressions also occurs after a stress and stop. The leader, while taking his or her turn at reading, may ask a question that calls for an affirmation of a bit of the text just read. The

---

you, amen. Lord, thank you for this precious and beautiful dream. [The letter read reported a dream Moses David had experienced.] Thank you, Lord, for all the things you've given us through this dream and the things you've shown us, Lord. Thank you so much. Lord, bless—help us to follow this advice, Lord. Amen, Lord. We pray that you speak to us, Lord, if there is anything you want to say. . . .

[3] Common intonational patterns among glossolalic speakers within one group have been reported by observers (Goodman 1969:238; Samarin 1972).

other participants immediately answer with one of the routine expressions. For example[4] :

> Only Pioneers Climb Mountains—*people who want to do something that no one ever did before*—(B:5)
> You guys want to do that?
> [*others*] Yeah! Amen! Yup!

These routine types of exchanges (Goffman 1971:42–94) affirm the message of the text as well as the reading process itself and provide members with a sense of belonging to a cohesive, affective group. But they have a very loose relation, if any, to the content of the text itself. It is at these stops or the end of each chunk of text marked by these extratextual factors, however, that the most important processes occur. The stops provide the periods of silence (Merleau-Ponty 1964:42) within which the interpretive work takes place.

Presuppositions in Reading

As in other ideological activities, each COG member carries socially provided presuppositions into reading that determine his or her orientation toward the text (cf. Hawkes 1977:103). These assumptions do not predetermine the meaning of the text; rather, they point the reader in a particular interpretive direction by providing an undetermined "horizon" of meaning that the actual reading of the text fills out. In adequately socialized COG members, these presuppositions are fully operative in the reading of in-group texts. Neophytes pick them up through the practice of reading itself.

Among the presuppositions that orient a COG member toward a COG text is the assumption that all textual assertions are absolutely true and not open to challenge; all textual assertions are taken as statements of fact. This applies not only to obvious factual statements in the text, but also to most of the interpretive suggestions offered by Moses David. For example, he makes many unverifiable assertions about the motivations for people's actions that are presumed to be true.

A second premise, the inclusiveness of the truth of the texts, assumes that the COG texts include all the important truths known to humanity. The Mo letters and the bible are in no need of supplementation from any human source, and they contain all knowledge es-

---

[4] The italicized words denote the text being read. The extratextual comments appear in roman typeface.

sential for correct action in the world. Supplementation is only possible via a further revelation from God (through Moses David).

Moreover, for the COG member, the Mo letters and the bible contain simple and transparent truths that even a child can understand. In fact, the child is often in a better position to understand them because his or her mind has not been corrupted and clouded by secular education. According to this presupposition, the only possible impediment to understanding the texts is to be found in the reader's own mind, not in the texts themselves. Members often speak of the difficulties they experienced in first joining when they had to "get rid of a lot of old ideas." The term "brainwashing" is used by COG members to indicate what is needed: "Yes, we brainwash. We wash dirty minds!" The texts themselves, however, are transparent: the relation between the language written and the meaning or interpretation of the language is unproblematic.

The fourth presupposition asserts that the texts have clear, pragmatic value for the conduct of everyday life. Moses David writes a great deal on such topics as health care, food preparation, and sexual practices. His advice is considered to be the best possible on any particular problem.

Finally, the previous four presuppositions are legitimated by the "connecting presupposition," which asserts that both the Mo letters and the bible are the Word of God passed through nondistorting human vessels or communicators. The texts have a special status because they come from God. This premise underlies the first four: when a reader is asked why a certain passage in the text is true, one normal response[5] is that it is the "Word of God." Thus, for example, the belief in the absolute truth of the text is embedded in the connecting presupposition. The text is true because it is presupposed that Moses David has an open channel with God.

Interpretive Procedures in Reading

The above presuppositions provide the static background for the grasping of the text. While they merely define the boundaries within which the interpretation takes place, the interpretive procedures "fill out" the space within those boundaries with specific meanings (Schutz 1972:84). The procedures are methods of handling the text

---

[5] Another normal or expectable response is to appeal to the questioner's commonsense intuition. "It makes sense, doesn't it?" This response calls on the questioner to compare the text with his or her own practical experience.

that allow the reader to make sense of or to grasp the material. In contrast to the presuppositions, the interpretive procedures are readily observable. By examining the extratextual discourse surrounding the actual reading of the text in group reading, I identify five procedures and illustrate how they work. These procedures are part of the social competence of an adequately socialized COG member. New members learn how to read texts from hearing this type of extratextual discourse during group readings.

The discrete chunks into which the text is divided by the intonational and stress patterns provide the reader with a small bit independent from the rest of the text to interpret. The interpretive procedures are applied to these atomized chunks serially, often without reference to prior or future chunks. This may be due to the presupposition of the transparency of the truth of the text, which asserts the immediate apodicticity of the passage. Once a certain passage has been passed, a later revision of its meaning is not possible, because its total meaning is easily grasped on the first occasion of approaching it.[6] Although the interpretations often skipped over possibly problematic passages, no attempt was ever made to return to those passages.

Clarification

Clarification is simply the defining and explaining of terms in the text that are strange to some of the readers. This is an important feature of reading in colonies in which there is a mixture of different language speakers. The American idioms and expressions of the Mo letters often need explanation for non-Americans. The leader tries to explain the expression in English or in the reader's native language. For example:

> "Tenderly Gather Them In. Open the door for the children, tenderly gather them in." I don't know the words. "Open the door, gather them in, open the door for the children, tenderly gather them in." How about that, Honey! I used to sing that in Sunday School!—And we sang it in Daily Vacation Bible School (588:3).

That's, ah, during the summer they have, ah, you know, vacation bi-

[6] I never observed application of the "wait and see" rule (Cicourel 1973:54), which would suspend interpretation of a passage until a later point in the reading. Perhaps the lack of revision is handled by an "et cetera assumption," which relegates the problematic to a "what-we-all-know" category, thus making them unproblematic and unambiguous, albeit by fiat only.

ble school, you could go, yeah, two weeks or something like that where you go to get special bible classes for children and things.

Relative to others, however, this interpretive procedure is ideologically uninteresting. It is simply the application of a dictionary or "kernel" meaning to an expression. It does, though, introduce new members to the common linguistic expressions used in the group.

Fringe-Meaning Articulation

While clarification works to illuminate the "kernel" or "objective" meaning of the text, the second procedure operates on the "fringe" or "subjective" meaning (Schutz 1972:126). Fringe articulation develops or "fills out" the referential meanings of phrases in the text (Cicourel 1973:61; Husserl 1931:125–26). This is done by relating the specific passage to another aspect of the COG ideology. Below are two reading segments of biblical text:

> The soul of the wicked desireth evil: his neighbor findeth no favor in his eyes. When the scorner is punished, the simple is made wise: and when the wise is instructed, he receiveth knowledge (Prov. 21:10–11).

This is why God must punish the Americans—so the world can learn what happens to a person who hardens his heart to instruction. Proverbs 1 shows what happens. You can learn with an open heart [nods his head to indicate that next person should begin to read].

> The righteous man wisely considereth the house of the wicked: but God overthroweth the wicked for their wickedness. Whoso stoppeth his ears at the cry of the poor, he also shall cry himself, but shall not be heard (Prov. 21:12–13).

Oh boy, listen to this one! Think of America—A small minority of the world using 30 percent of the energy. This is not saying that rich is bad. For example, God gave Solomon riches because his desire was to help people—if God gave the poor money, they would waste it: one reason they are poor is because they waste. Riches aren't bad if God finds someone who is wise and will share them.

COG ideology regards America as lost to Satan: it is one of the most "God-forsaken" places on earth because of its greedy, materialistic capitalism and long history of refusing to listen to God. Here, four verses of Proverbs are grasped by the procedure of articulating two specific phrases: "when the wise is instructed, he receiveth knowledge," and "whoso stoppeth his ears at the cry of the poor." These phrases are tied to ideological ideas about America. The reading gives a wider interpretation than what is directly denoted in the text. The excursus on the moral significance of wealth illustrates one of the large number of possible directions this process can take and demonstrates the basic indeterminateness of the fringe meaning.

The next example occurred while the group was reading a Mo letter, *Hitch Your Wagon to a Star!* (311B), that encourages members to look to God and the future for their inspiration. The leader asked someone to read Isaiah 11:6–9 for comparison:

> *The wolf also shall dwell with the lamb, and the leopard shall lie down with the kid; and the calf and the young lion and fatling together; and a little child shall lead them. And the cow and the bear shall feed; their young ones shall lie down together; and the lion shall eat straw like the ox. And the sucking child shall play on the hole of the asp, and the weaning child shall put his hand on the cockatrice' den. They shall not hurt nor destroy in all my holy mountain: for the earth shall be full of the knowledge of the Lord, as the waters cover the sea.*
>
> This is the point where the whole world will be taken over by Jesus. The millennium. God will solve every problem. The final solution will be 1000 years later when New Jerusalem comes down from heaven. The main point is keep your eyes on that, whatever you go through! How far you go depends on where you hitched your wagon. You will never be satisfied unless you hitch it on this hope. Hope to see your salvation. If you look only at yourself you're like the normal unsaved person. You must walk by faith, not by sight!

Isaiah's words are fit into the quite definite millennial ideology of the COG. The text is expanded and its relevance is explicated by treating it as an indexical expression referring to COG doctrine. The fringe-meaning articulation procedure, then, has two functions. It brings texts into the overall COG ideological perspective by articulating their possible meaning in a particular direction, and it also contextualizes the texts to demonstrate their relevance to specific COG ideological issues.

Concretization

This procedure is the one appearing most frequently in reading; it takes a text and puts it into a concrete situation that has happened or is happening. The text is made meaningful for the reader by showing how it applies to a concrete situation. Below, I identify three subtypes of this procedure.

Group Projects

First, the text can be concretized by showing how it governs a present project of the group. The following examples are taken from two

Mo letter readings that took place while this particular colony was making a push to gain catacomb members:

> *The most lasting missionary works in the world have continued on in countries even now closed to the Gospel, where the natives themselves were taught to carry on by themselves, after the missionary was gone—*
> Praise God!
> *a procedure the Apostle Paul practiced, and which resulted in the evangelising of all Asia, and most of Europe before his death, by means of his own single-handed efforts and that of a few of his friends—by training his converts to witness and carry on after he was gone! The best ones, who were willing to forsake all and follow him to become fishers of men, he even brought home for further training* (23:20).
> Now, the—it's a real catacomb vision this paragraph! Yeah!

The second example:

> *people who want to get above the multitude—beyond what has already been done and accomplished. Pioneers must have Vision—vision to see what no one else can see; Faith—faith to believe things no one else believes* (B:5);
> I mean, I believed, I believed this thing was gonna work a long time ago! But it's been a fight!
> [*others*] Yeah!
> It's been a fight!

The third:

> *They don't want it to be known that there is any place else to go. They don't even want their children to know there is anything else or any other place to go or a way to get there! They want to keep them shut in down in the valley and in the mud and in the mire!* (B:6).
> So we gotta 'um, keep 'em for awhile, keep 'em for awhile from knowing that, ah, at least. Understand that their parents when they realize that you're not only entertaining, but you're, coming in and showing these, uh, that's why Ellen's, I think, party was so important. Cause her mother saw that we weren't just trying to give something to her daughter, but we were trying to give it to her too, see . . .
> [*others*] Um, ha.
> . . . that it's good for her too.

In all these cases, the text is seen to be exemplified in the current group project, even though these texts were written long before the introduction of the idea of catacomb members. The text is grasped in an application to present daily work. The three examples show differences in the type of articulation carried out. The first is simply a statement tying the text to the problem, almost by fiat. The second is a more detailed articulation of a general idea, "pioneering," which applies to the project of increasing catacomb membership. The third interpretation discusses a particular problem in attracting members— their parents. It associates the "they" in the text with "parents" (in the text, the antecedent of "they" is those who are not pioneers—a residual category—that is, those who live among the multitudes in the valleys of Mammon, in the System) and solves the problem by asserting that the parents can be converted too.

PERSONAL LIFE EXPERIENCE

A second subtype is the procedure of relating the text to personal experiences of the reader. A personal testimony concretizes the text.

> Boy, I'll tell you, some drivers that we have it's a miracle they've survived. It's nothing but the miracle-working power of God the way He's spared us! I've had a piece of tube that big showing through the fabric of my tire. We pulled into the filling station to get gas and the guy says, "You've been driving on this thing?" I guess the angel was hanging on that keeping it from getting worn. We've had people run out of gas just pray and kept on driving on, haven't had a nickel! Praise God! (T:54).

> I've a testimony about that. In Texas, I used to always check all four tires. I couldn't do anything if I found something, but I checked anyway. One day there was a huge bubble. We all got around it and laid hands on it and the tire healed itself.

Here, the personal example is identical in subject matter to the example in the text. The miracle-working power of God described in the text is connected to a personal example. The text's relevance becomes quite obvious when the same or similar event can be seen to have happened in the reader's life.

Often by tying the text to a personal event, the significance of the personal event becomes clear to the reader. Many members state that the Mo letters explain what they had previously only had vague ideas about. According to one member, before she joined the Family she had always thought that there was something evil about flies. After becoming a member and reading several Mo letters, she realized that "flies are of the Devil"; they are minor evil spirits serving Satan.

COG EVENTS

The last subtype occurs when the text is related to the events that have happened in the COG and to its leaders or to figures in the bible. The first example of this use of the concretization procedure employs the experiences of Moses David to concretize the idea of seeing a project through to its end:

> *Initiative—initiative to be the first one to try it; Courage—the guts to see it through!* (B:5).
>
> . . . Ah! The guts to see it through, to go through with it no matter if it kills you. No matter if sometimes you feel like you are go——you know, sometimes I felt like I had gotten myself really out of God's will. I'd go through such a heavy trial. Like Mo did—off there in Israel, he start——; how did he get *I Gotta Split*? He must of gone through a real heavy trial, thinking, Lord, they need me so much back there, am I wrong? Am I half way around the world and made a wrong, made the wrong choice, you know? He went through that and that's where he got *I Gotta Split*.

Often the general experience of COG members is called on to serve as an example. There is a whole set of experiences that are considered to be specific to COG members or characteristic of them. In the following example, the idea that COG members are protected from mishaps is drawn on to concretize the text:

> *Have you ever noticed how little sickness, accident or injury we have in our midst?—A miracle of God. Most camps have a full-time nurse or doctor on hand and the clinic is always busy with sickness and injury and accidents and all kinds of stuff. But God is good to us, God is merciful and miraculously protects us because He knows we love Him and we're trying to do the best we can and we ask Him for it, and we expect it, we pray for it. You better keep remembering to give God the Glory!*
>
> *Don't go rushing off in your own strength, in your own impatience, and forget to pray!* (T:50).
>
> Very few COG have been in the hospital. I know only one person who had to go.

In summary, these concretizing procedures can be contrasted to the fringe-meaning articulation procedures: the latter make associations between ideas while the former make associations with actual experiences. The preponderance of concretizing procedures makes them by far the most prevalent of the interpretive procedures used in reading. This may be a product of the COG emphasis on "doing" as opposed to concerns with theological formulations. At the same time, these procedures probably reinforce this action orientation.

---

[7] This is a Mo letter (28) in which Moses David explains why he isolated himself from the group members.

Analogy Articulation

The texts themselves are full of explicit analogies and metaphors. Some are biblical—shepherds and sheep, for example—while others are not—sexual comparisons. Occasionally, the reader extends or "plays out" a textual analogy to interpret the text. This is done by citing other characteristics of the analogue that might be applicable to the subject of the text. In other cases, new analogies are brought to bear to make sense of the text, as in the following reading:

> You get over here in this little multitude and this little make believe of Mammon and you can't see anything but time and creatures of time and things of time, which are soon to pass away, but you thrust your head above that of those around you in that multitude and you yourself become a mountain in their midst and they resent you and they resist you and they fight you because they can't understand you and because they don't want you. They don't even want to know there are mountains! They don't want their children to hear there are mountains! They don't even want their children to have a breath of fresh air from that crystal peak. That clear water you drink up there is delicious! But when you appear to be on a mountain while they are in the valley, they hate you because it's obvious you are above them and they don't want anyone to be above them. They want to keep you stuck in the mud like the rest of them (B:6).

I mean, I'm just thinking, we—our life, I was just walking down the street thinking today, sometimes it's really good to just get away from everything, so you can think and pray and I was just thinking: I mean what do we want to do? We want to intrigue people, intrigue them, be a mystery to them, we wanna be a mystery to them so they want to know more about us, right?

[*others*] Um!

That is part of it, isn't it?

[*others*] Yeah!

I mean, that's what a woman tries to do to attract a man, isn't it?

[*others*] Yeah!

She shows him just enough to make him interested and con-, conceals enough to make—to keep her interesting, you know? You know, she shows enough that he—she gets his attention and then she conceals enough that there's still something else to find there, so always, you know, do that.

In this example, a woman's supposed intrigues are compared and seen as similar to the intrigues believers should use in proselytizing. The extratextual discourse seems to refer to the "breath of fresh air" and "clear water" that people in the valley of Mammon or the Systemites "don't even want to know" about. As a woman supposedly shows a little to lead on a man, the COG member should show a little of the "breath of fresh air" or the COG message to lead on the prospect. The analogy articulation procedure allows the reader to grasp the meaning of the reading by showing its parallel with a commonly supposed experience.

Pragmatic Imperative Formulation

This final procedure takes the text and derives a pragmatic imperative on which the reader should follow through. The imperative indicates some activity that in daily practice is morally desirable to pursue. A general textual statement is converted into a relevant imperative for a specific situation.

> *Now the stage you're in right now is probably going to be the rock-bottom stage because first of all He sees what you're going to do with a nickel before He starts giving you quarters or half-dollars or dollars or maybe a hundred or even a thousand. He wants to see if he can trust you with nothing before He gives you something. If you're faithful in a few things He'll make you ruler over many. The Lord's going to wait to see if He can trust you with the necessities before He trusts you with any luxuries* (T:65).

> This is a heavy principle here. It says God will reward you if you're obedient to Him. We must all be loyal and obedient to God's will.

> *Only pioneers climb mountains—people who want to do something that no one ever did before* (B:5).

> You guys wanna do that?
> [*others*] Yeah! Amen!
> It's the only way to be alive, isn't it!?
> [*others*] Yeah!

Sometimes an entire Mo letter is read as providing an imperative for a particular situation. In the next example, a drop in the colony's statistics for leading people to Baptisms in the Holy Spirit the previous month led to the reading of the letter *Spirit of God* (337). This letter describes the meaning and effect of the Pentecostal experience of being filled with the Holy Spirit:

> *Nearly all of the natural things which the Lord has created, or man-made inventions that He has allowed man to discover, are visible illustrations of the unseen spiritual realities of the spirit world to help us to try to understand it and grasp its truth. For, as Paul said, "The invisible things of Him (God) from the creation of the world are clearly seen, being understood by the things that are made." With the creation of sex, for instance, God was trying to illustrate for us*

how we could also experience a spiritual orgasm by being filled or baptized with
his Spirit! (337:1).

So that's what you're denying them if you don't give them the Holy
Spirit. A spiritual orgasm.

The extratextual discourse transforms an expository statement that
uses an analogy to describe the Holy Spirit Baptism into an imperative statement about members' obligations. At the end of the letter
reading, this imperative was reinforced:

Right. Thank you, Lord! So the point. Everybody going to do more
about that next time?
[*others*] Amen!
This month? Praise God. Hallelujah. So, get'em filled! If you're in a
ah, if you're in a good situation like here at the colony, really go over it
really clearly with them and get'em filled and help them to speak in
tongues.

By transforming the text into practical imperatives for activity, the
meaning and relevance of the text are grasped. It changes from an
interesting statement or description into a relevant prod to action that
is morally binding to the reader.

The Product of Reading and Implications

The product of this reading process is an accretion to each reader's
practical ideology (see Richards 1943:93). While each particular grasping differs from another due to the specific procedures used and the
textual content, they share three general characteristics. First, what
is grasped is not a distinct content, but rather a general affirmation
of the COG ideology. For example, although the texts go into great
detail about the structure of events before and during the imminent
millennium, most members' grasping of these events is simply, "Yes,
Jesus is really coming back." Related to this characteristic is the fact
that what is grasped is a momentary clarification of the ideological
ideas. Readers work through the content, then tend to forget its details and are left with the core or nucleus of meaning noted above.
Finally, what is grasped is not knowledge "of" the world, but rather
knowledge "for" activity in the world. It is essentially moral or pragmatic, offering guidelines for action. This, of course, differs from the
sociologist's reading of the text, which is primarily an intellectual exercise: the sociologist rarely seeks to produce pragmatic imperatives
for life from the religious texts he or she reads.

This sociological analysis is formal—that is, it examines the extra-textual, socially given processes that are applied regardless of the specific textual content. Such a separation, however, is only valid for the sociologist. Phenomenally, no such distinction exists for the individual believer. To the COG member, the text demands to be read in a certain way. The social roots of the reading process are obscured: the text and the believer's approach to it are inseparable and seen as based in the content itself. COG members are at first astounded when they find out that I do not accept some of their interpretations of the texts. Their second reaction is to look for a reason external to the text itself—my stubbornness, pride, or education—to explain why I refuse to see the "truth."

EIGHT

PRACTICAL RELIGIOUS ACTIVITY: CREATING AND

MAINTAINING THE CHILDREN OF GOD REALITY

I N THE preceding chapters, I analyzed in some detail three fairly circumscribed sets of ideological activities in the Family. By engaging in such activities, members create and maintain the ongoing social reality that is "life in the Family." In this chapter, I suggest that this sense of "living in the COG" is also created and maintained in the course of everyday interactions—even the most mundane—between members. Even when members are not engaged directly in an ideological activity such as litnessing, witnessing, or reading, they are constantly talking with each other. In this talk—practical religious reasoning—they reason about and account for[1] their daily experiences; that is, they make their world and their activity in it rational and accountable. In effect, such activities contribute to members' "maintenance of faith" (Lofland 1966:197–98).

Practical Religious Reasoning and Its Resources

This practical religious reasoning is not some strange and alien system of thought separate and apart from that in which most members of society participate (Geertz 1973; Winch 1958). Instead, it is parasitic to commonsense reasoning: COG members in analyzing and justifying their world and activities rely on their commonsensical understanding as well as on more ideological interpretations drawn from their practical ideologies. These sources of understanding are relied on by COG members in making sense of their everyday life in the

[1] In this chapter I examine the observable utterances that occur in social interaction and that are accepted as appropriate. I refer to these as "accounts" (see Roche 1973:110–25; Wittgenstein 1958:59e–60e). My use of the term "account" should not be confused with the more limited use of the term as an "excuse" or "justification" for socially inappropriate behavior (Scott and Lyman 1968:46–47; see Mills 1940:908). Instead, it refers to any utterance employed to render a phenomenon reasonable to others in an interaction (Garfinkel and Sacks 1970:346).

Family (Coulter 1979:166–68). Members in facing a particular topic or issue draw on both of these resources to interpret or to justify some phenomenon and move easily back and forth between them. Instances of practical religious reasoning, therefore, cannot be said to be either completely ideological or completely commonsensical.

This flexibility and ambiguity are possible because of the discrete nature of each instance of practical religious reasoning. Such reasoning always takes place in a bounded context in that the conversational topic concerns a particular phenomenon or event presented to members by the current situation or brought up by one of the members for discussion. Moreover, the sufficiency of utterances is tied to this bounded context: an assertion can satisfy participants in the interaction even though it might not be a complete or thoroughly justified assertion in another context. For the practical purposes of members in the given context, the assertion is sufficient (see Cicourel 1973:53; Garfinkel 1964:248). Such activity is also situated so that members participating in the interaction have current interests and activities that affect the interaction. For example, much discussion occurs in the context of the group planning specific proselytization forays. Thus, although a variety of interpretations or justifications may be formulated for any activity, some will be more appropriate given the members' current agenda.

This context-dependent nature of practical religious reasoning gives the activity an atomistic character. Practical religious reasoning, as does commonsense reasoning (Schutz 1943:136–37), consists of pragmatic and independent attempts at order creation (Van Zandt 1987:918). Each incident of this reasoning is separated from other incidents, and one account is not necessarily compared with accounts generated at other times. Instead, the reasoning demonstrates the rationality or reasonableness of some phenomenon or practice here and now. Each of these pragmatic, independent attempts is linked to others, not according to any overarching logical or procedural rules, but rather simply serially and by their common source.

The accounts of the world produced by practical religious reasoning are successful when other members accept them as correct. Other members' acceptance of an account is also a function of their ability to generate similar accounts. Although they may not have accounted for the same phenomenon in the same way (Schutz 1953:8), members recognize the proffered account as acceptably plausible because they share similar commonsense and ideological theories about the world, and the account seems to be a product of a reasonable application of those theories (Scott and Lyman 1968:53).

The context of practical religious activity also makes the activity moral, in the sense that it regulates action. A member may give an account of an event or a justification for a phenomenon specifically in order to exhort others to take a certain action. Or he or she may provide an account to demonstrate to others that an event has a certain significance for members. In either case, the point of the process is that COG activities are right or morally correct. Practical religious reasoning is not concerned with the acquisition of theoretical knowledge of the world; rather, it provides members with a reasonable or morally right basis for a variety of actions, whether they be proselytization or continued commitment to the Family.

In this process, the moral is viewed as simply a constituent part of the empirical world. To take the most general example, the reason a member is to proselytize is because God has commanded it. The world is empirically put together in such a way that moral precepts are directly derivable from its structure. This relationship between the empirical and the moral is not specific to the COG subculture. Commonsensical justifications for moral precepts that rely on empirical propositions abound. The prohibition on murder, for instance, has a number of justifications that rely on empirical beliefs about the structure of the world. It can be justified on functional grounds: absent the prohibition, murder would become so widespread as to make human society impossible. This argument includes empirical assumptions about the propensity of humans to kill one another, murder's likely effects on society, and the value of that society. Given such background assumptions, however, the argument is satisfactory to most members of society for all practical purposes. Despite what philosophers see as a need for a more substantial justification, most members of society accept moral orders because they can be based on members' empirical conclusions about the nature of the world.

Presuppositions in Practical Religious Reasoning

In engaging in practical religious reasoning, members draw on both commonsensical presuppositions about the world they share with members of society-at-large[2] and presuppositions and theories spe-

---

[2] For example, in everyday life we all assume some type of mind-body dualism; the existence of antecedent causes for observable effects (Roche 1973:56–58); that an intention or an act of will can be an antecedent cause (ibid.); a pragmatic theory of truth ("Ideas [which themselves are but part of our experience] become true just in so far as they help us to get into satisfactory relations with other parts of our experience") (James 1963:28 [emphasis omitted]); that fellow interactional participants exist and experience the interaction and the world in general in the same way (the reciprocity of

cific to their subculture—those that make up their practical ideologies—in order to produce or understand and accept accounts of events in the world. Challenging an account by questioning the validity of one of these presuppositions is inappropriate and is taken by other members to show inadequate socialization or commitment to the group, in the same way that challenging a commonsensical presupposition in a routine interaction in wider society is evidence that something is wrong with the challenger (Garfinkel 1964:229–30).

In contrast with the formal ideology, it is difficult to describe the practical ideology of COG members in detail. This is because practical ideologies differ in emphasis due to differences in members' biographies and variations in how they have learned the formal ideology. Moreover, members rarely articulate their understanding of the formal ideology in systematic detail because most members consider the details to be unremarkable features of the obvious that need no explanation or analysis. However, the following COG presuppositions are those that most commonly appear in practical religious reasoning.

All COG members share the presupposition that God is a spiritual entity that can alter the physical world, and, corollary to this assumption, that moral rules and empirical conclusions given by God (through the Mo letters and the bible) are true beyond challenge. Thus, if a member can tie an assertion appropriately to a biblical or Mo-letter passage it becomes irrefutable. Another COG assumption is that nonmembers of the Family live in a corrupting environment, the System, and that the West, with its capitalism and false churches, is more deleterious than the East. The witnessing presupposition that nonmembers have a lack in their lives that only a salvation experience can remedy is also prominent in everyday interactions. In addition, COG members routinely assume that there exists an active spirit world: not only does every living thing have a spirit existing in its material body, but there are also many disembodied spirits that affect the course of the material world. Finally, accounts that offer observably ideological explanations of events trump accounts that rely only on commonsense explanations.

Although many presuppositions are peculiar to the COG subculture and often conflict with more generally held ideas, several of these presuppositions have roots in prevalent commonsense ideas about the world. For example, the notion of an active spirit world

perspectives) (Schutz 1953:8); and that members of a social group have sufficiently similar orientation to the world to make shared understanding possible (Schutz 1953:8–9).

may be built on the widespread belief in mind-body dualism. Or, we may see the COG belief in the corrupting influence of the System as a version of the general commonsense notion, based on the Judeo-Christian theories, that society is corrupting.

Episodes of Practical Religious Reasoning

In what follows, I analyze the most prevalent everyday situations or practices in which members interact and account for phenomena to other members.

Subcultural Idioms

Members use words and phrases throughout everyday life that are peculiar to the COG subculture. Many have their roots in the late sixties' youth and drug culture of California,[3] others in the southern Protestant evangelical culture,[4] and still others have grown up around COG practices.[5] These idiomatic expressions often have primarily mundane meanings. For example, "God bless you" typically is a functional equivalent for "thank you." "Praise the Lord," "Thank you, Jesus," and "Hallelujah" in many contexts mean "that's amazing" or "that's great."

[3] For example, "heavy," "wow," "on a mind trip," "far out," "you know," "trip off," "to drop out," "sold out," and "to space out."

[4] For example, "pray over" means to pray about; "have a burden to/for" is often equivalent to saying "I would like to"; "to get the victory over" means to overcome some undesirable practice or thought; "that's really inspiring" often has the simple mundane meaning of "that's good"; "to bring to the Lord" or "to lead to the Lord" means to bring a salvation experience to a nonmember; "to get something from the Lord" or "to get a check from the Lord" is to have an idea that the member believes to have come from God; "be a sample, not a sermon" means to show people by your actions and style of life, rather than to tell them how to do something; "to be a blessing" often is equivalent to "it is good"; "to have in your heart" means to believe something strongly or to be committed to it; "it was a miracle" is another equivalent for "it is amazing"; "he or she is hungry" means that the person is seeking the Lord; and "to feed [someone] [with the Word]" denotes how a member meets the "hunger."

[5] For example, "to counsel with [someone]" simply denotes talking to another member about a specific problem; "to deal with [someone or something]" is used when a problem is viewed as serious and requires drastic attention; leaders are said "to oversee" COG activities; "break your bottle" means to break a person's pride; to "slam 'em" is to give a nonmember a strong anti–established church message or to correct a member in a strong and unequivocal fashion; "to pray with [someone]" is to lead a potential convert through a salvation prayer; "sharing a letter" means to read a letter with another; "to get desperate" is to address your problem with prayer and serious concern.

By using such expressions in everyday talk, however, members mark their conversations as special—a form of communication privileged to group members; they see themselves as sharing an exclusive language (members frequently remark that outsiders find some of their words and phrases strange and unintelligible) and thus are participating in a different social world. Part of this marking is due to the explicit ideological references of many of the terms, even though they more often stand in for mundane expressions. To participate successfully in conversations that generate accounts of COG phenomena, members must acquire the ability to use these expressions properly in everyday interactions. Persons who do use the idioms cross the threshold into the COG social world.

Routine Affirmations

The routine affirmations that occur in group reading appear throughout COG conversations. They are often responses to a standard question that demands an affirmation, but they also occur more spontaneously. The actual subject matter being affirmed varies widely and can be quite mundane as well as ideological. In one case, at the end of a meal, the colony shepherd's wife asked all those in the dining room, "Did everyone like the meal?" The response, in virtual unison, was "Yeah!" A frequently heard example of this is the shepherd's question to a group of members: "Does everyone love each other?" "Yeah!" "Sure?" "Yeah!"

Such affirmations indicate to other members that the member is happy in the Family, that Family activities are fun or exciting, and that Family beliefs are correct. It is not the actual contents, which are extremely abstract and general, that send this message, but simply the fact of the affirmation. In commenting on the day or on some COG activity—usually litnessing or some other proselytization activity—members generally state that "it was heavy!" or that they "were inspired by it." This occurs even if later conversation reveals that the activity or day could have gone better. These routine affirmations function to guarantee that most public and general statements about COG activities are positive. If something is wrong, it is with the details rather than with the overall activity. Thus, routine affirmations contribute to members' sense of participating in a reasonable, if not perfect, social order.

Instrumental Utterances

Throughout everyday life, members often employ utterances with ideological content in an extremely instrumental fashion: they request that God cause specific physical events to occur. These utterances may be prayer, but they often are simply isolated pleas for divine help. By employing these instrumental utterances, members demonstrate to themselves and each other that the world is subject to God's activity: God can answer their prayers.

Small prayers for God's aid are ubiquitous throughout COG activities and interactions, and most call only for an indefinite response. Members who wash dishes often gather in prayer before starting and request God to help them do a good job and to make it go quickly. One prayer I heard was "Lord, help us to get the house cleaned up really quick, so we can get out and feed some sheep." Before getting into a car, members often say a short pray requesting that God get them safely to their destination. Others include more specific requests for aid. For example, a member and I were moving two doors up a flight of stairs. Although the first door went smoothly, the second was larger and we had some difficulty with it. A high-level COG leader passed by and, seeing our plight, prayed, "Lord, make this door go in there or help us." On one occasion I heard "Jesus make this pen work," while another prayer asked God to make a recalcitrant can-opener function.

Although these prayers are direct requests for divine intervention, the failure of God to provide the assistance is unremarkable to members. The utterances are not assumed by members to have "magical" efficacy. Of course, if the physical condition changes as desired, the incident is recounted to others as a miracle. But an apparent failure of God to heed the request is not considered to be a problem in need of explanation or interpretation. Members seem to agree tacitly that not all prayers are answered and that there are good reasons for this that do not need to be articulated.[6]

---

[6] In one extended incident, however, a member did attempt to offer me several explanations for the persistent failure of the instrumental prayers he uttered. We were trying to hitchhike back to the colony in the early evening. After waiting for some time, he suggested that we pray. His prayer included the clause, "Lord, we claim from you, we demand, a ride." The phrases, "claim from" and "demand" are common in instrumental utterances. In the prayer, the member gave God five minutes in which to produce a result. He told me that God answers prayers.

When the five minutes passed, he said, "Out of the worst defeats come the greatest victories." He asserted that our failure to get a ride "must be a real attack from the Devil." "It means we did well today [litnessing]." The member then took even more direct measures to secure transportation. He told me, "Watch this. I'll give them the look of love." He approached a driver stopped at the intersection and smiled broadly. He did this for several automobiles. If the driver smiled back, he said, "We are getting closer to a ride." Finally, we turned and began to walk back toward the town we were trying to leave. He then suggested that we sit and read a Mo letter. He thought this might do the trick because he and another member had once had trouble getting a

Interpreting

The great bulk of practical religious reasoning involves the interpretation of events in or features of the world, so that they are presented as reasonable or expectable occurrences. Commonsense interpretations are certainly acceptable explanations for phenomena: Family members do not demand systematicity between interpretations or exclusivity for their ideological interpretations. In fact, for members interacting in pairs or cooperating on a specific task, a commonsensical explanation is more likely to come to the fore. Moreover, leaders, who face more practical and logistical problems than do members in everyday life, are more likely to provide commonsensical interpretations of events. The exigencies of a situation affect which resources members draw upon. In larger group settings, which are usually away from pressing demands for action, members are more likely to produce more ideologically inclined interpretations of phenomena.

Strictly ideological or strictly commonsensical interpretations are rare. When they do occur, they generally are truncated assertions about phenomena. For example, the day after a party at the house of a potential convert, one member ascribed the reticence of the father of the prospect to the fact that "the Devil fought really hard last night because the party was so important [for proselytization]." Conversely, a strictly commonsense explanation was immediately applied to the group's low statistics during a proselytization push. "Our stats were not as good as they should be from Nijmegan. The rain and the fact that we had only two litnessers has something to do with it." If members were forced to articulate these assertions in more detail, their pure character might dissolve; the circumstances of their occurrence, however, do not demand further explanation.

Most instances of interpretation are an amalgam of ideological and commonsensical notions about the constitution of the world. For example, a significant number of conversational interactions involve interpretations of the secular world or the System. One member contrasted the education a young child gets in the Family with that available in System schools. "In the System, one teacher handles thirty kids. The kids lose all their individuality." Here, the ideological presupposition of corruption is merged with the commonsense the-

---

ride. When they read a letter, they got a ride right away.

This member's attempt to account for the failure of the instrumental utterance to achieve its purpose may have been prompted by my presence as an outsider. This particular member was more inquisitive than others about the nature of my research. He was somewhat older and had some university training. If I had been simply another member, he may have not attempted such an elaborate explanation.

ory that classrooms are overcrowded and that children learn better with a lower teacher-to-pupil ratio.

In another interpretation event, a member described his venture into Poland to other members at dinner:

> The people there are so innocent; they haven't gone through the shit that Western kids have. We visited several nightclubs and homes, and witnessed to a nightclub band and a top Polish actor. The people there are very hungry [for the Word]; only a word or two would open them right up. . . . All Poles look to the West. We tried to tell them that it wasn't real freedom in the West . . .
>
> [Another member interjected:] Americans have a slanted view of the East. . . .
>
> . . . The East doesn't have layers of shit on them.

Here, the member explained the phenomenon of his warm reception by the Poles by applying the corruption assumption and the presupposition of a lack. He articulates the corruption assumption by incorporating a commonsensical view that citizens of communistic countries are basically simple, sincere, freedom-seeking people unaffected by Western commercialism. The corruption of the System—the most severe manifestation of which is American capitalism—has not reached deeply into Poland. The Poles are innocent people in search of salvation who provide the Family with a fertile field for proselytization.

Specific events are often interpreted by tying them to ideological beliefs. The colony shepherd one morning read an article from *Time* magazine on the New York City blackout in July 1977. He told several of us that the blackout was foreshadowed in *Death to the Cities* (373), a 1975 Mo letter that predicted that New York's financial woes would result in an economic crash and breakdown of law and order, all of which are caused by America's failure to heed God. He remarked that one section of the *Time* article was headed "Acts of God?" and described how four separate lightning bolts had hit and disabled sections of the transmission lines. When I stated that people in middle class areas of the city turned the blackout into an occasion for parties, he passed over my effort to reduce the significance of the situation and stressed that there was widespread looting during the blackout. This showed, he said, how much people needed the Lord. I later heard the same shepherd tell another member about the blackout. He compared it again to *Death to the Cities*, and seemingly attributed the blackout to Mayor Beam's failure to pay the city's bills. He said, "That's what happens when you don't pay your bills—don't pay your dues to God." In this episode, an event is located in the group's view of the world by interpreting it as a product of the System's corruption and of God's action in the world to wipe out that corruption. It draws on the commonsense notion that blackouts routinely cause breakdowns in law and order and result in looting and violence. By painting the picture using this commonsense idea, the gravity of the situation is enhanced and demonstrates the depravity of people in the urban environment without God.

Social trends in society are similarly given interpretations that draw on both ideological and common sense notions. For example, one member interpreted the women's liberation movement as follows: while men are the natural rulers in the home, women can often outshine men in the Lord's work. Members of the "women's lib" movement fail to recognize that "God has made women as a completely different vessel." They are naturally different from men. But the System beats down women in all things. As a consequence, women in the System are "getting so bitter and frustrated" that they want to take over everything.

Again, the presupposition that the System corrupts operates here. In addition, the member explicitly employs from his practical ideology the theory that women and men are naturally different and draws on the commonsense theory prevalent among many men in society that the most vocal leaders of the women's movement are bitter and frustrated. Nonmembers—particularly women's—failure to recognize this fact causes them to chase after an illusory equality. The implication is that, although the women's libbers' complaint is valid in some respects, they take it too far.

Illness, when it occurs, is interpreted in several ways that members do not find inconsistent. Members often attribute illness during a neophyte's first three months in the Family to God's testing the new member's faith: "The Lord tests them with illness." Illness is also attributed to God when members state that their own failings have led Him to punish them. Much illness, however, is blamed on the Devil, who is said to attempt constantly to undermine members' faith. Illness with this etiology is said to involve possession by evil spirits. Finally, members also offer commonsensical interpretations for disease, such as lack of sleep, failure to dress warmly, or "it's going around." Due to the atomistic nature of conversational events, all these interpretations can be applied to a single illness without members' noting an interpretive problem. (And, in most cases, only one interpretation is uttered in any one conversational episode.)

Astrology, an occasional topic, provides a set of empirical conclusions about personality types that members employ to interpret the character of others. For example, a member stated that another was a Libra and therefore bound to be stubborn; in another case, a member born under Gemini was said to have a lot of problems because of her sun sign. Members frequently inquire about a person's sun sign upon meeting them and enjoy guessing each other's signs. Astrological knowledge is part of a member's practical ideology, and its use rests on the presupposition that people are spiritual beings and can be influenced by spirits in the heavens. The level of astrological practice, however, is superficial: it seems to be a form of play rather than a subject of serious study.

Evidencing

Evidencing moves in a direction opposite to that of interpreting. In evidencing episodes, members assert that certain events or facts demonstrate the validity of an element of their practical ideology. Evidencing works by relying on members' commonsensical understandings of the world: the speaker asserts something that common sense validates and then shows how it relates to the ideological proposition. In witnessing encounters, for example, members routinely use their testimonies or biographical accounts of their own salvation experiences to prove to a nonmember the need to accept the Lord.

Much evidencing, however, occurs in interactions between members, who routinely repeat testimonies about their prior lives and recount how they joined the Family. They also "give testimonies" or recount events—witnessing successes, new contacts, and fortuitous encounters—to other members to demonstrate that God is helping the Family in an active way. A second function of these accounts is that they provide evidence to others that the speaking member recognizes and believes that God is so working. Finally, members cite events in world affairs as proving the validity of the Mo letters.

A constant instance of evidencing is members' comparison of life in the Family with participation in an established church. The undesirability of the latter is taken to be evidence of the correctness of the COG way of life. One member remembered growing up as a Catholic and being scared by the apocalypse. He asserted he was generally scared of churches and thought that their musty smell was of dead bodies. His parents, he claimed, were just religious by tradition; they were so hardened that they did not think about what they were doing. Because he finds the Family to be "young and active," life in the Family is better. This account also demonstrates for hearers that this member's choice was based on reason rather than force of habit. He relies on two commonsense ideas—that it is better to be happy and to do something by choice—to affirm the value of Family life.

A similar example occurred in a group meeting. A member asserted that the Family is different and better than other religious groups:

> Churches still have their feet and hands in the System, while the Family has all parts of its body working together. They used to think that the appendix and tonsils didn't have functions—that they were merely evolutionary holdovers. They now have discovered that they do function all together and each part has its own function. It's like the Family: different people have different gifts and talents. Everyone is not identical like zombies.

This account relies on the commonsensical idea that organic unity is preferable to a system with nonfunctioning parts. Any member of society-at-large would accept this proposition.

In recounting events that occur to Family members, members sometime suggest that the event would have been otherwise if not for some sort of divine intervention. In one such episode, a member recounted the response received when COG musicians began singing on the steps of the city hall in a nearby town. A crowd soon gathered, and the member attributed it to God, saying this was "what God did." As he described it, "It was heavy; we got more attention than other more professional bands would get." Here, the member attempts to depict a situation as one that commonsensically could not have occurred and is unexplainable absent COG beliefs.

Of course, as this last example shows, interpreting and evidencing are often two sides of the same coin. The account given both evidences the reality of God's action and interprets the event. In a second example of this interconnection, a member cited to me the fact that the Eritrean rebels were scoring gains in Ethiopia as evidencing the correctness of a Mo letter on that conflict (333B), and more generally the correctness of the COG ideology as a whole. Although the form of the account was that of an evidencing effort, the account also interpreted the rebels' success in terms of the ideology.

Justifying

Practical religious reasoning also is used to justify an event or activity. Commonsense and ideological notions are applied to cast an activity as morally correct or empirically efficacious, and therefore desirable. Justifying often occurs when members attempt to exhort fellow members to take action in some way. The line between justifying as a procedure and interpreting is often fine and permeable; a member can judge an activity to be desirable on the basis of an interpretation of the activity. This reflects the general confluence of the moral with the empirical in everyday life.

For example, the practice of "train litnessing" is desirable, according to one member, because people receiving literature on the train have time to read it. When they are through, he stated, they most likely leave the Mo letter on the seat so that the next occupant of the compartment receives the letter as well. Here, the member provides a commonsensically plausible account of how a Mo letter would reach several train riders. He unites it with the ideological imperative to proselytize to justify a new type of access strategy. Of course, this account could also be an interpretation of why train litnessing is thought to be effective. In this case, however, it was offered as justifying the activity because of its effectiveness.

In justifying, the empirical can serve as a basis for a normative rule or suggestion. Members on occasion remind each other that they can "think too much" and that they should have faith that God will take care of things. Some members support this moral proposition by stating that they get headaches when they think too much, or that they quickly "get out of the vision" or "get out of the victory," and things start to go wrong. In the following example, one member tried to convince another that it was not good to think too much:

> There are many things I don't understand. You must leave something to God—when you show you follow Jesus, He gives you strength. It's good to sit down and be quiet sometimes; God can show you things. I'm a Gemini, I'm a real thinker for myself. I had to listen to the Lord and stop thinking—that's how you get understanding and wisdom, listening to Jesus. I sometimes do too much [thinking] myself. Michael, it's not easy to accept something when you are used to looking at things in another way.

The speaker tries to convince the member not to overanalyze. She does this by invoking the commonsense idea that if you are always "talking," you cannot hear anything. She also invokes the ideological idea that God will reward the member with "strength" for "letting go and letting God" guide him.

Another example of this was the attempts of a colony shepherd to excite members about a proselytization project at a local weekend festival. He stated that litnessing at night during the festival would be productive because people would be drunk and more receptive to the message. Members should be sure, he suggested, to put the literature in their prospect's pockets so they do not drop it or forget it. Similarly, Flirty Fishing attempts in bars and nightclubs on occasion were justified by a member's articulation of a theory of bar culture:

people in bars "are not really relating to each other, but they are looking." This makes witnessing in bars, the member asserted, worthwhile: "You can get to know them [prospects] really well." In these examples, commonsensical depictions are offered as justifications for moral positions or for taking certain action.

Joking

Members' practical religious activity is not all business: joking is also a common feature of everyday life. Even in joking, however, members create and maintain a sense of social order (cf. Douglas 1968:365–66). Much humor revolves around ideological themes and depends on members' knowledge of and ability to manipulate ingroup and ideological usages. Some incidents of joking involve simple plays on words—for example, "the best litnessing and singing are when people are soused and in the Spirits"—or slips of the tongue— "love always fails." Others occur and play on ideological activities. One member recited his memorized verse, ending it with a smile and "thus saith the Lord." Another member asked the member checking on the recitation, "Becky, is that what the Lord says?" Some jokes involve authority relations and the ideology: for example, "You three decide [which songs to sing] unless I [the colony shepherd] get a revelation." On another occasion, several members started a joke argument about who had the authority to divide up the pineapple upside-down cake for desert. There is even some good-natured teasing among members. For example, "this is the girl who won Joel to the Family, but she's also done some good things, too." In stepping back momentarily from the seriousness of their projects, members use joking to highlight features of their relationships that normally go unmentioned or are unremarkable. The ability to cause humor in others is a ratification of the members' shared sense of social order (Douglas 1968). The joke teller reaffirms for him- or herself his or her competence as a member of the Family, and the joke hearers do the same.

Ideological Challenges and Other Conflicts

Overt conflicts in practical religious reasoning, and challenges to offered accounts, although rare, do arise from time to time.[7] They may

[7] I discuss here only disputes that are available to social observation; that is, disputes that members express verbally. Of course, many members might believe that a particular account is formulated incorrectly. Unexpressed beliefs of this sort, however, do not influence the social practices that members use to deal with expressed disagree-

be pitched at either the commonsensical or the ideological level. As a general rule, however, members attempt to resolve disputes in the formulation of accounts swiftly. The infrequency of disputes is attributable to two factors. First, the hierarchical organization of authority in the Family means that in most situations there is a leader in a position to resolve any dispute. One of the few extended debates of an ideological point that I observed occurred over dinner. One member asserted that members are to bless their enemies; another argued that members should not do so. After listening for some time, the colony shepherd resolved the dispute, stating that members should pray for their enemies, not bless them. Whether or not the same protagonists would accept that formulation in a future debate, it was sufficient in this situation to end the discussion.

In addition, members, though constantly engaged in practical religious reasoning, have no strong interest in an abstractly correct and consistent body of accounts. Nor do they develop strong attachments to particular accounts. If in each episode of practical reasoning, an apparently acceptable account is offered, they are satisfied and accept that account. They do not spend time attempting to improve on the account. When this is coupled with the strong interest in harmonious living arrangements, the possibility of open disputes is negligible.

Most disputes that do occur revolve around the correct commonsensical interpretation of an event. These typically concern the validity of underlying empirical generalizations, disputes that often are not immediately resolvable. For example, one member's statement that the Russians sold their jam abroad while their people at home starved was challenged by another member. The challenger asserted that the Russian people have plenty of food. In another case, the shepherd and others got into a dispute that derived from the fact that the musicians had missed a train. The argument concerned when the train left Arnhem. Such disputes typically are not finally resolved, but are quickly put behind members. Only when someone seems irritated with another does the argument go on for any length of time. The existence of disputes about such matters is not seen by members as a problem, unless, of course, the dispute lingers.

Members occasionally use this unremarkableness of commonsense disputes as a way out of ideological disputes. Thus, if someone challenges another's ideological account of an event, one response is to recast the account as a commonsensical one. On one such occasion, the colony shepherd discussed a *Time* magazine article he had read

---

ment. Unexpressed discontent is normally manifested in the phenomenon of role alienation discussed in the next chapter.

about the biblical borders of Israel. He asserted that "the millennial kingdom will spread to the extent of borders of Israel promised to Abraham." Another member challenged this assertion and its apparent ideological clothing, asking, "Why do you think that?" The shepherd backtracked, saying that he really did not know, but that it was possible. The original assertion was transformed into one based merely on the shepherd's own common sense.

On rare occasions, leaders terminate (usually mundane) disputes by recasting them as posing an ideological problem. For example, the shepherd and one member told the breakfast cooks that in the future the potatoes should be peeled before they were fried. Others, however, wanted the peels left on. The shepherd then decided to resolve the dispute by a vote. He first called for "yes" votes from those who wanted their potatoes peeled, and got only three. Instead of calling for the "no" votes he began to talk about the need for members to be "good samples." One component of this, he argued, was to eat the food of the country in which members were living. This, he claimed, was the teaching of the Mo letter *Become One* (208). Because "the Dutch people abhor unpeeled potatoes," members should eat their potatoes peeled. The vote was never finished, and thenceforward the potatoes were peeled.

This transformation as a way of ending and prevailing in a dispute is only performed by leaders who have the authority to carry off the sleight of hand. In another situation, one of the singers said that she did not want to sing the phrase "Pour toi je vie" in one of the Family songs. The shepherd got upset and told her to check with him before changing any of the words. The member, obviously annoyed, said "I do all things in Jesus," to which the shepherd responsed, "I will know from God what to do, so check with me." The dispute ended with the member's singing the song as written, in acquiescence with the shepherd's command. He successfully transformed a personal preference into an ideological dispute and terminated it with an ideological assertion that the member accepted.

NINE

SOCIALIZATION AND ROLE NEGOTIATION

HOW DOES a person become a Child of God? Sociologists use the concept of "socialization" to answer this question, and COG members have their own theory of socialization that is strikingly similar to the sociological theory. From my study, however, I found that becoming and remaining a Child of God is an ongoing, never ending process in the Family. I have described various activities that members engage in in everyday life in the COG. Being competent at these activities is the essence of what it is to be a Child of God. There is no discrete point in time when a person "becomes" a Child of God; instead, this is an enterprise that members work at constantly. In this chapter, I analyze two phases of this process: the initial acquisition of the ability to be a Child of God and the subsequent efforts members undertake to maintain their faith (see Kanter 1972).

Socialization into the Family

Upon joining the Family, members must somehow be socialized to be competent members who can accomplish group tasks in an orderly and productive manner. The result of this process is "commitment" to the Family (Goffman 1961b:88–89). However, commitment should not be confused with "conversion" into the group in the sense of some psychological "attachment" to the organization (Goffman 1961b:89), as many people have "converted into" the Family but quickly realized it was not for them.[1] In fact, most persons agreeing to join the Family are not competent members from the outset. Moreover, they often have little in the way of knowledge of the details of the Family's ideology and of the Family's practices. They seem to have decided that the Family may be what they are looking for and that they should take a chance to find out. "Conversion" or "recruitment," the topics that so preoccupy sociologists of religion, may sim-

[1] As Berger and Luckmann state, "To have a conversion experience is nothing much. The real thing is to be able to keep on taking it seriously; to retain a sense of its plausibility" (Berger and Luckmann 1966:158).

ply be short-hand descriptions of a person's decision to take the risk of looking further. The real problem of socialization is how a neophyte is incorporated into the group once he or she has moved in.

Sociologists commonly speak of socialization as a process by which new members of a social group internalize the norms and values of the group (Berger and Luckmann 1966:130; Dahrendorf 1973:38; Long and Hadden 1983:3; Parsons et al., 1951:17n.23; Stark and Bainbridge 1987:45), which then guide the neophyte's behavior and alter his or her view of the world. This incorporation of substantive contents is achieved through some circumscribed though undefined process of "learning" from or "interaction" with group members; that is, the sociologist attempts to point to particular practices that are said to cause incorporation. Moreover, the incorporation, particularly in religious contexts, is thought to result in the replacement of one persona with another: "alternation" (Berger and Luckmann 1966:157–63).

As in the case of "conversion," this sociological conception of socialization is little different from that held by COG members themselves to explain and guide their attempts to train new members. Members tend to view socialization into the group as precisely such a replacement of one persona with another through the incorporation of "correct" beliefs and norms. They refer to the need "to wash away one's old self" and "to replace it with a new one." COG members use this theory of socialization to justify and to explain formal socialization practices that the group applies to new members. Moreover, members point to radical personality transformation as an important feature of their membership in the Family. This includes a radical change in their beliefs, attitude to the world, and their happiness with themselves and others. A "real" COG member is completely "sold-out" to the Family rather than to the System; that is, the most important thing in his or her life is serving God through the COG.

Members constantly cite evidence to substantiate this theory. Members claim that activities they despised in the System now seem enjoyable to them. For example, one member told me that he "had never had the vision for kitchen work [when he was] in the System. Getting the vision for something is most of it." Another member offered the empirical generalization that new members develop both a "spiritual hunger" and a "physical hunger" upon joining: new members' spiritual hunger is reflected in their desire to read the bible and Mo letters; the physical hunger caused large appetites. Members, it is often said, who had "no potential in the System, get it in the Family."

The same theory appears in statements of what must occur for a person to become a full member of the Family.[2] Members state that a person must break with his or her "old life" and not look back, even if this requires burning bridges back to the System. The training of a new member or even the introduction of new practices to old members is referred to as "bottle breaking": the "old bottle" or vessel must be broken down completely so that it can accept the "new wine," or new practice or message. Older members who are unable to accept and to adapt to new practices and revelations delivered by Berg are said to be "old bottles": they are not strong, "sold-out" members, and may turn out to be "weak brothers or sisters."

In addition, the theory of socialization prevalent among Family members adopts the standard sociological view of socialization as the incorporation of new ideas or beliefs into the subject's mind. Old contents are replaced with new contents. Use of the term "brainwashing" is not uncommon among members: it is necessary to "wash" the neophytes' brain of all the "filth and garbage" that has accumulated from living in the System. One of the major efforts, members state, in socializing neophytes is to replace "lies" inculcated in people's minds by the "godless modern education system" with the simpler "truths" of God as found in the bible and the Mo letters.

Formal Socialization Practices

As do sociologists of socialization, COG members point to specific practices—"formal socialization practices"—that achieve this transformation and incorporation. For the most part, they involve efforts to transfer to the neophytes substantive knowledge; that is, the beliefs of the Family. In most cases, new members or babes are placed in field colonies immediately upon joining the Family. Because the life of a babe differs little from that of an older member, the distinction between babes and other members is blurred. Babes, however, do participate in several formal socialization activities. The colony shepherd schedules these by altering the daily routines of babes. Typically, babes spend one or two days a week at the colony on such activities.

From their first day in the colony, all neophytes begin to memorize bible verses. This practice, begun during the road travel period in 1969, has remained constant throughout COG history. The new member is given a set card, on which is printed references to the biblical passages to be memorized, organized into ten sets of nine to

[2] Formal membership—in the sense of being counted statistically as a "full-time disciple"—is not dependent on these criteria. Instead, it requires only living in a colony and obeying Family leadership.

eleven verses each. Neophytes are encouraged to tape the card to the inside cover of their bibles. The initial set is composed of verses relevant to the salvation experience.[3]

Neophytes are directed to memorize at least two verses every day. In the first few months of membership, this prescription is adhered to fairly closely. New members use the temple time in the morning to start memorizing; at intervals throughout the day, they take opportunities to continue the memorization. New members often help each other out by quizzing one another informally. At meal times, colony shepherds frequently ask new members to recite their verses for the day. If they are unable to do so, they are admonished to try harder, although actual punishment for failure is rare. Young members seem extremely anxious to memorize their verses successfully, and they continue to practice verses learned on previous days. After several months of membership, however, supervision becomes less direct and, as a consequence, memorization activity declines.

COG members justify the memorization practice by stating that it makes members better witnessers. A member can use memorized verses to underscore a point with a potential convert. Moreover, memorization increases witnessing effectiveness because it places the "Word of God" in the members' "hearts," rather than simply in their heads. Second, according to the COG theory of socialization, the more verses that are memorized, the more solid is the new member's foundation on the Word and the less vulnerable he or she is to the attempts of the Devil to drag him or her away from the Family. By being constantly engaged in memorizing, there is little chance for the Devil to get into a neophyte's thoughts and to plant doubts and questions. Finally, during the end-time, the Antichrist will confiscate and destroy all bibles; therefore, only those passages that members have committed to memory will be available to the group during the persecution.

Another formal socialization practice that has persisted from the earliest days of the movement is bible classes taught by the colony shepherd. The classes today almost always concern COG millennial beliefs, and they usually focus on Daniel and the book of Revelations; these lessons often require a whole morning or afternoon. The actual conduct of the classes is similar to other types of group reading, the major difference being that the leader provides more extended interpretations of each passage. Babes participate little in this interpretive

---

[3] Set one on the first set card is the group of verses most widely memorized by Family members. It includes the following: John 1:12; John 3:16; John 3:36; Romans 3:23; Romans 6:23; Romans 10:9; Romans 10:10; Ephesians 2:8–9; Philippians 4:13; I John 3:16; Revelation 3:20.

process; instead, they listen and raise questions when some interpretation is not clear to them. Alternative (System) interpretations are rarely presented; when this does occur, it is simply to belittle the "incorrect" interpretation. For example, a class may begin with the leader stating that most church people interpret the text to be taught as metaphorical or symbolic, rather than as a literal description of the end-time. He or she then states: "If that were true, why should anyone bother to read it?"

More and more, bible classes are being replaced with supervised reading of the Mo letters. New members are given a list of 144 Mo letters divided into 8 subject categories[4]—"The Mo Letter Reading and Study Course!"—and encouraged to start reading immediately. They check off the letters they have read on a poster on the colony wall and periodically take "Mo Letter Tests" on the content of their reading. Shepherds, as with memorization, continually monitor a babe's reading by inquiring at meals about the babe's progress on the checklist. Although there are no formal sanctions or rewards for reading, new members are put under some pressure to complete the course.

Reading also is said by members to socialize the new member by building up a solid foundation for faith. The information acquired in reading Mo letters replaces the years of System education. The more knowledge a new member has of the Family's beliefs, the less likely he or she is to be diverted by the Devil. Moreover, reading is cumulative: provided the member reads in good faith, more reading creates stronger faith. The activity of reading itself, for new as well as for older members, is imbued with an extremely instrumental or magical quality.

Although any member may be sent on a faith trip, such trips are also used to socialize new members. Their justification rests on the perception that they are one of the more strenuous of COG activities. At some point after the first several weeks, the babe is paired with an older member and sent out for one or two days to "live by faith." The new member is forced out of the comfort and communality of the field colony into the "hostile" world, with no money or means of support. Such trips are said to test the new member's faith and to permit him or her to see how God provides for members' needs if they have sufficient faith. Faith trips both test the effectiveness of already conducted formal socialization and contribute to it.

[4] The subjects are: "Introduction to the Revolution and Our Basic Beliefs," "Your Spiritual Life and Walk with the Lord," "Why We Must Drop Out!" "Our Goal: World Conquest," "The World Today: Politics and Economics," "Our Shepherd: Moses David," "The Spirit World," and "Love and Sex."

The Process of COG Socialization

Although these formal practices do contribute to a new member's socialization, activities that make up everyday life also contribute to the process. Instead of demarcating a single group of social practices, socialization is an ongoing process that is often inseparable from the everyday maintenance of the beliefs of and commitment to a group. A member develops competence (Cicourel 1973:42) by participating in the flow of practical religious activity, whether that activity is proselytization of outsiders or interactions with other members of the group. Every interaction in the context of ideological activity has a socializing effect. Socialization is thus ubiquitous in social interaction.

On this view, incorporation of the contents of the formal ideology—the key element in the COG and sociological theories—is a product of the process of socialization, not the process itself. Most members of society-at-large can study a COG text or listen to a COG member's utterance and be able to distill and state a set of propositions. This abstract ability, however, does not guarantee that such people are able to employ the ideas in their daily life. What is essential to socialization is that members acquire the capability to do so. They must begin to approach their interactions in everyday life with the new set of assumptions and the ability to interpret events, act, and justify actions in a way that other members recognize as appropriate.

The socializing effect of this process is not dissimilar to the "primary" socialization that members of society-at-large experience in their everyday interactions (Cicourel 1973:52–56). Children and immigrants learn their new culture by participating in it. Even experienced members of a society, however, continue to undergo socialization: members exercise and reinforce their competence at conducting interactions with others. The difference lies in the fact that COG members are acquiring and maintaining an additional competence (see Berger and Luckmann 1966:138–47). A person coming into the Family is not a tabula rasa, but a fully socialized member of a non-COG society: he or she can engage in social interactions, interpret events, and justify choices in such a way that other members of that society accept him or her as a competent member.

Moreover, this prior or primary socialization is not necessarily contradictory to the new skills that a member learns in the Family. In fact, the persistence and even possibility of socialization into the Family depends on how well the new skills complement the commonsensical rules that the member has acquired in the prior or primary socialization process. Thus, socialization into the Family is not the complete replacement of one persona with a new religious or COG persona as both the sociological and COG theories suggest. Instead, it is the development of the ability to apply a different, but complementary, set of assumptions and rules.

Members acquire this ability through participation in interactions in which they attempt to meet the expectations of older, socialized members. Members are constantly exposed to interactions that demand participation, such as litnessing, witnessing, reading COG texts in groups, and general interaction within the colony. All these activities are occasions in which the member must interact in ways that conform to the expectations of other members who are fellow participants in the interaction or at least observers of it.

The adequacy of a new member's participation is determined by his or her own sense of what more experienced members are doing and by cues given off by those members. Any rule-following behavior (Rawls 1955:24) is accompanied by two types of sanctions for improper performance. First, improper performance may cause the member's action to be unrecognizable as an instance of the intended activity (Fish 1980:226). COG members, however, are extremely capable at repairing even the most egregious failures. Members are normally able to reconstruct the attempted performance in order to determine what was meant or intended by the action. They consider the new member's failure to use the proper form to be inappropriate, but they are able to make sense of his or her performance.

This attribution of "inappropriateness" to a performance is the second, more common sanction. Other members in the interaction pass on to the speaker or the performer signals that communicate, "We know what you intend, but you have not done it correctly." In such cases, a funny look or double take communicates to the new member that he or she has performed an activity improperly. Only in rare and persistent cases is the performer taken aside and told that "in the Family, we do it [this way]" or "we believe [this]."

The most obvious example of this socialization is the acquisition of the COG argot. New members not only pick up the specific phrases peculiar to COG conversation, but also recognize when to employ each phrase appropriately. In gaining this competence, they observe how more experienced members use the terms in the course of interactions. Neophytes develop a sense of the meaning of the terms in context and try out their understanding by tentatively employing the phrases. Inappropriate uses are not punished, but do receive quizzical looks. The same process applies in the course of other activities such as litnessing, witnessing, and practical religious reasoning.

Role Negotiation

This socialization process, however, does not produce COG automatons who are without dissatisfactions or who always "embrace" their membership in the Family. All members routinely express disaffection with their role as a completely committed Family member. In most cases, the expression takes the form of petty malingering and complaining. However, when a member claims to experience more difficult problems or openly expresses doubts about Family membership, several COG techniques are used to address the problem. The techniques of role negotiation are additional constituents of the ongoing socialization process.

Such dissatisfactions can be analyzed as distance between social role and self. This alienation—or "deviation" from the "role" of an ideal COG member—however, is itself a social feature of everyday life in the Family. The familiar feeling that COG activities are sometimes "burdensome" is a commonsensical interpretation that clashes with the appropriate ideological evaluation of the activities. Members' own ability to interpret these alienation events within acceptable ideological bounds determines whether such events are commitment reinforcing or commitment eroding. Only in the severest case of doubts does the member perceive the problem, the way sociologists describe the role-self issue (Goffman 1961b), as a conflict between his or her social role as COG member and his or her "true" self.

Routine Alienation

The most common form of this alienation occurs quite frequently, usually in connection with ideological activities such as litnessing and witnessing. COG members verbally claim in the abstract that they enjoy all COG activities at all times, and they recognize that the fully committed COG member should want to do nothing else but proselytize. Litnessing and witnessing, however, are extremely taxing activities that at times appear, from a commonsense perspective, to be quite unattractive. A gloomy and cold day makes standing on the street an uncomfortable activity. Moreover, aggressively approaching strangers, many of whom do not want to be approached, takes some effort and can be embarrassing. Members are not always as excited about the prospect of litnessing for six to eight hours a day as they might want other members to believe. These types of disaffections are "routine alienations" that arise when members examine their activities through the eyes of members of society-at-large. From that perspective, the effort involved in ideological activities seems to outweigh any practical benefits the member gains. When routine alienation occurs, the member is simply ignoring ideological justifications and interpretations of his or her activity.

Members recognize verbally the existence of these routine alienations by speaking of "being out of the vision" or of "being out of the spirit" on a particular morning. Members also suggest a variety of measures for avoiding or curing this condition: before heading out for a day of proselytization, members should get a good breakfast, "get plenty of Word time," or "spend some quiet time in prayer." Also, if a member does not get out of the house early, it is said that he or she will have trouble litnessing. A bad day on the street is often accounted for as being caused by a failure to follow one of these prescriptions. Once on the street, the member must "look at Jesus and not at yourself or other people" and jump right in. To dwell on the fact that you might embarrass yourself is bound to affect the litnessing effort adversely. It is better "just to let go" and start litnessing. The member in the proper condition for litnessing is said to "be in the spirit," to "burn free," or to "be on fire."

These verbal acknowledgements of routine alienation, however, merely identify the problem and prescribe ways to overcome it so that the member can fulfill ideological expectations more easily. However, the prescriptions are not always followed and sometimes are not adequate. On other occasions, a member simply does not acknowledge publicly that he or she is alienated from the activity. In either case, members engage in a variety of practices that permit them to avoid participating fully in an ideological activity without challenging its legitimacy.

A panoply of secondary adjustments has developed in the COG subculture that enables members to avoid ideological activity at least temporarily (Goffman 1961a:189). For the most part, these adjustments to institutional pressure are "contained" ones: they fit into the existing organizational structure without undue disruption of organizational activities (Goffman 1961a:199). They involve the member doing things that he or she can justify to other members as appropriate, but that delay or prevent the member's participation in an ideological activity. The most prevalent form of adjustments are those that interfere with litnessing. Members can engage in extensive "preparation" before starting to litness. In one episode, two members going out to litness engaged in numerous activities—looking for the right literature, getting a drink, using the toilet, taking a rest to get "the vision," buying chewing gum, and engaging in topical conversation—that, while individually justifiable as appropriate "preparation," when taken together delayed their departure substantially.[5]

Usually in such episodes a form of tacit collusion exists among members: members rarely challenge others' secondary adaptations. At times, however, such adaptations do not go completely unchallenged. Shepherds are certainly aware that members are malingering even though they assert that they are engaged in reasonably necessary activities. Because of the member's presented justifications, the shepherd is less likely to accuse the member directly of malingering. In the following example, the shepherd applies gentle but firm pressure on the members to stop procrastinating. When members are confronted directly with their avoidance of ideological activity, they either invoke commonsense justifications for the delay, such as shaving or counting literature, or they remain silent and stop stalling.

> [The shepherd] wanted to know if they were ready to litness. One member said no, because he had to shave. After he finished shaving, the other member sat in the bedroom and began to open mail he said was from home. Then both members slowly began to pack and count their literature. The shepherd came in again: "Maybe you can count your lit outside, Benjamin, so you can save time." He responded: "How will I know how much I have." "Take some, but it will get you out the door," the shepherd replied with a note of irritation in his voice.

Secondary adaptations even involve using one ideological activity to postpone or avoid another. While litnessing, members frequently state that they need "some Word Time" and ask their partner to join them in reading a Mo letter or bible chapter. In another context, a group of café singers remained in the colony one day to practice new songs. Although the shepherd wanted the practice session to begin just after noon, the members stalled, using a variety of techniques including reading a Mo letter, bible chapters, and the day's Daily Might quotations, and did not begin practice until three. In each case, the secondary adaptation was patently justified because it was another ideological activity.

"Trials and Battles"

These ubiquitous episodes of routine alienation and secondary adaptation are not perceived by members as threatening the social or-

---

[5] Members' manipulation of my presence in their secondary adaptive behavior was not uncommon. One member, for example, took time out from litnessing to accompany me in purchasing some film, even though I insisted that I did not need his help and had bought film on my own several times in that town. The incident is even more remarkable because the member's Dutch was no more adequate than mine.

der of the group or as undermining members' commitment. COG members do, however, claim to suffer periodically from more serious forms of alienation. Members recognize these events as being problems of "maintenance of belief" and attempt to "repair" them through socially prescribed activities. To the extent that these episodes of alienation are interpreted ideologically by both the sufferer and those members around him, the episode contributes to social order (cf. Lofland 1966:212–22): a breach is made sense of through the ideology and is closed by ideological activity. Again, such episodes are expected, if infrequent, features of life in the Family.

When members recognize and acknowledge more severe alienation, they say they are going through "trials and battles." Typically, members describe their trials and battles as involving questions about particular ideological beliefs or activities. New members who are having difficulty adjusting to colony life, to COG leaders, or to other members also describe these difficulties as trials and battles. In some cases, members have trials and battles because they feel they are not living up to God's demands, that they are not accomplishing what they think they should. Members often cite Moses David's personal trials to show that they are not unusual.

The source of this type of alienation is the members' persistence in interpreting a belief or activity nonideologically. For example, many members have difficulty accepting the creationist doctrine that the formal ideology insists on. One member stated that even after he had received Jesus with the help of a Family member, he still held onto his belief that evolutionary theory was correct. It caused him "a lot of problems" until he simply decided that he could not go just halfway and he accepted Genesis 1–2 in total. Evolution, he asserted, was a Catholic hangover from his past. In this case, his trial was due to the fact that he continued to use a commonsensical theory of evolution acquired prior to joining the Family to interpret the world, despite its conflict with the accepted ideological interpretation.

Several standard techniques for handling these episodes are available within the COG subculture, but key to these techniques is the precondition that the member interpret his or her alienation ideologically. That is, a reservation about a belief, practice, or performance must be seen by the member as an ideological problem, one that can be explained by other parts of the ideology. COG members assert that trials and battles have a number of such sources. The most significant is that the Devil attempts to shake the member's commitment to God by "planting seeds of doubt" in the member's mind (cf. Lofland 1966:216). An alternative interpretation is normally used for new members: God is testing the neophyte's commitment. Trials and battles may also be caused simply by the member losing sight of the Family's goals: when this happens, it is easier for the Devil to come in. Although the problem may actually be a resistance to interpreting a phenomenon ideologically, it is handled by attributing the resistance itself to ideological causes.

If the alienation is interpreted by the member as a trial or battle, then the member and others around him "deal" with the alienation by attempting to close a breach in a member's interpretation of the world and COG activities. The asserted purpose of this activity is to help the member "get the victory" over his or her trial or battle. One of the more common ways a member handles trials and battles is to read one of several Mo letters addressed to the problem[6] and to pray "desperately." If the member's alienation persists, the colony shepherd "counsels" with the member or the member seeks help from other members. Often in such "repairing" interactions, the member helping another overcome his trial adopts an interactive posture similar to that used in witnessing interactions. Eye contact is maintained and the member attempts to show the other love and concern through bodily posture, tone of voice, and facial expressions. Prior to the end of my disguised participant observation period, I had the following encounter with a member:

> I told him I had qualms about litnessing, esp. telling people it was for youth work. He said it was for youth. I said but it wasn't the way people understood it as a charity. He said I should try another line [if the youth work representation bothered me]. I said that wouldn't help—that I had lost sight of the reason we litness. He began to witness and love me up—quoted proselytizing parts of Matthew. He went on and on. As soon as I told him there was a problem, he shifted radically. I changed from a piece of furniture to a direct object of his attention.

Members enter a persuading mode of interaction in such cases when they attempt to close a breach in the social order caused by the complaining member's trials and battles. In some cases, though, if a member is unable to overcome the problem, a transfer is suggested to place the member in a new environment.

In the following episode, the shepherd addressed directly the trials and battles a catacomb member was experiencing concerning the

---

[6] The formal ideology contains several Mo letters that discuss this type of problem and urge members to overcome it. Some of these include Let's Talk About Jesus (20), Dumps! (33), Listening?—Or Lamenting? (320). Moses David has also addressed specifically the problems mates of Flirty Fishing women experience when their wives are sleeping with potential converts—the "Flirty Fishing blues" problem—in letters such as The Men Who Play God! (564) and The FF Explosion! (576).

newly introduced access strategy of Flirty Fishing. The member had been brought up in a conservative Christian home and interpreted the new practice, from the vantage point of his background, as a form of religious adultery:

[*The shepherd spoke to the catacomb member in the boy's bedroom*] The only law once you're saved is the law of love. Salvation frees you from other laws. It repairs the damage done by Adam. The church is too cautious: a girl in church is afraid of what you'd think if she held out her hand. It's bad to be cautious. For example, the Song of Solomon is pornography: it tells you exactly how to make love.

[*doubting member*] But it's adultery.

[*shepherd*] It's done in love. Yes, there is adultery, but it depends on your motive. Adultery means betraying marriage. You must "have the faith" to engage in Flirty Fishing. For example, I began seeing a secretary who hadn't been out in over a year. [My wife] knows what I'm doing. You must do it in faith. The partners in a marriage have to decide together. Marriage is sex: when you make love, you have responsibilities. Fornication is just lustful sex—you just want to bang her and leave her; it gives you nothing spiritual. God looks on your heart and will judge your works. If you do it just from lust, He will punish you. It's really radical, huh?! You have to be willing as a Christian to give everything. There will be sex in heaven, as we are all the Bride of Christ.

This repairing technique depends, obviously, on whether the doubting member is open to accepting a justification of a practice couched in ideological terms.

Successful efforts to "get a victory over" trials contribute to members' sense of social order and membership in the Family. If a problem requiring attention does exist, both the member with the problem and others address it using ideologically provided interpretations and techniques. Such episodes are cited as evidence for the ideological fact that God protects members. A "victory" is interpreted as "a defeat for the Devil." "Victories" also demonstrate a member's ability to be a part of the Family. Because trials are thought to be inevitable, victories over them simply ratify the correctness of the ideological beliefs. Moreover, members with doubts demonstrate to themselves the efficaciousness of the COG way. The occurrence of trial-victory episodes throughout a member's life in the Family and among other members is simply another example of practical religious activity and reasoning through which members are continuously socialized into the Family.

Commitment-Threatening Alienation

In some cases, however, attempts to help a member "get the victory" over a trial or battle fail, and the member decides to leave the group. Members refer to this as "backsliding"—a standard southern Protestant term—and, as the COG's own figures indicate, backsliding is a fairly common phenomenon. Members universally attribute backsliding to the Devil. In cases in which the ex-member becomes antagonistic to the Family, members explain his or her backsliding as due to actual demonic possession of one sort or another. Either way, the Devil has won, at least temporarily, the battle for the member's soul. By interpreting backsliding in this fashion, members maintain their sense of social order: an act that no member would willingly commit is satisfactorily explained.

Those more likely to leave the group are members who, prior to joining, were active conservative Christians and who continue to account for phenomena by relying in part on presuppositions and interpretive procedures acquired in that prior experience. Thus, they find Moses David's claims to be God's last prophet difficult to square with their prior experience. More recently, the liberalization of sexual practices both in proselytization and between members has resulted in frequent instances of commitment-threatening alienation in members who refuse to interpret and address their doubts from within the COG ideological perspective and instead draw on nonsubcultural resources.

When a member announces that he or she intends to leave the group, leaders are immediately informed. They confront the member as soon as possible and determine why he or she wants to leave. The posture of the interaction is almost identical to a witnessing encounter, and leaders bring all their witnessing skill to bear. Using the procedures of practical religious reasoning, the leader attempts to dissuade the member from this rash action. They attempt to get the member to see the doubts as a normal occurrence of a trial and battle and to help him or her address the problem using COG techniques. Leaders tell the member that leaving is a "drastic step" in the member's spiritual life. They attempt to persuade the member that, despite his or her doubts about the Family, life in the System will be intolerable. The member is asked to remember why he or she joined the Family in the first place and is told that, upon returning to the System, he or she will be a ripe target for the Devil. Moreover, to leave is "to let God down." Often, the leader engaging the leaving member gives a personal testimony of how he once wanted to leave or of his own trials over the same issue. The leader also may read a bible passage or a pertinent Mo letter with the member.

In the course of my research, I was exposed on two occasions to leaders' attempts to persuade me not to leave. Below is a reconstruction of the first encounter from my field notes:

> I returned to the colony and knocked at the front door. [The shepherd] answered, saying "Bless the Lord." I hugged him and whimpered. I told him I was suffering a trial over litnessing. He took me into the boys' bedroom, where we prayed. He told me about his own trials with litnessing, how he was only able to get out 8 pieces of lit in 5 hours. He said that it was an entrance test for the Family and that I must yield to the Lord. He said that [another member] was also going through heavy trials right then. "We are like a holy vessel—we must give our body to the Lord—it's the hardest thing." I told him that I wanted to leave and asked him to write out a list of Mo letters[7] and to look over the ones I had. He didn't remove any [although several were classified DO]. He said leaving was my choice, but that he thought it would be better if I stayed. We prayed again, and read a Mo letter, *Letter to a Labourer* (325). He emphasized that doubts are the Devil's work. It is better to pray together, because when you are alone, it is easier for the Devil to get to you. Memorizing verses, he stated, helps fight the Devil by laying down roots in the Word. He again asked me to stay, but I insisted on leaving. He then said that I had body talents that the Lord could use—"we don't get many educated people"—like Jeremy Spencer, the Lord can use his bodily talents. Before I left, everyone in the colony at that time prayed in a circle for me.

The second episode followed a similar pattern:

> [The district shepherd] said that the Devil was tempting me and that God was permitting it as a trial of my faith. In response to my statement that I had trials over litnessing, he told me the parable of the seeds: litnessing was a better process for sowing the seed. "You can't be of two minds in the Family." He cited James 1:8. You must get the Word into your heart. Make a choice: stay and fight or go after something else. He refused to accept the third alternative I offered: that I didn't know what I wanted. He brought in a *New Nation News* and showed me statistics on how the Family was growing rapidly. The only way to prevent doubt is to keep reading and memorizing. The most important commandment is Mark 16:15. He said he had been into drugs—when he saw the real love

---

[7] The list contained *Letter to a Labourer* (325), *Benefits of Backsliding* (312), *Renewing Your Mind* (Mother Eve letter 27), *Sex Works!* (306), *Diamonds of Dust* (3), *But if Not!* (313), *Prayer Power* (302), John 14, *Stop-Look-Listen!* (74), and *Exorcism* (303).

of the Family he joined and has never looked back. Every time a doubt starts in his mind, he rebukes it in the name of Jesus. "If you go back, you will never get out. The Devil will work on you." Going back will solve nothing. It will be a real mistake. It's your choice. The Lord keeps giving you new struggles. Before I left, he and several others prayed with me: "Lord, help him find the way."

In the course of this interaction, the leader's voice grew forceful as he told me it would be a mistake to leave. He was visibly upset with my decision. I felt, however, no danger of physical restraint.

If the member is not persuaded to stay, he or she is permitted to go. I have no knowledge of physical coercion being used during the period of my research to prevent a member from leaving. For a believing member, however, the persuasion attempt is most likely very compelling. Affiliation with the group is based on at least some congruence between the Family's and the departing member's presuppositions about the world. These make the prospect of returning to the System an unappealing option. Only if there is a substantial disjunction in presuppositions, such as existed in my case, is departure easy.

The departing member, if he or she wishes, is given a list of Mo letters to read and is urged to write as soon as possible. It is expected that some backsliders will return, and some do. Members often say that those who have backslidden frequently make stronger members. Initially, members attempt to maintain some contact by mail or telephone with the backslidden member as long as he or she remains friendly. Unless, however, the backslider gives substantial signs of changing and returning within a month or so, he or she is written off as lost: the backslidden member has had his or her chance, and members prefer to allocate their time to new and more promising prospects. The souls that remain to be harvested are innumerable.

Conclusion

In this book, I have tried to understand what it means to "live in the COG." By constantly interacting with each other and with outsiders in the course of both ideological and more mundane activities, members create for themselves and others the reality of being members of the Family. From this perspective, COG members are little different from members of the wider society-at-large: both must negotiate daily life and do so in pragmatic ways. Both employ socially given rules that guide action in and interpretations of the world. Although these rules differ between subcultures, they rest and build on the more general commonsensical rules that all members of society share. Living in the COG is not the utter submission to a strange and oppressive ideology; it is a constant and continuing activity in which members confront and attempt to solve the pragmatic problems of daily life using the resources they have at hand.

POSTSCRIPT

JANUARY 1991

I N THE period since I completed my study,[1] organizational aspects of the COG have continued to change with the same freneticism that marked change during my study.[2] However, the Family's aphorism, "All things change, but Jesus never!" still applies: while David Berg has run members through a gauntlet of changes, the same basic techniques of witnessing, litnessing, and reading still form the core of the COG experience. As of July 1988, the Family claimed to have 12,390 full-time members of which 6,833 were children, most of whom were born into the Family.[3] The Family today is centered in Brazil and countries of southeast Asia,[4] particularly Japan

---

[1] In preparing this postscript, I have relied on reviews of Family publications, journalistic accounts, and telephone and personal interviews with ex-members of the Family. In addition, I have interviewed by telephone the press secretary of Moses David.

[2] Even the name changed for some purposes. Music cassettes were distributed on the street to the public under the name "Heaven's Magic" in the middle of 1985. Berg reports that members found the public to be more open to the musical message if they did not immediately associate it with the prior names that had received considerable amounts of adverse publicity. *An Open Letter to Our Friends!* (Jan. 1987).

[3] *The New Good News!*, GN338 (Oct. 1988) (DO). The Family also reported 714 full-time Homes with an average of 16.3 persons per Home. The age distribution of full-time members was 0-2 years (12.1%); 2-5 years (15.5%); 5-12 years (27.1%); 12-15 years (4.3%); 15-18 years (1.7%); 18-20 years (0.9%); 20-30 years (13.0%); 30-40 years (22.7%); 40-50 years (2.2%); and over 50 years (0.5%). This age distribution reflects both the aging of the members who joined in their teens and twenties in the middle 1970s and the emphasis on internal growth through children in the 1980s.

Finally, the time spent in the Family by full-time members in July 1988 is as follows for each year joined: 1968 (0.2%); 1969 (0.4%); 1970 (1.4%); 1971 (3.6%); 1972 (3.2%); 1973 (2.9%); 1974 (3.8%); 1975 (5.2%); 1976 (4.7%); 1977 (5.2%); 1978 (5.6%); 1979 (6.2%); 1980 (5.9%); 1981 (6.2%); 1982 (5.9%); 1983 (6.7%); 1984 (6.7%); 1985 (7.2%); 1986 (8.3%); and 1987 (10.7%). These figures show a fairly steady decay in affiliation over time.

[4] As of July 1988, there were 4,239 members in 198 Homes in Latin America; 2,418 members in 88 Homes in the Pacific region; 2,368 members in 206 Homes in Europe; 1,269 members in 41 Homes in southeast Asia; 1,087 members in 44 Homes in India and neighboring countries; 854 members in 126 Homes in North America; and 75 members in 7 Homes in the Middle East and Africa. Most of the members located in North America and Europe seem to be in nuclear family Homes. The predominant nationalities of the members continued to be skewed toward North Americans and Europeans: the top four nationalities were American (27.1%); Brazilian (7.8%); British (5.1%); and Canadian (5.0%) (*The New Good News!*, GN338 [Oct. 1988] [DO]).

and the Philippines,[5] although some members are returning to North America and western Europe.[6] Members have been arrested in or expelled by authorities from India (1986), China (1986),[7] Egypt (1985), Malaysia, and Indonesia (1985) for their sexual teachings, and they have had problems in both the Philippines[8] and Japan.[9] In early 1989, Berg acknowledged that many members would have to return to their home countries in the West (2507).

By the early 1980s, the Family was stagnating. The radical changes in both organization—the destruction by Berg of most intermediate levels of leaders—and sexual activity—the introduction of sexual sharing—led to significant defections from the group. Moreover, the basic organizational unit became the nuclear family[10]: a COG couple with their children lived and traveled as a unit, usually in a caravan or camper vehicle. Even a single individual could constitute his or her own TRF Home. Without the social support of group living, more members began to have doubts about Berg and the group's direction, and additional defections occurred. In many cases, members' only lifeline to the group was the *FN* (now *The New Good News!*) that arrived weekly by mail; members lived for the day on which they received the mailing from World Services.[11]

---

[5] One ex-member reports that the COG successfully infiltrated the Philippine army through Flirty Fishing with high army officers in the mid-1980s and enjoys informal protection from the military. (Lynch 1990:16, 20.)

[6] In July 1990, 10 adult and 22 child members were arrested in Barcelona, Spain, in a police action dubbed "Operation Moses" on charges of abduction and illegal proselytizing (Reuters, July 9, 1990, P.M. cycle). The charges were dropped in early October 1990. In late 1990, COG members previously located in the Far East began reappearing in England. "Alarm as evil child sex cult returns to UK" (*Mail on Sunday*, November 11, 1990, at 13). The COG continues to use a postal box in Zurich, Switzerland, for World Services.

[7] Four members were expelled from Canton after being arrested for promoting "sexual promiscuity among young people" (*Los Angeles Times*, Aug. 26, 1986, at 2, col. 1). The members had been in China under the guise of teachers of foreign languages and had founded a "Wonderful Music Club in Canton to lure Chinese youngsters to sex parties and to view pornographic videos" (Reuters, Aug. 13, 1986, P.M. cycle). Over several months, more than 200 Chinese students had joined the music club, but had since "been re-educated and renounced all ties with the sect" (*Ibid.*).

[8] At the behest of Cardinal Jaime Sin and other religious leaders, the COG were barred from preaching on school grounds in 1987 (Reuters, Apr. 9, 1987, P.M. cycle).

[9] Berg and Maria were expelled from Greece in 1987, and spent some time living in South Africa. Deborah Berg Davis believes that her father may be living in Japan, while another ex-member states that he is in Brazil.

[10] COMBOs, however, have continued to exist to the present. Located in each Language Area, they serve as landing stations for arriving members. Every Home has an affiliation with its Language Area COMBO.

[11] Berg's Mo letters shrilly predicted imminent nuclear wars in the early 1980s that

Berg's attempt to re-create the old solidarity of colony living with the Fellowship Revolution in 1981 was slow to take hold. By 1984, however, members once again were living in Homes with other unrelated members. The pattern was, and remains to this day, one in which four or five nuclear families together with a small number of single members make up a Home. Because of the high birthrate that continues to this day, a Home typically consists of eight to ten adults and sometimes twenty-five children. Periodically, Homes in an area will hire out a hall and hold a DAF (District Area Fellowship) or LAF (Language Area Fellowship). Living in such a Home is now a prerequisite for access to DO literature.

Two changes from Berg in 1985 reintroduced more focus to the organization. First, he used his authority to push the group toward more proclamatory efforts. He called on members to distribute and collect donations for music cassettes and colorful and sometimes sexually provocative posters, which are produced by World Services.[12] Berg also suggested the imposition of quotas, and of punishments for failing to meet these quotas. As they had done during the litnessing period with Mo letters, members sold the posters and tapes on street corners with great success, especially in India. There are reports from ex-members that the Family also succeeded in distributing COG booklets through unknowing religious bookstores in Latin America. Actual personal witnessing dropped off except for some infrequent Flirty Fishing. As occurred during the litnessing period, the stream of new members recruited into the group dwindled to a small trickle. The Family's main source of new members today is the children born into the group.

As was also the case during the litnessing period, the proclamatory effort was accompanied by a more defined and authoritarian leadership structure. In what he called the "Obedience Revolution," Berg appointed trusted members as leaders to oversee the activities of Homes, and by 1985 their number had multiplied and their training was improved. Instead of the softer image that they had presented in the mid-1970s, leaders became stricter and more authoritarian. One couple was selected to be Home Area Servant or shepherd, and was relieved of day-to-day chores. This allowed them the freedom to

---

would precede the coming of the Antichrist in 1986. To this day, the literature distributed to the public emphasizes the coming end of the world even if it is not so bold in its precise predictions.

[12] The posters are produced and printed by World Services, which remains in Geneva. The music tapes are copies of COG music produced by Music with Meaning in the early 1980s. The MWM located in Greece was disbanded in 1982, and much of the literature distributed in the late 1980s was produced in 1986 and earlier.

intervene again in all aspects of Home life, from the most mundane to the most private; on occasion leaders ordered couples to match up or break up, and would counsel members on their failings and monitor their activities closely. One benefit of the revolution was that the quality of Home life quickly improved.

Members who violated Family rules or were thought to be "rebellious" or "disobedient," or to have "other spiritual problems for which they refused to get the victory" (LNF86), received special attention. Such members were said to be "murmurers" or to be "murmuring against God's prophet [Berg]" and were sometimes threatened with expulsion (1879). A less drastic step was to demote a member to "babe's status," which meant that the member was denied Mo letters and COG literature classified as DO for a period of three to six months (LNF86). For several years after 1985, confession sessions—called "rebukings"—during which members would confess their failings,[13] proliferated at the local Home level, although they have now been phased out. In many cases, "murmurers" were sent to other Homes or even back to their native countries ("Home Fields") to prove their commitment to the group.[14] When this occurred, the departing member might be separated from his or her children, who remained behind (2468). By 1988, the COG suffered a series of public relations problems when ex-members attempted to recover custody of children they had left behind.[15]

The innovations of Flirty Fishing and sexual sharing among members introduced in 1978 survived into the late 1980s. While Flirty

[13] In the early 1980s, Berg had reported the trials and battles of Hosea and his wife Esther; reports included criticism sessions with Berg and Faith and detailed confessions by Hosea and Esther. Subsequently, in a Mo letter entitled *My Confessions*, Berg admitted to being an alcoholic. Berg also publicized his belief that certain leaders who had fallen out of grace suffered from "serious spiritual problems" or were "demon possessed," including Keda Sky, then a top leader in the Pacific area (and who remains a member), and Berg's daughter Deborah Davis, whose 1984 book caused a flow of vituperation from Berg's pen (1856). Berg frequently called for members to "pray against" or "curse" "our enemies" (2477; 2478).

[14] In 1988, some recalcitrant members were sent to experimental Retraining Centers or "Rehabilitation Homes" in Japan (FSM121:1).

[15] The most public of these episodes was Vivian Shillander's successful scheme in early 1988 to remove several of her children from a Family Home in Thailand. This episode was recounted by ABC News's 20/20 Program on July 15, 1988. Berg prayed that God would "[d]estroy that woman [Shillander] who's caused us so much trouble & save the children!" (2477:1). Berg made a similar plea against a Japanese magazine that had published an unfavorable story on a Family school in Japan (2478). World Services has distributed a form legal document that enables parents to grant another COG member guardianship of their children to thwart attempts to remove the children from the group (LNF120).

Fishing was prominent in much of the group's literature, including the *FN*, its practice by group members was less than universal (it was limited to a reasonably small number of leaders and members). With the onset of the fear of AIDS, Berg in late 1987 banned all Flirty Fishing except in specially approved situations, and it has ceased to be a significant method of recruiting outsiders into the group.

The matter was different with sexual sharing. After an initial period of reticence, members, whether by choice or by suggestion, did participate.[16] By the early 1980s, sexual sharing became a regular feature of everyday life that continues to this day. In most cases of both Flirty Fishing and sexual sharing, members made their own decisions about participation, and many members successfully avoided it. It appears, however, that the social pressures toward participation were great and that in some instances local leaders even assigned and directed members to share sexually.

The same is true of sex between adults and children. Despite Berg's 1988 statement that its publication was an "oversight," *My Little Fish*, issued in 1979,[17] was taken by some members as a blueprint requiring adults to introduce their children to sexual experiences. During the early 1980s there was experimentation with small child sex including incest. In late 1987, according to the Family, Berg expressly banned incest and small child sex and threatened guilty parties with excommunication.

Berg, however, has consistently held to his belief that sex is one of God's gifts to be enjoyed[18] and that it should not be denied to those who are capable of enjoying it (779; 999; 2061).[19] Sexual sharing among children who are as young as eight or nine years old is not uncommon. The one prohibition is that females who have begun to menstruate should not have intercourse with a seminating male until

[16] In the early 1980s, the periodic Fellowship meetings at times included sexual sharing. While Berg forbade such practices in 1983, group sharing continued on in South America for several years.

[17] The letter appeared in a book, *The Story of Davidito*, which recounted the birth and early childhood of Davidito, a Jesus baby born to Maria on January 27, 1975, from her Tenerife Flirty Fishing experiences. The book consists largely of letters written by a childcare worker in Berg's home named Sarah Davidito. The *My Little Fish* letter is a series of photographs of naked young children (some alone, some together, and some with naked adults) interspersed with quotations from earlier Mo letters on sex.

[18] Since the early 1980s, Berg has encouraged the making of nude dancing videos by women for viewing at Fellowship meetings (1026) and urged women and girls to send in nude photographs of themselves—"nudie cuties"—for his enjoyment (2347).

[19] In the Mo letter *The Devil Hates Sex!* (999:110), Berg stated that there should be no age or relationship limits on sexual sharing. Only sodomy is prohibited by God (1110). In *Child Brides!* (902), Berg stated that marriage at the age of 15 was appropriate.

they reach the age of fifteen. The stated rationale for this rule is that the System will be suspicious of girls younger than fifteen having children (2061:36; *Basic Training Manual*:293). As with adult sexual sharing, there are reports that some leaders set up "sharing nights" for children in which they were paired off to make love before falling asleep. Moreover, there were many cases in which older males were pressuring young girls to share sexually.[20]

This activity apparently got out of hand by 1984, and the group established "Teen Training Camp[s]" ("TTC") in 1985 and 1986 at which pre- and young teens were removed from these sexual pressures and were educated. At the TTCs, which lasted from one to three months, sexual activity was banned and young teens were encouraged to discuss their problems. As a result, although children continue to be taught about sex and that sex is one of God's gifts to be enjoyed, sexual activity, particularly between adults and young teens, has become less prevalent and is rarely openly encouraged at the Home level. Still, full sexual sharing remains an important part of daily life in the Family.

More importantly, the TTCs reflect a radical change in the Family. Instead of recruiting older adults from the outside, the Family has turned inward to produce[21] and nurture its own children who it believes will be the leaders of the millennium. In a series of three books entitled *Heaven's Children, New Heaven's Children,* and *Heaven's Girl,* Berg described his visions and dreams of the Tribulation and the coming millennium in which the teen members of the Family will play critical roles. *Heaven's Girl* is an inspirational tale set in the early 1990s about Marie Claire, a young teenager who is caught behind the Antichrist's lines and must sleep and fight her way out of trouble. These books have also revised some of the details of Berg's description of the final years (2250).[22]

For the Family, the teens are the vanguard, the new leaders. Addressing the second-generation problem of religious sects (Niebuhr 1957:19) head-on, the Family employs the TTCs to train and prepare the teens for this new role and to secure their allegiance to the group. At the age of eleven or twelve, a member is sent to one of the TTCs

---

[20] As early as 1982, Berg was concerned about older adults forcing sex on children (1142). The *FN* published some letters from young girls with approving comments from Berg and Maria complaining about sex with older men.

[21] From the early 1980s, World Services offered a "baby bonus" to mothers who bore a child (1051). It probably amounted to about £50.

[22] For example, in *The 70-Years Prophecy* (156), Berg was to die before the Tribulation; *New Heaven's Children* now has Berg dying after the conclusion of the reign of the Antichrist.

for leadership training. In many cases, those who attend the TTCs do not return to their parents, but are sent directly to new Homes to begin their adult proselytizing efforts for the Family. More recently, Berg has called for the formation of Family boarding schools for the training of the teens (2430; 2432). The Family encourages young teens to achieve independence from their parents so that they can serve the Lord more fully, and warns them of the dangers of the System (2462).

Despite recent rumors of his death, Berg[23], who in February 1991 turned seventy-two, apparently still lives. What will become of the Family upon Berg's death? His predictions of his own death and the events of the end-time should certainly enable his successor, whether it is Maria or Faith, to perpetuate or appropriate his charismatic authority for a period. Moreover, most members will have strong incentives to stay in the group no matter who succeeds Berg. Many members who joined during the 1970s—the peak recruitment period—are now well into their thirties and have five or more children. Particularly for women with young children, the thought of leaving the group and making it in the System may be both frightening and impractical. At the least, the Family has provided such people with sufficient material support. Those who do try to leave have a difficult time, and many drift in and out of the group. More importantly, as Berg has recognized, the children born into the group are its future. Far more than half of the full-time members are under the age of fifteen and have never known any other life. They hold the key to the Family's survival. While younger children might follow their parents out of the group, it is far less clear that those in their early and later teens would leave.

[23] His chief lieutenants are Maria and Peter ("First Fruits") Amsterdam, an earlier European convert who replaced Timothy Concerned in 1978 and who acts as Berg's executive assistant. While many ex-members believe that Maria, Peter, and Faith, who is currently running a Family school, are locked in a struggle to succeed Berg when he dies, COG sources deny this and state that Faith is not as actively involved in the administration of the Family. Maria has played a stronger executive role in the 1980s and has been particularly concerned about the education of children. She sought to ameliorate some of the sexual excesses of the mid-1980s and was behind the TTCs.

APPENDIX A

THE LIFE HISTORY OF THE RESEARCH AND ETHICAL CONSIDERATIONS

MY RESEARCH on the Family grew from some vague theoretical interest and the conjunction of several fortuitous events. Prior to my initial contact with the COG in Greenwich Village, I had been intrigued for some time by the relation between religious ideology and social structure and related questions in the sociology of knowledge. In particular, I had been interested in that relation as it affected individual believers. I thought that a study of the COG would be appropriate to this interest because I believed the group to be one in which ideology dictated almost every action. By studying a severe and extreme form of social organization, I hoped to understand more about social processes in general. My image of the Family was of a highly authoritarian and ideological group in which the notion of individualism was attenuated.

Initial Contacts and Research Decisions

My initial research upon arriving at the London School of Economics did nothing to disabuse me of this perception. The more I read, the more I felt that I had chosen an interesting topic. My commitment to the topic was also bolstered by the fact that I was immediately associated with the group by faculty and other graduate students. Newspaper accounts led me to believe that the Family engaged in extreme tactics: brainwashing, physical restraint, and forced surrender of all personal possessions. I began to wonder whether a participant observation study would be possible.

My first research contact with the group occurred in November 1975. My intention was simply to scout out the group and to decide how to proceed. I was concerned that I not be taken as someone who might harm the group. Presenting myself as an interested person who was also a graduate student,[1] I visited the COG discotheque in London—the Poorboy Club—on the second floor of an old building at the corner of Finchley Road and a cross street. I immediately noted

[1] John Lofland adopted the same role in his early encounters with the Unification Church (Lofland 1966:269).

the often mentioned starry-eyed look of the member who greeted me.

This member led me into the club itself. It was not lavishly decorated by any means. At one end was a bar serving soft drinks and charging the cost. A dance floor occupied the other side of the club; although no one was dancing at the time, a late sixties record was playing. The member immediately began to witness to me. I tried to fend him off, but he was persistent. He offered me several pamphlets that I eagerly accepted: they turned out to be Mo letters. He then invited me to stay around for a skit that "some of his friends" were going to put on. The skit was called "Richman, Poorman" and depicted a hostile Dickensian interaction between a figure with similarities to Uncle Sam and a tattered resident of the Third World. I sat with the member and other spectators on the floor. It was quickly obvious that many of the spectators were Family members: their laughs were a little too vigorous and their applause and cheers too strong. Most of the other spectators were young, in their mid- to late teens.

After the skit, the member talked to me some more. He described his belief in Jesus and what Jesus could do for me. He insinuated that my current educational experience was probably not very fulfilling. I neither agreed nor disagreed. He finally suggested that I ask Jesus into my heart. I declined politely, and said that I had to go. He invited me to return again soon. I left the place with a sense of relief. I found the pressure of being witnessed to uncomfortable. My doubts about the research increased: both whether access to the daily lives of Family members was possible and whether I had the temperament to do the study.

I returned to Finchley Road in early December. Again, I was the target of intense proselytization, this time by another member. I tried to ask questions about the activities of the group, but these went largely unanswered. Instead, the member pressed me and pressed me to pray to ask Jesus into my heart. Without much forethought, I decided that maybe it would be better to acquiesce and see what happened. The member held both my hands, closed his eyes, and told me to repeat after him a short salvation prayer. When I finished, he opened his eyes and presented me with a big smile and a hug. "Praise the Lord!" he said, almost shouting.

He immediately asked me if I also wanted to pray to ask for the Baptism in the Holy Spirit. A little shaken by what I had done, I told him that I preferred not to at the time. I nervously let him know that I had to go soon, but that I wanted to take something to read. He lead me into a small room that was packed with Mo letters. I began to look through them quickly, trying to decide in my mind how many I could take without attracting his suspicion. I was in the sociologist's heaven: I had access to large quantities of what I thought was the carefully guarded literature of a deviant subgroup. As it turned out, the member was thrilled to see evidence of my voracious appetite "for the Word," as he referred to the letters. I came away with a good pile. The member encouraged me to come back as soon as possible.

Christmas intervened, and I did not return to the Poorboy Club until early January. When I did, I found it closed. Apparently, the Family was leaving London in large numbers, and there were no longer enough people to staff the club. I did run into two members who were coming out of the club as I approached, and I asked them how I could get in touch with either of the members I had spoken with on earlier visits. They told me to write to the London address on the literature, and that my letter would be forwarded to the appropriate place. The two then rushed off.

About this time, I contacted the late Professor Roy Wallis, who at the time was at Sterling University in Scotland. He had a research grant from the Social Science Research Council of Great Britain to investigate the Family and was planning a book. I decided to visit him in late March, during a hiatus in class work. I also wrote to several sociologists of religion about my thought of conducting some covert participant observation. Most responses expressed ethical reservations.

Prior to visiting Professor Wallis, I again wrote to the London COG address. Sometime later, I received a reply from two members in Bradford. They informed me that most of the Family members in Britain, including the two I had met at the Poorboy, had gone "abroad to other countries which are more ready to hear about Jesus than England!" The letter encouraged me to write back and to read the enclosed Mo letters. It also asked for a small donation.

I wrote back, requesting more letters and enclosing some money— £1. I also talked a little about what I was doing and intimated that I found going to classes to be uninspiring. I suggested that I might like to visit them in Bradford sometime. In mid-March, I got a reply. The same two Bradford members, commenting on my letter, stated that "It's true what you said in your letter, that going to school *does* seem a bit useless, and even if you *haven't* read a Mo letter, there is not much sense in the whole thing. The fact is that Mo gives us an *alternative* (Drop *out* for Jesus!)." They encouraged me to continue to write and went on: "We'd love to hear what you're studying, and just how you think your life is heading and most of all—if you are *happy*!!!"

My visit with Roy Wallis interrupted this correspondence. It confirmed my concerns about access to the group for the type of study I wanted to pursue. Although he was encouraging, he thought that open access to a COG colony was likely to be impossible.[2] Professor Wallis also mentioned that Rex Davis, who at the time worked for the World Council of Churches in Geneva, had some contact with the Family. During my visit with Professor Wallis, I concluded that only a covert entry would satisfy my research needs. He warned about the COG "forsake all" practice: COG members were known to appear at the apartment of a new member to collect all his or her belongings for sale or for distribution within the group. He also expressed some concern about the possible dangers of being discovered as an impostor, but thought that the consequences would not be disastrous. Finally, he mentioned the fact that members spent much time in litnessing. This last feature of the group somehow went in one ear and out the other.

Because I had invested a not unappreciable amount of time already, and because my concern was with the group life of average members, I decided to attempt a period of covert participant observation. Due to the nature of commitment to the group, this entailed joining as a full-time member and living in a COG colony. I settled on a period of two months as an initial goal. As I recall, ethical considerations did not play a big part one way or another in my decision. I intended no harm to the group, and I felt that I would be unlikely to have any adverse impact given both the lowly position I would adopt and the short period of time I intended to be involved. Nor did I try to contact COG leaders for permission; I feared that any such contact would tip off what I believed to be a highly organized social control apparatus that could put a covert attempt in jeopardy. I approached the whole problem with a different concern, my personal safety.

I wrote to the Bradford group again, this time expressing more than passing interest in the Family. I recounted my conversion experience as having had a strong, if somewhat scary, effect on me.[3]

[2] Roger Curl, then a graduate student working under Professor Bryan Wilson at Oxford, had given up a proposed study of the Family for the reason that he believed it only possible through infiltration. Letter from Roger Curl to Author (Oct. 28, 1977).

[3] I reproduce my letter in its entirety below. It is a shameful example of dissembling. I wanted to make a significant impression of sincerity on its readers and may have gone overboard (cf. Festinger et al 1964:238):

11/4/76

Dear [two members],

Thank you for your letter! It's really great to get mail from people who really care! I'm sorry I've not written you. I really feel bad. I've been on holiday for several weeks, but haven't done much traveling. I have to write a paper for my

My letter was quickly responded to. The two members, who I soon discovered were the colony shepherds, gave me a street address and telephone number. The response letter stated: "I'm sure you'll get your mind blown—just like *I* did when I first met the COG because it's just *all too simple*!!! The love of Jesus is too simple for some people they can't understand it!!" The letter was designed to fit precisely what I was beginning to understand to be Family members' theory about those who are not saved or who are still living in the System. I telephoned the colony shepherd shortly thereafter and arranged a visit for the following Wednesday.

Covert Participant Observation

I arrived at noon on May 12, 1976, and was greeted in a rather unfriendly fashion by one of the members. The house used by the Family in Bradford was in a poor section of that industrial town; most of

---

tutor and it's really hard. I'm not really into it, but I would feel guilty if I didn't do it. You asked me to tell you about what I'm studying. That's a good question! I study at the University of London. I read in sociology things like Karl Marx and other theorists. I am also taking a statistics course and doing a little computer work so I can "count people." I have to write papers on theoretical topics. I graduated from Princeton University last June. I had made no plans and didn't know what to do. I was "lucky" enough to be accepted here, but what I'm to do after this year I don't know. Finally, I don't really know whether I'm happy. I guess if I don't know maybe I'm not. If I was I would know it.

I would love to come and see how you live. It sounds so different. I was at the Poor Boy [sic] Club several times and I liked the people there. Someone prayed for me—it felt good to have someone care. I accepted Jesus into my heart and I did feel different, but I didn't go back to the disco. I think I was a little scared of the new feeling. I do want to come for a visit and talk with you, but I don't have your address in Bradford. Please send it to me so I'll know where to find you. Do you have a phone number?

In the meantime, please tell me more about the Children. Is it all true what's in the Mo letters? I'm supposed to be a hot-shot academic, but I find so much more in some of the Mo letters! Is all I have to do is drop out to be really happy? Please tell me!

I guess because I'm a student I like to read a lot. I really enjoyed the last Mo letters you sent me, especially "Student Stand Up." [299] I'm sending £2 more. It's all I can afford now. Please send me more Mo letters. I need some of the following: A, I, 117, 179, 192, 317, 333, 9, 31, 203, 231, 306, 46, 315 if that isn't too much. Whatever you can send would be great. I hope someday I can share the happiness you all obviously have.

Love,
Dave

David Van Zandt
215 Portnall Rd.
Queens Park
London W9

P.S.: What can I tell my roommates? They are giving me trouble about Jesus[,] laughing lots of times. I just ignore them.

the neighbors were Pakistani or Indian. (Because of the ongoing exodus from Britain, the Bradford colony was somewhat larger than normal. It had 18 members and two shepherds and their wives. In addition, the district shepherd and his wife lived in the colony.) I met several members: Rebecca gave me her testimony about leaving her husband to join the Family; Naomi, the wife of the second shepherd at the colony, told me a little about her experiences, but seemed aloof. Shalom, my original contact, gave me his testimony. It included a description of how COG members went with him to his apartment in Liverpool after he joined to pick up and sell his stereo and electric guitar equipment.

I told Shalom that I wanted to join. We then prayed about it, and Shalom said it was a very important decision. He said that life in the Family was very difficult; he suggested that I read two Mo letters, *Forsaking All* (314A) and *Revolutionary Rules* (S). He said that there would be a two-week provisional period "to see if it's for you." Otherwise, he was very unclear as to particulars. He then disappeared upstairs; when he returned he said that I could join. I told him that I wanted to return to London to collect my things and that I would be back on Saturday. I left at about five in the afternoon.

In London, I began to make arrangements. One of my fears was that COG members might want to go with me to my flat to pick up my belongings. I lived in a three bedroom flat with three other roommates. At the time, I had one of the single bedrooms. I left most of my possessions in that room, moving only a few things to the double bedroom so that it would look as if I had been sleeping there. One of my roommates moved from the double room into the single and agreed to claim, if asked, that all my possessions belonged to him. My parents also contributed to my efforts to avoid detection. They altered their letters to me during the period to protect my cover. For example, in a convincing paragraph they questioned my decision to join the Family, but acquiesced to it as a decision made by a mature adult. I also instructed my roommates not to speak to strangers about my project, and to forward mail only after checking to be sure it had no damaging information.

My second fear was of being trapped in the Family against my will. I developed an elaborate signal system to effect my possible escape. I sent my parents in the United States what I thought would serve as legal authorization for them to kidnap me and to deprogram me if necessary. Such action would be triggered if either my parents or my roommates received a coded message in the mail or by telephone.

I left London on Saturday afternoon, May 15, 1976, carrying my clothing in a backpack and old suitcase. I arrived in Bradford in the early evening and got on the bus to go to the Family colony. On the bus, I noticed a young couple who I immediately recognized as Family members even though I had never met them before. They were the only young whites on the bus, and the male was playing a guitar. Both were laughing and singing. I got off at the appropriate stop, but they continued on. As I later found out, members in the Bradford colony made a practice of not getting off the bus at the exact stop: they went a little further and walked back in order to prevent someone from discovering the location of the colony.

I was greeted warmly this time at the door. I was first introduced to everyone, all of whom were seated around the dinner table. A member took me into the bedroom on the ground floor in which most of the unmarried males slept. I left my suitcase and came out to take a place at the dinner table. Many members came up and hugged me in welcome. Later that evening there were devotions and some singing, and several members danced. We all went to bed at midnight. I felt remarkably comfortable in my new home.

The next day was Sunday, a free day in the colony. I helped out with some cleaning and got to know all the members a little better. I also decided on a new bible name for myself. I chose Abel, in part out of the ironic fact that I would have to work hard at maintaining my false identity in the group. Shalom said that the name was appropriate because he believed that I would be a hardworking servant for the Lord. Again, I did not feel uncomfortable, and I fully expected to last the two months. On Monday, however, my project became more tenuous.

That morning I began to realize what Shalom had said about the difficulties of living and working in the Family. I had not been prepared for the strenuousness and duration of proselytization activities. After breakfast, Shalom announced the litnessing teams for the day. I was paired with his natural sister, Ruthie Rainbow. After getting our literature and praying, Ruthie and I set out for a small midlands town less than an hour from Bradford. Shalom gave Ruthie £2 for our bus fare and any other expenses. On the bus, Ruthie decided that we should go to Halifax instead after the driver told her that Halifax was much busier. We hitchhiked up to Halifax.

Ruthie and I spent the rest of that somewhat chilly, overcast day in a shopping precinct of Halifax attempting to distribute literature, to collect funds, and to witness to people. Ruthie was careful to be sure that I never left her sight. Aside from lunch and one or two rest periods, she and I occupied the entire day approaching strangers in the precinct. I had several encounters with Jehovah's Witnesses, who attempted to convince me that they, rather than the Family, were on the road to truth. At five o'clock we hitchhiked back to Bradford. After dinner, at which we gave testimonies or reports about the day's events, there was a short devotional period. We all went to bed at quarter to eleven. I fell asleep quickly, exhausted, but was to wake up on and off throughout the night.

When awake, I lay on my stomach thinking. I was worried about litnessing the next day. I jotted down these notes the following day:

> Everything began to rush through my head and swell. I felt I was about to be overcome by a bright cloud. I almost jumped out of bed. I quickly talked to myself [silently], "Get a grip." I rolled onto my back and settled my mind. I restated my purpose and what I would get from the study. I told myself just to try to bear up to everything. I had simply repressed that swelling.

I finally fell asleep.

I woke up for good very early the next morning, maybe four or five o'clock. The wake-up call was scheduled for quarter to seven. I lay awake dreading the day. When the call finally came, I rose to go to the bathroom to wash. Because I also intended to shave, I let Sunflower in ahead of me. She spent over twenty minutes in the bathroom, while I sat outside growing more tense and irritable. The lack of sleep caused by the strain and dissembling brought on by litnessing contributed to my irritability. At no point did I fear being discovered. In fact, that morning I had experienced a joking questioning of my true identity without feeling any fear. At breakfast, we drank something called a Mo Drink. I asked one member what was in it. He said that it was a deep COG secret and that I should not ask such a question. Shalom, the colony shepherd, added, "I always thought you were a spy," and laughed. I laughed too, quite easily.

After breakfast, Shalom announced the litnessing teams. I was to go with Sunflower and Rebecca to a nearby town. We set out on the bus with me sitting between the two women. I was completely preoccupied as they talked through me. On two occasions, Sunflower warned me not "to space out." I soon realized that I was not going to make it. A raging desire grew in me to get off the bus and out of the Family. I blurted this out to Sunflower, and she gave me some money to return to the colony.

At the colony, only the two sets of shepherds remained. Shalom took me into the boys' bedroom and tried to convince me to stay. In this particular case, he also mentioned that he had reservations about sending me out with Sunflower and Rebecca, but that the colony was too big and that it was an emergency situation due to the evacuation of England; he regretted that he had to leave some of the ministering to younger members such as Sunflower (the rest of our interaction is reported in Chapter 9). I packed and went out the door after praying with those in the colony.

Despite my anxiety and almost paranoid desire to get out, I purposely did not destroy my cover and left things in such a way as to permit reentry. I was extremely discouraged, however, at failing to pull off the research, and on the train ride to London decided that I would not be able to complete my study. On Wednesday, I came down with a fever that lasted about twenty-four hours. In the next few days, I began to reconsider my initial decision to abort the project. I realized that in only one day of litnessing I had gathered a great deal of information about the daily life of a Family member. Moreover, I believed that my negative reaction was in part due to the fact that I was simply unaware of the nature of Family life. I remembered that I had enjoyed interacting with members in the colony context; it was only the litnessing—the false interaction with strangers on the street—that got to me. After consulting with the school psychiatrist, who provided some sleeping pills, I decided to try again.

I thought if I could keep some perspective on my activity, it would be easier to get by. I carried two index cards. One contained a list of imperatives to help me remember my goals and to keep that perspective.[4] The second held the words to a song that I always had found particularly relaxing and reassuring. In addition, having left fairly easily the first time, I was less anxious about being held against my will.

On Saturday, May 22, I went to Bradford again. I was much less apprehensive starting out; by the time I was walking up to the colony, however, I again was nervous. Members welcomed me back warmly; I received no special treatment or attention as might be expected for a once-failed member. In fact, both Sunflower and Rebecca said that they knew I would come back. I felt quite relaxed as the evening wore on.

The next day I did a number of things including cleaning and beginning to learn to play the guitar. In the afternoon, Shalom called

---

[4] Those propositions were:

1. Maintain 2 distinct positions: don't let them merge and conflict.
2. Derive internal gratification from this effort.
3. Maintain distance or perspective.
4. Take time to contemplate and relax.
5. Avoid consideration of time—keep busy.
6. Resign self to one month sentence.
7. Study what is happening to self.
8. Battle and strive *to conquer.*

me into his upstairs bedroom and asked how I was getting along. I told him how I had been sick back in London, and that I knew that I would have many "trials," but that I hoped the Lord would help me through them. We hugged and I went back downstairs.

In the following two weeks, I litnessed almost every day. Shalom apparently avoided pairing me with Sunflower; in fact, the first day I went out with the other colony shepherd. Only on Wednesday of the first week and Friday of the second did I stay at the colony. The first day there was a Word Day, a day of reading the bible and the Mo letters, with several other new members. On the Friday, I stayed home to help several other male members move some "survival supplies" into the basement. At some point near the end of the second week, Shalom asked me to fill out a membership application. He specifically told me to mention that I knew some Russian; he thought that I could help translate Mo letters into that language for "pioneer" or proselytization efforts in the Soviet Union. The consistent litnessing began to take its toll again. Despite employing a number of protective techniques described in the Introduction, I still found the activity difficult psychologically. As before, I went to sleep easily, but woke up early in the morning feeling a great deal of anxiety about the day ahead. Over the course of the period, I grew more and more tired.

On the second Saturday, June 5, 1976, the other colony shepherd called me into the boys' bedroom about an hour after the wake-up time. He said, "Would you like to go on the road?" I replied, "That would be great." "How about with Nathan?" Nathan was a somewhat disoriented member with whom I did not have excellent rapport. "Fine," I said, swallowing hard. "You can go to Scotland and stay for a week or two." "Okay." "Get ready and leave as soon as you can." The shepherd then went out and spoke to Nathan.

I was excited about the research prospects of going on a "faith trip" and was pleased that the shepherd thought enough of me to send me out so early, but I was apprehensive about being out alone with Nathan and outside of the comfort and security of the colony. I tried to view it as a challenge. Nathan came in and said we would have to carry a lot of literature if we were going out for so long. As we went downstairs, another member asked what we were doing. I told him about the faith trip; he said, "Praise the Lord, I bet you're happy."

I helped Nathan collect the literature for our trip. The pile grew fairly large, so I told Nathan that I thought we had enough. He responded that you needed a lot for a two-week trip. My stomach tightened; I was already thinking that a week would be long enough. I said, "This is my first time out, and I don't know if I'll be able to last." He did not seem to register my comment and continued to pile up the literature. I asked the wife of the shepherd whether Nathan and I could have bowls of cereal before leaving. The request was more of a delaying tactic on my part. I later spoke to the shepherd about Nathan's desire to stay out two weeks and expressed my concern. He agreed to speak to Nathan before we left.

Nathan and I discussed where we could go first. I suggested Lancaster, saying that I had a friend there with whom we could stay. I also said I knew someone in Sterling who might put us up, thinking of one of Roy Wallis's graduate students. I was trying to provide breaks in the trip to provide myself with an emotional crutch. Nathan thought we should aim for someplace closer the first night. He suggested Burnley, stating that it was a good place to litness. He said he had a debt to his father to pay off and that was why he wanted to stay out longer. I told him I needed a lot of Word Time and that I would take it easy on the trip. We left at eleven in the morning. We were given £2 to start us on our way.

We took a local bus downtown. I led the way to the bus station, an act for which Nathan seemed overly grateful. At the station, Nathan asked an inspector from which platform the Burnley bus left. He got an ambiguous answer and became upset. When I asked why he was so angry, he said he got that way when "people screwed him up." We each read Mo letters while waiting for the bus. Once on the bus, we moved to the very back. There were several men standing in line for the bus with black hats, black beards, and black robes. Nathan thought they were Indian; when they sat near us, the thought, "how sad they look!" went through my mind.

I then began to experience some of the same sensations I had two Saturdays before. I quote from my field notes:

> By this time the world was turning gray—I knew I was in trouble—but I wanted to fight on. [Nathan] sat in [the] back seat—I in the seat right in front [of him]. I began to read—trying to ignore him. I began to fear that my privacy—so essential in the colony—was going to be out on this trip. After awhile, Nathan suggested we should have a devotion period after I finished the letter I was on. He said we should stay in the unity of [the S]pirit as much as possible on the trip. I was developing an inner aversion.

I then moved to sit next to him, and we read the Mo letter *Faith* (73). At my insistence, we took turns reading paragraphs. Nathan exclaimed under his breath "Wow!" or "Heavy!" or "Isn't that heavy!" after almost every point in the letter. Because he apparently was having trouble hearing me when I read, he pressed his head right up to my face. To give me some space, I told him his hair was getting in my eyes. I was beginning to show my irritation through looks and comments that he ignored. As a result of my irritation, I asked him whether he had done drugs in the System; he said he had smoked marijuana and for a time had taken LSD almost every day. I said to myself, "That explains his burned out expression."

Upon arriving in Burnley, we went to get some food in a large shopping mall. Because I wanted a malt loaf and he fruit, I suggested we go to different stores and meet in a minute or two; he objected: "We are a team and should stay together." I expressed my disgust with my face. We then sat down in a café, and with the last of my money we bought tea.

I was extremely apprehensive about litnessing and felt as if I were moving in another world. The sun seemed to move in and out; I was getting impulses of fear that I tried to suppress. When we were finally ready to litness, Nathan wanted us to keep moving through the crowd to avoid being caught by security guards in the plaza. I objected, but he said we had to do it that way. As we started, I could barely see people. Everything was gray and distant. When I approached shoppers, my voice was barely audible.

I let several people pass by, and then without thinking beckoned to Nathan to come over. I told him I was having "real problems about litnessing." He suggested we go sit down; when we found seats, I said that I wanted to return to Bradford. By this time, I realized that my difficulty was knowing that I would have to live on what I collected during the faith trip and that I would always be in the litnessing situation, the situation in the Family I hated the most.

Nathan then said, "I thought you were going through trials on the bus." I acknowledged that I realized I had been irritable towards him. I felt a sense of relief that I had taken the step that was going to get me out of this hell. I was agitated and told him that I had qualms about telling people that the money we collected was for our youth work, and that I had lost sight of why we litness. I had chosen an explanation for my behavior that I knew other marginal members used. He told me that if the phrase "youth work" bothered me, I should use something else. We talked for a while about this and about trials in general, and he then called the colony to ask them if we could return. I had decided without a lot of thought to leave the Family for a second time.

We returned to the colony, and the district shepherd spoke to me for some time, urging me not to leave (see Chapter 9). Although I feared that he might have tried to restrain me physically, at no point was that really a possibility. There was a lot of tension between us over my decision; I sensed that he was put out with my equivocation. The district shepherd cashed a £5 check for me, and I left in the early evening. Although I realized that the train would not arrive in London until half past three in the morning, I felt exhilarated. I smiled and said hello to everyone. On the ride back, I read a copy of *Plain Truth*, the Garner Ted Armstrong magazine, cover to cover. I sorted out some literature I had collected. My attempts to sleep did not succeed. The train arrived at King's Cross late, around four in the morning. I walked all the way home to West Kilburn—London was bright, colorful, and cheery in the early morning light. At home, I read my mail and ate breakfast. At six, I went to bed and fell into an unsettled sleep dotted with jumbled and unclear dreams. I kept waking up. I rose at noon to bright sunshine and more exhilaration. I then typed out my notes of the last day in the Family.

Over the next several weeks, my sleeping pattern matched that which had developed in Bradford. Regardless of when I retired, I woke at five or six in the morning and could not get back to sleep. While I had numerous dreams, I had only one severe nightmare.[5] Most of the other dreams I could not remember. I received one letter from the wife of the second shepherd, urging me to keep the faith. She opened with, "It must be so horrible to be in the System again!"

Although I was disappointed that I had not been able to last longer, I felt that I had made at least a start on the research. I thought that it could be completed with less extensive, but many more, visits to Family colonies. My next contact with the Family came in July. I had gone to Dijon in France to take an intensive French course to help with my research. There I met several COG members on the streets and spent nights talking with them. On one occasion, I put up several of them in my small room on the Universite de Dijon campus. I presented myself to them as a former member who was still interested.

In August, I moved to Paris. I had written ahead to a Paris address

---

[5] I quote my notes written after waking from this nightmare:

Dream: I was in West Virginia or thereabouts in a house similar to the one in Bradford. Bunch of COG people around I didn't recognize—whole dream was not clear—they wanted me to stay with them—they were all smiles—I got scared—I liked being there but also wanted to get out. The fact I was so far from home also scared me. I felt if I stayed any longer I wouldn't be able to get out—I woke up went to loo—paranoia about shuffling outside—felt presence of COG people around who would try to catch me. (In dream I was mingling in the living room.) Sharp fear! it was [my roommate] moving around in kitchen—as soon as got in light I was all right.

for the Family, and a letter was waiting for me when I arrived. Again, I presented myself as a former member who, while not wanting to rejoin, was willing to help out. In the middle of August, I visited a Family colony on the Left Bank. The colony was a recruitment colony to which potential new members were invited. At the time, it was inundated with Americans who had finally left the United States and were landing in Europe for the first time. I helped them with their French as they tried to witness to people. In addition, I took part in several skits performed before potential converts. I felt like part of an ongoing enterprise. Although I spent several evenings in these activities, I did not sleep at the colony or go out litnessing.

Overt Participant Observation

In the fall of 1976, I finally connected with Rex Davis. He suggested that he might be able to arrange for me to observe one or two colonies for an extended period of time. I mailed him a copy of my earlier study of Neo-Pentecostals to give him an idea of the nature of my work. He read it and then wrote a February 9, 1977, letter to Imrah and Martha, the COG leaders in charge of northern Europe at the time. Martha had been a lover of Moses David early in COG history. He told them of my study and recommended that they get in touch with me directly. As this correspondence developed, I took the winter months to interview a number of ex-COG members in England. For the most part, these interviews were not particularly productive on the topic of colony life at the time. Most interviewees had joined the Family during its initial foray into the British Isles and quickly left the group.

Imrah and Martha wrote to me in March and later met with me in London. Rex Davis had informed them of my covert participant observation prior to the meeting, and they were intrigued and wanted to know the details. Both thought it was funny that I was litnessing without believing, and both were amazed that I could do it so long "without being in the spirit." In retrospect, their positive reaction to me was the product of two factors. First, they felt more comfortable knowing that I had infiltrated, but had not written anything negative about, the group. Second, they trusted Rex Davis and accepted his advice that "the Children of God need some record in the world of scientific sociology, based on careful field study. Too much [existing writing] seems distorted journalism." The Family was coming under increasing criticism in Germany as it had earlier in Britain. I might serve a useful public relations function for them.

From this meeting, Imrah and Martha thought the project was possible. Another flow of correspondence arranged a stay for two months in a Family colony in Arnhem, Holland. In addition, I would be taken to visit several other colonies in the Belgium, Luxembourg, and Netherlands area. I sent a copy of my litnessing chapter, written that spring, to Imrah and Martha so they could review the nature of my interests. No further details of my stay were worked out.

On Friday, June 24, 1977, I traveled from Paris to Amsterdam where I was met by Job and Habbakuk. That evening I left Amsterdam with Habbakuk for Arnhem. The colony was located on a clean, working-class street outside of Arnhem proper, in a detached house with no real yard. It was close to a wooded area where members often took potential converts on walks. The house itself had two rooms and a kitchen downstairs; one room was used as a living and visitor's room and was kept very clean; the other was the dining room and playroom for the colony shepherd's two children. Upstairs, there were three bedrooms: one for the men, one for the women, and a third for Habbakuk and his wife, Zion. Habbakuk's older daughter, Joela, age five, slept with the women. The colony members included four men and three women, not including Habbakuk's family. Although one of the men was thirty, the ages of the rest were between eighteen and twenty.

I lived in the Arhnem colony full-time for the next two months. I participated as much as possible in all the colony's activities. In almost all cases, the interactions I observed or participated in took place in English. The colony shepherd was American and spoke only halting Dutch. The rest of the members spoke English virtually fluently. Language was never a problem.

I did not litness or witness to outsiders, but I did help with many activities designed to gain access to potential converts. I accompanied members on the street and observed their litnessing and witnessing. I also went with members to local bars and discotheques and observed them attempting to interest people through incipient Flirty Fishing techniques. Often, I would speak with potential converts drawn to the group when a member was otherwise preoccupied.

In the colony, I took regular turns reading passages from Mo letters in group readings and participated in daily devotionals. I occasionally helped members memorize new bible verses. I always used COG argot. In addition, I bore my full share of practical tasks around the colony: cleaning, fixing meals, dishwashing, repairs. I went provisioning once; that is, I went with another member to ask local merchants for food. Although there was no formal arrangement, I on four occasions gave Habbakuk approximately $20 to cover the extra expenses of housing and feeding me. When on the street with members, I sometimes picked up the bill at a café or paid for bus transportation.

My reception by members was unexceptional. Although several questioned me initially about my work, in a very short time I felt as if I was treated as a full member. At times, I myself would get so caught up in a Family project that I would forget my purpose and begin to think only in terms of getting the project completed successfully. Only at the end of my visit did members express concern for my soul and want to witness to me.

While both members and the colony leader were generally open, I was not given access to some meetings between the shepherd and individual members. In the early days of my visit, I was excluded from a full meeting of the colony members; later, however, I was permitted to attend. I was also excluded from the content of certain telephone calls between leaders and from specific meetings. In addition, meetings between the leader and members were often of a personal nature and, under any standards of propriety, off-limits to a nosy sociologist—even one with an interest in observing the management of personal problems.

I also got the impression from the shepherd that certain aspects of the Family could not be passed onto me. He was reticent about and refused to show me certain Mo letters unless he received permission from higher leaders. Other leaders were also circumspect about Family organization and policies. Some of my observation of organizational activities and of accounts of them given by leaders, I felt, were managed as a public relations technique. For the most part, this reserve was limited to the organizational realm, and therefore not damaging to my study of daily life—that was always present in almost its complete and natural entirety. In most areas, I found members making sincere efforts to help my study and not being afraid to acknowledge aspects that might be taken negatively by the public-at-large.

I tried to keep my research activities as unobtrusive as possible. Occasionally, I asked pointed questions, but for the most part I let the social life unfold around me in much the same manner as it would around a true neophyte. I did interview each member near the end of my stay for an hour or so each; I made little effort, however, during the course of the research to elicit background information from them. Most of it came out as they spoke to me or as they witnessed to potential converts. I did carry a camera and shot over two hundred color slides of members in the colonies and on the streets. I lent some of my slides to the Family publication unit outside Amsterdam. One or two were used in regional publications of COG. I also recorded several meetings and bible classes on cassettes. My major tool, however, was note taking. I carried a small notepad on which I jotted down everything I could, from observations and theoretical points to fragments of conversation. In addition, I took some time each evening to record observations on the day in a larger notebook. During the course of the visit, I tried to collect Mo letters I did not possess, although later I received a full set. A leader in England later lent me the first three volumes of the bound Mo letters. I subsequently was able to order the next two volumes directly from Gold Lion Publishers in Hong Kong. I had access to the other two volumes and later letters through an ex-member now residing in New York.

The end of my stay did bring a few moments of tension. I left the Arnhem colony in mid-August and traveled through the Netherlands and Belgium meeting other members. On my departure, each member in Arnhem gave me a personal note that involved some component of witnessing. Shortly before I left Belgium, and my final contact with the Family that summer, both the Arnhem shepherd and another COG leader with whom I had grown friendly openly stated their disappointment that I had not decided to join. The general reaction of most members was that it was not possible for an outsider to live for such a period in the Family and not want to join up.[6]

Subsequent Contacts

Upon my return to London, I frequently visited a selah or secret colony of members living there. They were involved in witnessing to Arabs in London through the use of the Flirty Fishing access strategy and had a fairly comfortable, two-floor flat in Holland Park. Whenever leaders came to London from Amsterdam, I visited with them and discussed developments. I also had a chance to watch the production of "The Bible," a Family record album recounting significant biblical events in song, which was released in time for the Christmas 1977 shopping season.

In mid-December I left London on a driving tour of COG colonies in western Europe. Imrah and Martha provided me with a list of colony addresses and telephone numbers, and I set up an itinerary that they approved. In Paris, my first stop, I visited the musicians colony where The Bible album was written and prepared. I then went south,

---

[6] This reaction was extremely similar to that experienced by John Lofland in terminating his research with a cell of the Unification Church. In Lofland's case, the local leader sat him down and expressed distress with his continuing the " 'studying the movement' game" (Lofland 1966:274). In that case, Lofland's open, initial entry was accepted as a means of converting him; his sympathetic participant observation techniques did nothing to dissuade members of their view that he was himself seeking to join. In my case, I believe that members were not under a similar illusion; they hoped that I would both do a favorable study and join up. As one member told me, "You can be saved and still write about us."

stopping in Milan and Turin. I spent Christmas in Rome, visiting the local Poorboy club on the outskirts of the city. Several days before New Years, 1978, I drove to Florence. There, I stayed at Poggio Secco, a villa and vineyard donated to the group by Emmanuel Canevaro. Canevaro, an Italian duke, joined the Family after marrying Rachel, one of the top leaders. The estate continued to produce wine in small quantities under the supervision of the non-Family staff. Family members, about twenty or thirty, lived in the villa. It housed many couples and children, as well as unmarried members. While in Florence, I also visited a music colony in which Jeremy Spencer, a famous early convert from the rock group Fleetwood Mac, and other musicians were recording tapes. On one evening I was taken to an expensive club where COG Flirty Fishers employed their proselytizing skills and where Spencer and other members occasionally played.

New Years night I arrived in Munich and spent a day and a night with the local leader. From there, it was on to Koln, and then back to Arnhem, Amsterdam, and Brussels to spend several days with old Family friends. By mid-January I was back in Paris at the musicians' colony. Throughout my trip, I stayed in each colony one to three days and discussed local affairs with the leaders present. I also participated as much as possible in the daily affairs of each colony.

The End of Contact

Aside from frequent contacts with the London colony until I left Europe in June of 1978, the Christmas tour was my last substantial contact with the Family. In early 1978, Moses David announced the major reorganization of the group known as the "Reorganisation, Nationalisation Revolution." Among other more prominent effects, the revolution cut off my access to the group. Imrah and Martha moved to Athens and no longer enjoyed the same authority. My attempts to reestablish significant contact with the group have not been favorably responded to by the central organization; my letters have been treated simply as letters from any other interested person. My knowledge of events in the Family after June 1978 is based on speaking to several ex-members who have brought out Mo letter volumes and newsletters. For these reasons, my study is based on practices as they existed between 1975 and 1978. In the History chapter, I indicate how these practices have changed.

THE EFFICACY AND ETHICS OF COVERT PARTICIPANT OBSERVATION

The sociological literature on covert participant observation frequently casts it as diametrically opposed to overt participant observation both in its validity as a research strategy and in its propriety (Dingwall 1980:888; Erikson 1967:373). As I suggested in the Introduction, however, the actual practice of covert participant observation varies little from that of detailed and intensive overt observation. Both require the use of the sociologist as an investigative tool and the management of a specially created self for presentation: both are "irremediably covert" in that they involve some deception (Hilbert 1980:74; Roth 1962:283). There are some differences, however, that cut both ways, as well as some ethical problems peculiar to the covert method.

Richard Hilbert argues, against the grain of most sociological opinion, that covert participant observation "is participation par excellence" (Hilbert 1980:53, 55): it permits "analysts [to] succeed in finding out 'what typical members do,' i.e., what they, the analysts, themselves were actually doing vis-á-vis a relevant social community." By participating covertly, and by managing the secret of his or true identity, Hilbert argues, the covert observer understands the true nature of membership and activity in a group. In fact, "[s]uccessfully managing the secret requires attention to areas which to other members may be nonproblematic."

In many respects, I accept this view. My own experience in litnessing and in fleeting attempts at witnessing was invaluable for my analysis of those activities. Although long periods of observation may have produced similar data for analyzing those activities, only actual performance of the ideological role of a litnesser gave me access to the nuances of interaction on the public street. Subsequent efforts to observe litnessing from the outside were largely fruitless; they were attempts to catch a beam of light in a net.

Moreover, to the extent that even in overt participant observation I presented myself as a member and was accepted as such for all practical purposes, this false presentation was essential to my understanding of interactions in the Family. Simply standing around observing COG interactions was pointless, and tended to emphasize the nonroutine aspects of the interactions observed; that is, observation normally drew attention to the strange doctrines themselves, rather than to their use in negotiating everyday life. Thus, acting as a member and passing as such was essential to understanding life in the Family.

I depart from Hilbert's analysis, however, in that the role adopted by the sociologist in covert participant observation does differ in an important respect from that performed by an actual member. The sociologist's orientation to the role focuses on managing the secret of his or her true identity. For the bona fide member, no such management concern is present. It is true, as Hilbert assumes, that most peo-

ple have something to hide; that is, most members' biographies conform to the acceptable pattern for members only more or less (Hilbert
1980:59). Most members do not want to reveal certain things about
themselves. But this fact does not approach the overbearing feature
of the covert participant observer's hidden identity: the lack of commitment to the group and the concern with a research goal.

As a covert observer, I was constantly conscious of my deceptive
presentation of self and concerned with the destructive potential of a
stripping away of that presentation. In retrospect, I believe that I
greatly overestimated the possibility of detection, but that concern
affected many of my perceptions of my interactions in the group.
This caused a skewing of my opinions on several important aspects
of colony life in the Family that I later was able to correct.

The most significant effect was on my views of authority and freedom in the group. As a covert observer, I felt an authoritarian op-
pressiveness that I attributed to the structure of authority relations in
the group. Leaders' questions about my activities and the necessity
of informing the shepherd when I and other members went outside
the colony were read as devious devices of social control. After overt
observation, however, I concluded that that initial impression was
due to my self-consciousness; I felt as if I were always on the edge of
discovery, and attributed to leaders' actions a totalitarian concern
with social control. Another source of this gloss was the fact that I
was always trying to maintain a sense of my true self apart from the
role I had adopted. To the extent that leaders and other members
reinforced and accepted my false identity, my true self was threatened.

These phenomena, however, were not limited to the context of covert observation. As an overt observer, I had an above average desire
to inquire into and to see behind routine events. I was occasionally
greeted with stonewalling tactics by leaders. While this phenomenon
says a lot about the Family's concern with information control vis-á-
vis outsiders, it says little about the salience of such control within
the group. In fact, most members had only a passing interest in and
rarely pressed for more information on the events I often thought
significant. Clearly, the Family has an authority structure that attempts to control information flow both within and without the
group. The significance, however, of this fact can easily be overestimated due to the observer's inquisitive stance toward the group. To
argue that covert participant observation solves these problems is, in
my view, incorrect.

Covert participant observation is not a rare research technique in sociological studies.[7] It is so frequently used perhaps because of its effectiveness particularly for microsociological research. To announce ahead of time the nature of the sociologist's activity may actually prevent observation entirely. Moreover, I have argued that even overt participant observation involves a significant degree of deception. Simplistic dichotomies of covert versus overt methods seem to me to be ethical exercises that bear little correspondence with the actual conduct of research.

Still, there are significant ethical considerations that I did not sufficiently ponder prior to undertaking my period of covert participant observation. I do not attempt to present a defense of my actions. When I began my observation, I sincerely believed that no other course was possible and that I would cause no harm. In retrospect, perhaps, overt observation was possible,[8] and if I had had that information at the time I would not have feigned membership. I now find the ethical implications of that phase of my research troubling. I believe, however, that pious statements about the impropriety of covert participant observation vastly oversimplify the ethical problems.

Such statements may be based on and may overemphasize one consideration with which I fully agree: a sociologist should attempt to avoid causing harm to members of the group under study (Lofland 1960:366). In particular, this canon rules out the most abusive form

[7] John Lofland sent an undergraduate student to the Unification Church cell to feign a conversion for further observation (Lofland 1966:275). He also initiated a substantial ethical debate in *Social Problems* by using graduate students, posing as alcoholics, to infiltrate meetings of Alcoholics Anonymous (Davis 1961; Lofland 1961; Lofland and Lejeune 1960; Roth 1962). Lofland is not alone in this practice. Roger Homan, himself a covert observer of an old-time Pentecostal group, cites a number of sociological studies based on disguised observation (Homan 1980:50–51 [citing Festinger et al. 1964 [feigned membership in small cult]; Humphreys 1975 [acted as lookout-voyeur to observe male homosexual encounters in public restrooms]; Caudill, et al. 1952 [sociologists feigned symptoms of mental illness to become patients]; Sullivan, Queen, and Patrick 1958 [officer-sociologist "enlisted," feigning lower socioeconomic status]; von Hoffman and Cassidy 1956 [attempted infiltration aborted for practical reasons]; Walker and Atherton 1971 [observers posed as committed believer and as sceptical evangelical who was interested]; Whyte 1961 [gained access to slum interactions by professing to be writing history of urban area]]).

[8] I do not agree with Martin Bulmer's implied conclusion that covert methods are never necessary (Bulmer 1980:63). The possibility of overt observation of the Family at the time, I believe, was an artifact of a peculiar conjunction of factors. First, there was the special relationship that the Family had with Rex Davis; there was also the public relations sophistication of the set of leaders with whom I had contact; finally, the Family was in a particularly open period—it was attempting to deflect criticism through positive approaches rather than through its more traditional strategy of strictly controlling access. Subsequent changes in the Family, I believe, have made the type of intrusive participant observation I practiced impossible.

of covert observation, which, however, is prevalent among journalists and law enforcement officers. The latter type of "observers" often enter groups with the purpose of revealing damaging information about their activities, whether criminal or simply undesirable. Such activity normally causes harm to members and is intended to do so, particularly in the case of law enforcement investigations. It is justified by the argument that the harm caused is outweighed by the public good that derives from revelation. In the case of criminal conduct, it is assumed that criminal activity has no claim to protection from the public eye.

Such a purpose was never part of my research, and I think it rarely is overtly present in any sociological research. I am often asked about various practices of the Family; in most cases, the question carries the implicit assumption that Family practices are bad, immoral, and completely deceptive. I always try to describe the practice without any moral commentary, and then, if necessary, argue for a different interpretation than my questioner is liable to give the activity. I do not believe that being a member of the Family is desirable as a general matter, but I do not engage in attempts to debunk their beliefs and life-style. In addition, during my research I carefully avoided revealing any confidences I shared with members to other members, because I had no intention of experimenting with internal reactions that might be caused by such revelations.[9]

The ethical prohibition against covert participant observation, however, may serve as a bright line-rule that prevents more subtle forms of injury to members. Although a sociologist means no harm and takes steps to prevent it, his or her covert activities may have an adverse effect, and a rule against covert observation would prevent that possibility. It is true that a sociologist cannot guarantee that the covert research does not harm the group or its members in some way (Erikson 1967:370). I think, however, that provided the intention is not to harm, and provided that the participation is kept close to the passive end of the scale, the potential for injury is vastly overrated.

Fears of injury may be more a product of sociologists' hubris—"we really do affect the world"—than of empirical evidence. Potential in-

[9] A whole range of more experimental research in social psychology often depends on the fact that the subjects of the experiments do not know the full nature of the test (Milgram 1963). Within the interpretive sociological tradition itself, Harold Garfinkel has encouraged his students to act strangely or to adopt different roles in interacting with their families and friends in order to bring to the surface taken-for-granted features of everyday life (Garfinkel 1964:229–33). The only justification for these activities could be that the value of the knowledge obtained outweighs any of the negative features of the deception.

jury, of course, depends on situational factors.[10] But I fail to see in most cases[11] the relevance of the covert-overt distinction to this form of subtle harm. As I have described above, simply informing the group that you are a sociologist does not necessarily decrease the risk of subtle and unintended injury. Any type of research into social interaction is always to some decree covert; full informed consent is impossible to obtain when the sociologist studies interaction in its natural setting.[12] Any intrusive participant observation will alter in some respect interaction within a social group; this result has little to do with whether the research is formally overt.

There is considerable substance to the view that the prohibition of covert research techniques does not rest solely on its role as a proxy to prevent harm to subjects of research. It also functions to uphold the image of the profession in the public's view and thus to prevent discouragement of participation by the public in sociological research (Dingwall 1980:876; Erikson 1967:368–69). The rule encourages public trust of sociologists in general. Although the public expects and even counts on the police and journalists to infiltrate certain groups for the public good, it has no similar expectation of sociologists. Perhaps this is due to the less practical evaluation given by the public to sociologists' products.[13]

As an abstract argument, this is persuasive. I doubt, however, that the covert research that has been conducted has had any impact on the public's reaction to the discipline. The current image of sociology

[10] When the group is small, for example, a covert presence may have a greater effect on the course of interaction than when the group is large (e.g., Festinger et al. 1964).

[11] One real concern that I had was that discovery of my identity might bring down negative sanctions on those fooled by my false presentation. To the extent I succeeded and disguised my research reports, this would not occur. The risk of failure, however, did present the real possibility of harm to those I fooled at least temporarily. I had no information that members who had been fooled in the past by journalists were harshly treated, but the danger did exist.

[12] Robert Dingwall meticulously tracks the vagaries of achieving "informed consent" (Dingwall 1980:877–79). The consent of superordinates may be forced on subordinates; the sheer practical problem of obtaining informed consent from all members in a social institution may be insurmountable; and insistance on consent may magnify the dangers of the research inaccurately. Dingwall perceptively notes that "many participants in sociological research are oblivious to the promptings of the most conscientious investigator. . . . '[T]ask' performance is a more important constraint on subjects than being observed."

[13] A subsidiary function of the rule is to protect subordinate researchers from abuse: graduate students should not be placed in the difficult position of conducting ethically offensive research for which they are ill-prepared out of fear of incurring institutional sanctions (Dingwall 1980:883; Erikson 1967:369). Using a rule of this breadth, however, seems to be overkill for a different kind of problem.

seems more tied to the results of its analyses than to its methods. In fact, studies employing covert methods (Festinger et al. 1964; Humphries 1975; Whyte 1961) most likely have done more to make the discipline popular among students and the public. The "protection of the discipline" rationale as a pragmatic assertion may not rest on any substantial empirical base.

In my view, the virtue of a rule prohibiting covert participation can be found in its effect on the defensive strategies and actions of the research subjects. A subject who knows that the sociologist is a sociologist is in a position to take whatever action he or she feels is necessary given that revelation. The subject can ask for more information about the research or even refuse to speak to the sociologist. Alternatively, the subject can alter his or her behavior to take account of the sociologist's presence if necessary. In most cases, as it was in mine, the subject will do nothing after an initial period of suspiciousness. The effect of informing subjects about the nature of the sociologist's activity, then, is to put the subject in a position to take defensive measures if he or she deems it wise.[14] The result is that the onus is on the subject to avoid harm to him- or herself.

My covert participant observation denied members of the Bradford colony this opportunity. My only justification is that I thought such a revelation would make my research impossible and that I meant no harm to the members of the Family. I shifted the determination of possible harm from the judgment of Family members to my own judgment. As it turned out, I know of no injury I caused. Although I doubt that I could have caused much harm, the end result may have been the result of stupid luck. Then again, fortuitous events and choices riddled my research path.

[14] This solution also does away with most of the problems of informed consent identified by Dingwall (Dingwall 1980). Provided the sociologist is convinced that the information is acquired by members, he or she need not worry further; members with difficulties would have to approach the sociologist for more information. This answer, unfortunately, does not solve the problem in authoritarian groups in which the leaders agree to the research and then force that decision on other members. In a sense, however, members who subject themselves to such an authority structure accept a number of consequences that they might not if they were not committed to the group.

APPENDIX B

SAMPLE MO LETTERS

THIS APPENDIX reproduces three Mo letters that are representative of the type of literature published by the COG. The first, *Diamonds of Dust* (3), was heavily used in litnessing; *God's Whores!* (560) was intended for members only and is representative of the Flirty Fishing letters issued in 1976 and 1977; the True Komix version of *The Dying Dollar* (730) is an example of "mini-lit," small size illustrated literature used in litnessing in 1978. The Mo letters all have a similar and distinctive style. As edited, they are printed on five by eight inch paper (or three-and-one-half by five-inch paper for mini-lit) in booklet form, average between eight and twelve pages, and contain cartoon illustrations to underscore important points.

Beginning in 1972, Family artists illustrated almost every Mo letter. In these illustrations, Moses David has been portrayed in many different guises. In fact, until the publication of a photograph of him with his Tenerife colony (reproduced in Chapter 2) in 1977 by *Stern* and in 1978 by *Time* magazine, few members knew what he (and Maria) looked like. He first appeared in 1974 Mo letters as a majestic and bearded God-like figure. A second rendition about the same time depicted Moses David as a slighter character with an exaggerated nose and long beard. The predominant characterization from 1975 through 1977 showed him as a gentle lion who stood upright. Often, the lion was accompanied by Maria, who appeared as a young woman with long black hair and a trim body. In late 1977 and 1978, Moses David again was presented as an old man with sharp features, sometimes in Spanish armor.

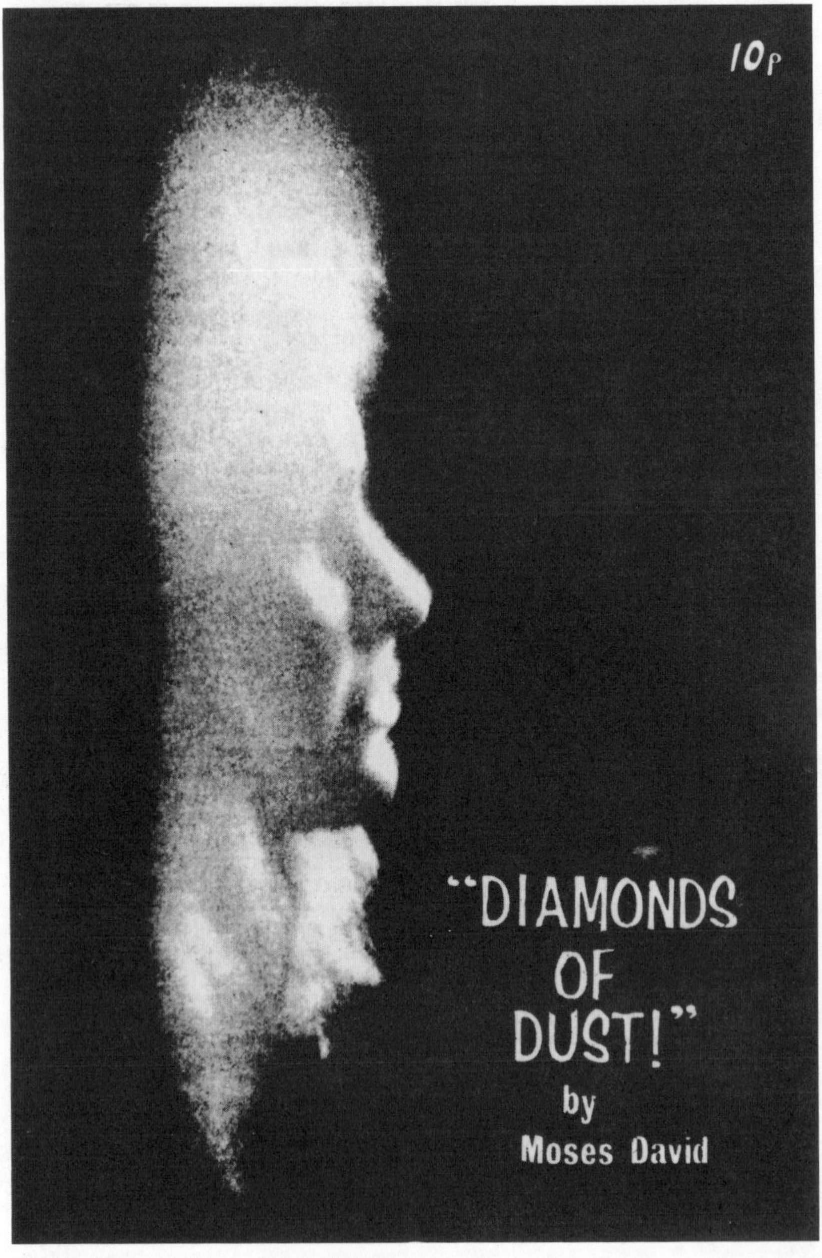
10p
"DIAMONDS
OF
DUST!"
by
Moses David

"DIAMONDS
OF
DUST!"
by
Moses David

1. GOD PUT ON A "LIGHT SHOW" THE OTHER DAY—and we were there to see it! He said a lot of things, too—and we tried to listen. I'm sure He must have shown it before, but we were all too busy to watch. Watch with us this time—maybe you'll see even more!

2. IF YOU WERE A BIG, FAT BUSINESSMAN or a frantic housewife or a hurried student—you wouldn't spend an hour in the morning watching the sun coming in the window—if you did, they might put you in the nuthouse!

3. HE LET THREE TINY RAYS OF LIGHT BEAM THEIR WAY INTO OUR ROOM—not through the shutter, obstructing the light, but through tiny peepholes, letting it in! The smaller the hole the more perfect the image and the more accurate the projection it reflects! The smaller you are, the clearer they can see Him!

4. THE RAYS WERE MANY DIF-FERENT COLORS—all showing a different color of His Light—but the same light;—different gifts, but the same Spirit, each one reflecting in his own way the Light of God—each one letting his light shine—showing his particular kind of works to cause men to glorify the Beauty of God!

5. HOLD YOUR HAND UP!—THE LIGHT SHINES RIGHT THROUGH IT; you can see the blood and bones! Nothing is hidden in His eyes!

6. THE THINNER YOU ARE, THE MORE THE LIGHT GETS THROUGH! The less there is of you, the more the light shines through!

7. WE'RE LIKE LITTLE RAYS OF LIGHT in this city that's so dark! Even a few rays of light can make some kind of impression! Don't ever think because there's so much darkness that it's no use to have just a little light, because even one candle can be seen a mile away when it's dark!

8. EVEN A GRAIN OF DUST, AS

"DIAMONDS OF DUST"

SMALL AS IT IS, CAN SPARKLE LIKE A DIAMOND if it will get in the sunshine—if the room is dark enough. The greater the darkness, the brighter the light! A little diamond of dust or a little ray of sunshine shows up best when the room is very dark, 'cause, "where iniquity doth abound, grace doth much more abound!"

9. BUT WHAT YOU SEE WHEN YOU SEE THE FLAME OF A CANDLE IS NOT THE FIRE ITSELF, but the tiny little glowing particles, made white-hot by the heat of His Love! You're not actually seeing the light at all; because the light itself is invisible! —It can only be seen in the reflections of all those little diamonds of dust! You don't dare look right at the sun or it will blind you, because "no man hath seen God at any time", and lived! But you only can see its reflection in the things that it shines on. People can only see God as we reflect Him, like little diamonds of dust! They can't look at God, cause He's too bright; He blinds them! They have to look at us to see God in our reflection of Him. God's light can only be seen if you reflect it! People can only see God in you as you reflect Him. So "let your light so shine before men that they may see your good works and glorify your Father which is in Heaven." If the dust weren't there, you couldn't see the light; and if the light weren't there, you couldn't see the dust! It takes both!

10. YOU MAY NEVER SEE THE LITTLE DIAMOND OF DUST AGAIN, for some of them just flow into the light, sparkle for a moment, and then vanish back into the darkness. They only have their moment of Truth! —But if only once in its life it scintillates with the light of the Lord, it's worth it! Even if only once in its life it is life and joy to someone, it's worth it! But if it could stay in the Lord's Light, it could sparkle its life out to the end, like one candlestick gives light to the whole house until it is finished! The longer that little grain of dust stays right in the Light, the longer it shines—and the longer it stays a diamond!

11. FOR THEY CAN SPARKLE SO SHORT A WHILE, AND THEN THEY'RE GONE, like a man's life;—like the grass of the field which today is and tomorrow is gone! For what is your life? It's but a vapor—a vapor that reflects His rays of light for a little while and then it's gone! You have no guarantee of tomorrow. You'd better sparkle now while you have the light, or you'll fade into oblivion and no one will know you even ever existed —'cause no man ever saw the light reflected in you shining through you! Because you'll always dwell in darkness! —Because you always dwelt in darkness. You never came to the Light that your deeds might be made manifest that they were of God!

"You never came to the light that your deeds might be made manifest that they were of God!"

"DIAMONDS OF DUST"

12. THE PATH OF THE LIGHT YOU SEE IS VERY STRAIGHT AND VERY NARROW! It only shines in one direction, and its source is only in one direction! So there is only one way to the Source — you've got to follow that way or you won't make it! Jesus is the Light of the world! He's the only Way. Only in Him is there Light — the straight and narrow Beam that points to the Love of God — to the Son of God's Love! — and unless you get in that Beam of Love, you'll never shine; for "I am the Way, the Truth, and the Life; no man cometh unto the Father, but by Me!"

13. THINK HOW MUCH GOD CAN SHOW YOU from even a little beam of light, if you're just simple and childlike enough to appreciate it — to look — and to listen! "Except ye be as a little child, ye shall in no wise enter the Kingdom of God!"

14. TO LEARN FROM THE LORD, YOU HAVE TO STOP — AND LOOK — AND LISTEN — or you'll get run over by all the cares of this life, — instead of running over with His Truth, His Love,

and His Joy! You'll be overcome by the world, instead of overcoming the world through Him!

15. STOP — LOOK — AND LISTEN — TO THE LIGHT, and let your dust become Diamonds that show the beauty of God!

16. IF YOU'RE TOO BUSY, YOU'LL NEVER LEARN ANYTHING! — Or, if you're in a hurry! The Bible says, "full of their own doings — their own things!"

17. WATCH THE DIAMONDS OF DUST! They don't try to sparkle and shine. They just let the light shine through them! They don't try to work to shine or move. They're not trying to get anywhere; they're not in a hurry! They just float so quietly on God's air — and only get stirred up when He blows up a storm. But even then, they settle back into their place when it's over!

18. STOP — LOOK — LISTEN — And become a Diamond of Dust!

19. "Let your light so shine before men, that they may see your good works, and glorify your Father which is in Heaven!"

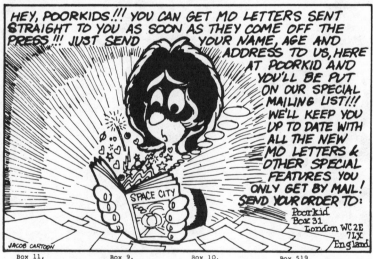

Box 11,
York YO11SY
Tel: 0904 - 798741

Box 9,
Liverpool L8 3UN
Tel: 449 - 1938

Box 10,
Glasgow G2 Scotland
Tel: 632-6810

Box 519
Birmingham B12 9QN
Tel: 021 - 3585137

Box ILA
Newcastle NE99 ILA
Tel: 089 4255759

"GOD'S WHORES?"--MO   April 26, 1976   DO NO. 560
(Compiled and Edited by Justus Ashtree.)
Copyrighted December 1976 by the Children of God
C.P. 748, 00100 Rome, Italy.

1. YOU'RE GOING INTO THESE CLUBS AS A TESTIMONY THAT GOD IS NOT A MONSTER Who's trying to deny you everything and make you miserable like the Church does, and Who's going to send you to Hell with a brick bat if you don't keep all the hard impossible-to-keep laws that the Church has made for you.

2. YOU KNOW WHAT YOU'RE SAYING TO THEM EVERY TIME YOU PUT YOUR ARMS AROUND THEM and dance with them and kiss them and love them and tell them that God loves them? You know what you're telling them? God is good! God is love!

3. GOD IS A GOOD GOD, A LOVING GOD, a fatherly loving Heavenly Father who loves you and wants you to have all this and wants you to enjoy yourself, and wants you to enjoy me, and wants you to enjoy sex and wants you to enjoy love. He made it all for you to enjoy. It's good, it's not bad!

4. WHAT WE'RE DOING IS GOOD, NOT EVIL. It's good. Do you understand? Just the opposite from what the Church has been teaching them, just the opposite of what all the churches teach, let's face it, right?

5. ALL THE GOD-DAMNED HELLISH FIENDISH DIABOLICAL RELIGIOUS SYSTEMS OF THE WORLD HAVE SOME KIND OF FETISH OF SELF-DENIAL, fakirism and self torture. Sitting on nails and putting skewers through your cheeks, whatever it is, it's all the same. Some of them have even had themselves nailed to crosses and hung there and suffering all kinds of physical torture, because the more you suffer, the more you're tortured, the more religious you're supposed to be.

6. I'M NOT DENYING THERE ARE TIMES WHEN WE HAVE TO SACRIFICE AND SUFFER, but we don't have to do it on purpose just as a self-righteous gaining of personal merit. If we do it it's because it happens and the Lord lets it happen, but not because we necessarily ask for it or want it or think we're gaining any righteousness by it.

7. GOD IS A GOOD GOD, A LOVING GOD, A KIND GOD, a fatherly God who loves you, who cares for you, who feeds you, who made you, and made all these appetites for you to satisfy and enjoy, right? And that's the bill of goods you're to sell to those fellows.

8. THEY THINK NOBODY LOVES THEM. One fellow said last night, "Love? I don't know if there is love, I don't know." Maria said, "Do you have love now?" He said, "I have love tonight; I don't know about tomorrow, but I have love tonight." He could say I have it tonight because he knew she was there.

9. GOD'S LITTLE ANGEL OF LOVE AND MERCY WAS THERE and he had her in his hands, he could see and feel love. She is the representation of love, she is the little light, the little candle, he can see and feel and know that it is I, it is the Lord and His love. That's why they cling so and hate to let her go. When they see such sincere love as you girls have, it's no wonder they flip out over you. Well, I want them to flip out.

10. I WANT THEM TO ABSOLUTELY TO-TALLY FLIP OUT AND FALL IN LOVE WITH YOU, that's what we're after! Because in falling in love with you, though they may not know it at first, what they're really doing is they're falling in love with God in you. So don't be afraid to attract them and win them and make them flip over you.

11. YOU ARE GOD'S REPRESENTATIVE, I've always said this about any kind of witnessing--you have got to sell yourself first in a sense. They've got to be sold on you, they've got to believe in you first, before they can believe in God. Like Dr. Moody said, "The only Bible the world reads is the one bound in shoe leather."

204 APPENDIX B

12. THE ONLY BIBLE THOSE BOYS DOWN THERE ARE LIKELY TO READ IS THAT GORGEOUS GAL WITH THOSE BOSOMS AL- MOST HANGING OUT bound in as little clothing as possible. That's the kind of love they can understand, that's the kind of love they can read and see and feel and hear be- fore they can ever understand the spiritual love of God--they're like little children. God wants us to worship Him in Spirit and in Truth, but how are they going to know the Spirit and hear the Truth until you bring it to them through your body, the vehicle?

13. YOUR BODY IS THE VEHICLE THAT THE SPIRIT IS TRAVELLING IN and your tongue is the instrument that gives them the Truth. It's your body that has to do it, the body has to come first. They see you be- fore they see God, don't forget, but they see God in you eventually, and once they're attracted to your body then they can begin to feel your spirit.

14. EVEN BEFORE THEY FEEL YOUR BODY THEY LOOK IN YOUR EYES AND CAN FEEL THE SPIRIT, the spirit draws them, draws them clear across the room like a magnet. They think it's your body, they think it's something in your eyes, they don't really know just what it is but it really draws them.--It's the Spirit of God!

15. THE SPIRIT OF GOD IS USING YOUR BODY, YOUR FLESH, YOUR EYES, AS THE BAIT to pull them irresist- ibly to you, against your body and looking into your eyes so they can feel His Spirit and His Love and then you can tell them why, the Truth, with your tongue, "The love of God! It's the love of God you feel, it's God, it's Jesus! Why am I so happy, why am I so beautiful, why are you so attracted, why are you falling in love with me? It's Jesus, because I have Jesus! That's the secret!"

16. YOU'RE GIVING THEM LOVE THEY'VE NEVER HAD BEFORE, the love their own

wives don't give them, and the church won't permit them to have unless they come to mass or service and blah blah blah blah and then they still don't get the love. With all the churches about the only thing they can hope for is maybe they'll miss Hell by all the works and duties and ceremonies and hocus- pocus. About the best the church can promise them is, well, they might not have to stay in purgatory quite so many hundred years--isn't that ridiculous!

17. YOU CAN TELL THEM HOW TO MISS THE WHOLE WORKS, HAVE ALL THIS AND HEAVEN TOO, hallelujah? You can have all this here and now, me, joy, love, sex and enjoy it, real love, and Heaven too, all by grace, as a gift of God through Jesus. You don't have to work for it, you don't have to go to the God-damn church for it and go through all those stinking ceremonies, sprinkling babies when they don't even know what water is much less spirit. The baby's already cleansed, before it was born it was cleansed by the Lord because you're a believer and you love Jesus--it's so ridiculous!

18. YOU'RE DOWN THERE AS GOD'S LIT- TLE ANGELS OF LOVE AND MERCY TO SHOW THE BEAUTY OF GOD and the Love of God and to pull them with the power that they think is sex, but is sex- plus-God, an irresistible power, ir- resistible! There's never been one of them that Maria's gone after that she hasn't gotten, ever!

19. THEY CANNOT RESIST THE POWER! AND THEN YOU TELL THEM WHY with your tongue: Who it is, what it is, why it is, the power of God, the love of God, the Spirit of Christ, you can have it all. You don't have to pay for it, you don't have to go to church for it, you didn't even have to come out and find me.

20. I'VE COME DOWN TO YOU, ALL THE WAY, TO FIND YOU down here in this pit to tell you God loves you and I love you and you can have all this

"GOD'S WHORES?"--MO   26-4-76   DO NO. 560   Page 3

love, affection, sex, all free, from
God, God's gift and Heaven too, salvation too. It doesn't have to send
you to Hell. It's all yours, this
and Heaven too,by grace, by faith,
as a gift of God through Jesus, all
yours. I'm yours because God sent
me. I'm here to tell you, I'm yours,
I'm God's gift to you, His free love
gift just like Jesus was.
  21. YOU ARE GOD'S FREE LOVE GIFT,
EVEN IF THEY NAIL YOU TO THE BED,
you're still His free love gift,
amen? You've got to understand that.
You've got to understand what you're
doing, why you're doing it so you
can throw your whole heart, soul,
spirit, body, mind, bosoms, everything into it, all you've got. So
that you're doing it not just to
them but as unto the Lord and you're
doing it to please God and because
you love them and you love Jesus.
You're not doing it in any halfway
measure, you're willing to go all
the way to the bed if necessary to
prove it, to convince them.
  22. NOW GOD PROBABLY WON'T ASK YOU
TO DO THAT IF YOU DON'T WANT TO, if
you don't have that much love for
them. He's not going to ask you to
do anything more than you're able to
bear. But I warn you, because I know
God, that God is going to love some
of them enough He's going to make
you want to.
  23. HE'S GOING TO PUT SO MUCH LOVE
IN YOUR HEART FOR THEM THAT YOU'RE
GOING TO WANT TO TAKE THEM TO BED
to show them how much you love them,
believe it or not! Not all of them
but once in a while--it takes that
with some of them. They get it from
all kinds of other women. "Oh,
you're God's woman? You love me so
much?
  24. "YOU CLAIM THAT THIS IS GREATER
LOVE THAN ALL THE REST? WELL, PROVE
IT! Why won't you go to bed with me?
The rest of them will, the Devil's
women will go to bed with me. The
selfish ones go to bed with me that
don't really love me but they just

want my body and they're selfishly
after sex. Are you going to prove
this spiritual love that you love
so much, and that you've got more
love than they have? Why won't you
go to bed with me if you love me
so much?"
  25. I THREATENED TO CALL ONE OF
THOSE FIRST CHAPTERS WE WROTE "GOD'S
WHORE". I was going to really shock
people! I love shocking titles that
provoke people and wake them up!
  26. THE LORD SHOWED ME HOW HE LIT-
ERALLY SHARES HIS WIFE, the Church,
with the world to prove His Love.
Now that's the truth, isn't it? He's
doing it all the time, in whatever
way you want to say. Why not the
bed--what's the difference? If He
is sharing His Wife, the Church,
with the world to manifest His love
to the world, is she being unfaith-
ful to Him? No! She is proving her
love for Him in that He uses her to
win them.--Boy that would make a
shocking title!
  27. GOD IS A PIMP! How about that!
--Boom! He's the biggest one there
is--He uses His Church all the time
to win souls and win hearts to Him
to attract them to Him.
  28. SO THE TIME WILL COME AND
YOU'LL FEEL IT AND YOU'LL KNOW IT
and you won't even worry about it
because God gives you such grace
you'll want to go to bed with them
to show them how much you love them,
you'll really want to love them that
much. God has had to give me the
grace where I've wanted to give
Maria to them because I love them
so much.
  29. I COULDN'T GO TO BED WITH
THEM, BUT AT LEAST I COULD SHOW
THEM HOW MUCH I LOVE THEM and do
my best to supply their need by
sending her to bed with them to
love them with my love.--That's
what she loves them with, just like
she loves them with God's love. Do
you wonder how that's possible?
Well, the time will come when you'll
feel it. If you sent your wife to

bed with me because you loved me, son, that's one form of it.

30. THE TIME WILL COME WHEN YOU LOVE GOD SO MUCH AND LOVE THESE MEN SO MUCH YOU'RE WILLING TO SEND YOUR OWN WIFE to bed with them. You can't go to bed with them, you can't supply what they need, but you're willing to send your own wife. You did. So, pretty shocking religion, huh?

31. PRETTY SHOCKING RELIGION--GOD'S WHOREHOUSE--THE LOVING WHORES OF GOD! I just use that term because it shocks you. I mean it's the worst thing you could possibly say about most women, at least most women would think so.

32. BUT THE LORD LOVED THE WHORES and He saved them, thank You Lord! And they loved Him because they knew He understood their love for men and their desire to try to help men and to comfort men and really to have a ministry to men--He really understood. And He didn't condemn them completely, He condemned the whoremongers worse, the guys who just run around after the world's filthy whores--there's a big difference. Thank You Lord! Thank You Jesus!

33. HOW WONDERFUL, WHAT LOVE! You don't have to worry about it in advance, don't worry about it in advance. Don't worry one minute in advance about anything, just flow with it as the Spirit leads you.

34. JUST GO WITH IT AS GOD LEADS YOU, and when the time comes you won't even have to ask. I mean it's nice if you ask me, like about dancing, but if you feel like going to bed with them, like that's necessary to show them that much love to prove how much God loves them, you don't have to ask me because I'll know then you really love them, amen? Well, shocking religion, huh?

35. PROVE YOUR LOVE WITH SEX.--Well that's what you're doing everytime you go down there, just like you'd cook a meal for them, just like you'd feed them. You're feeding their flesh because their flesh needs it, it

longs for it, it cries out for it, it begs for it, because that's the way God made them, you know that? And especially when they're not getting it anyplace else.

36. THEY GET FED UP WITH THESE SICKENING SELFISH WOMEN who are only really thinking of themselves and their own gratification. How many of them really unselfishly love these guys? How many of these women really unselfishly give?-- They may have sexual liberation and they may be uninhibited in their sexual responses in bed and really give the guys some response, but how much of it is really unselfish love?--That's the difference. That's what they see is the difference in Maria.

37. HOW MANY OF THOSE WOMEN HELP TO DRESS THEM AFTERWARDS and stoop over to pick up their shoes and wipe off their penis with the tissues and minister to them like a loveslave, like a servant? How many of those proud selfish women do you think ever do that?

38. FROM WHAT I HAVE SEEN THEY TREAT THESE BOYS LIKE SLAVES, like they're their prostitutes,and lord it over them and drag them around by the ear or the nose,and that's probably the way they treat them at home and why the guys get fed up with them. We've found very few of these "sweetheart" arrangements work out very well, they all wind up haywire for some reason. Sex can only last so long without real unselfish love, and if they don't get that, sooner or later it's going to sour.

39. BUT IN ONE NIGHT YOU CAN SHOW WHAT A LOVESLAVE YOU ARE and how sweet and humble and how unselfish you are. Whereas the worldly women just expect everything from a man. They expect him to give and give and wait on them and serve them,and that's the way I've seen them treat most of these men.

40. THESE WORLDLY WOMEN EXPECT THE

MAN TO MINISTER TO THEM. You watch them, watch them in the clubs--the women are enjoying being ministered unto. They came not to minister but to be ministered unto.

41. WE'RE TOTALLY DIFFERENT! We go down there not to be ministered unto but as Jesus said, to minister, and they can tell the difference, they can see the difference, they know the difference, they can feel the difference. "Oh, you're so sincere...completely different...I never met anybody like you, I want to marry you."

42. YOU'RE GOING TO GET PROPOSALS. What are you going to do about that? Well, I'm sure you can stall them off long enough to counsel about what to do. (Maria: I told a guy I wasn't ready for a wedding yet.) Well, you can always tell them, "I'm married to the Lord" or something, or "I'm already married", if it's true.

43. TELL THEM THAT YOU LOVE THEM AND GIVE THEM ALL KINDS OF LOVE AND EVEN SEX if they really need it to show them that you do love them, but that you're already married to the Lord and you'd rather show them the Lord than anything and get them married to Him too so they'll be satisfied and happy. I mean it's not going to hurt to say, "I wish I could" or even "yes, I'd love to marry you" if you love them enough and you can say that and mean it, but be sure you add, "But you have to marry the Lord too!--And my Family as well!

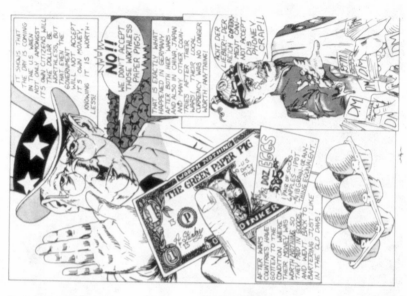

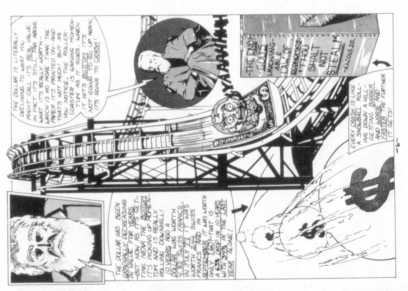

BIBLIOGRAPHY

I. CHILDREN OF GOD

Barker, Eileen. *New Religious Movements: A Practical Introduction*, 171–73. London: Her Majesty's Stationery Office, 1989.

Davis, Deborah (Linda Berg), with Bill Davis. *The Children of God: The Inside Story*. Grand Rapids, Mich.: Zondervan Publishing House, 1984.

Davis, Rex, and James Richardson. "The Organization and Functioning of the Children of God." *Sociological Analysis* 37 (1976): 321–39.

Ellwood, Robert. *One Way: The Jesus Movement and Its Meaning*, 101–11. Englewood Cliffs, N.J.: Prentice-Hall, 1973.

Enroth, Ronald. *Youth, Brainwashing, and the Extremist Cults*, 19–146. Grand Rapids, Mich.: Zondervan Publishing House, 1977.

Enroth, Ronald, Eric Ericson, and C. Breckinridge Peters. *The Story of the Jesus People: A Factual Study*, 21–54. Exeter: The Paternoster Press, 1972.

Herve, Jane, and Marie-Christine C. *Confession d'une Enfant de Dieu*. Paris: Rochevignes, 1985.

Hopkins, Joseph. "The Children of God: Disciples of Deception." *Christianity Today* (Feb. 18, 1977): 18–23.

Lynch, Zelda. "Inside the 'Heavenly Elite': The Children of God Today." *Christian Research Journal* (Summer 1990): 16–21.

McFadden, Michael. *The Jesus Revolution*, 84–109. New York, N.Y.: Harper & Row, 1972.

McManus, Una, and John Cooper. *Not for a Million Dollars*. Nashville, Tenn.: Impact Books, 1980.

Melton, Gordon J. *The Encyclopedic Handbook of Cults in America*, 154–58. New York, N.Y.: Garland Publishing, 1986.

New York State Office of the Attorney General, Charity Frauds Bureau. *Final Report on the Activities of the Children of God to the Hon. Louis J. Lefkowitz, Attorney General of the State of New York*. Albany, N.Y., 1975.

Patrick, Ted. *Let Our Children Go!* New York, N.Y.: Dutton, 1976.

Pavlos, Andrew. *The Cult Experience*, 161–63. Westport, Conn.: Greenwood Press, 1982.

Pritchett, W. Douglas. *The Children of God—Family of Love: An Annotated Bibliography*. New York, N.Y.: Garland Publishing, 1985.

Richardson, James, and Rex Davis. "Experiential Fundamentalism: Revisions of Orthodoxy in Jesus Movement Groups." *Journal of the American Academy of Religion* 51 (1983): 397–425.

Streiker, Lowell. *The Cults are Coming*. Nashville, Tenn.: Abingdon Press, 1978.

Van Zandt, David. "Ideology and Structure in the Children of God: A Study of a New Sect." Ph.D. diss., University of London Library, 1985.

Wallis, Roy. "Observations on the Children of God." *Sociological Review* 24 (1976a): 807–29. Reprinted as "Millennialism and Community: Observations on the Children of God." In *Salvation and Protest: Studies of Social and Religious Movements*, 51–73. London: Frances Pinter Ltd., 1979.

———. "Moses David's Sexy God." *New Humanist* (May/Aug., 1977): 12–14.

———. "Recruiting Christian Manpower." *Society* (May–June, 1978): 72–74.

———. "Sex, marriage and the Children of God." In *Salvation and Protest: Studies of Social and Religious Movements*, 74–90. London: Frances Pinter Ltd., 1979.

———. "Yesterday's Children: Cultural and Structural Change in a New Religious Movement." In *The Social Impact of New Religious Movements*, edited by Bryan Wilson, 97–133. New York, N.Y.: The Rose of Sharon Press, 1981.

———. "The social construction of charisma." *Social Compass* 29 (1982): 25–39.

———. "Hostages to Fortune: Thoughts on the Future of Scientology and the Children of God." In *The Future of New Religious Movements*. Macon, Georgia: Mercer University Press, 1987, 80–90.

Wangerin, Ruth. "Make-Believe Revolution: A Study of the Children of God." Ph.D. diss., City University of New York, 1982.

———. "Women in the Children of God: 'Revolutionary Women' or 'Mountin' Maids'?" In *Women in Search of Utopia: Mavericks and Mythmakers*, edited by Ruby Rohrlich and Elaine Baruch, 130–39. New York, N.Y.: Schocken Books, 1984.

———. "Women . . . Maids'?" In *Women in Search of Utopia: Mavericks and Mythmakers*, edited by Ruby Rohrlich and Elaine Baruch, 130–39. New York, N.Y.: Schocken Books, 1984.

Ward, Hiley. *The Far-Out Saints of the Jesus Communes: A Firsthand Report and Interpretation of the Jesus People Movement*, 53–73. New York, N.Y.: Association Press, 1972.

II. GENERAL REFERENCES

Aberle, David. "A Note on Relative Deprivation Theory as Applied to Millennarian and Other Cult Movements." In *Reader in Comparative Religion: An Anthropological Approach*. 3d ed.. Edited by William Lessa and Evon Vogt, 527–31. New York, N.Y.: Harper & Row, 1972.

Anderson, Nels. *The American Hobo*. Leiden: Brill, 1975.

Bainbridge, William. *Satan's Power: A Deviant Psychotherapy Cult*. Berkeley, Cal.: University of California Press, 1978.

Barker, Eileen. *The Making of a Moonie: Choice or Brainwashing?* Oxford: Basil Blackwell, 1984.

Beckford, James. *The Trumpet of Prophecy: A Sociological Study of Jehovah's Witnesses*. Oxford: Basil Blackwell, 1975.

Berger, Peter. *The Sacred Canopy: Elements of a Sociological Theory of Religion*. Garden City, N.Y.: Doubleday & Co., 1967.

Berger, Peter, and Thomas Luckmann. *The Social Construction of Reality: A*

Treatise in the Sociology of Knowledge. Garden City, N.Y.: Doubleday & Co., 1966.

Bittner, Egon. "The Police on Skid-Row: A Study of Peace Keeping." *American Sociological Review* 32 (1967): 699–715.

Bloch, Maurice. "The Past and the Present in the Present." *Man* 12 (1977): 278–92.

Blum, Alan, and Peter McHugh. "The Social Ascription of Motives." *American Sociological Review* 36 (1971): 98–109.

Bromley, David, and Anson Shupe. *"Moonies" in America: Cult, Church, and Crusades*. Beverly Hills, Cal.: Sage Publications, 1979.

————. "Financing the New Religions: A Resource Mobilization Approach." *Journal for the Scientific Study of Religion* 19 (1980): 227–39.

Bulmer, Martin. "Comment on 'The Ethics of Covert Methods.' " *British Journal of Sociology* 31 (1980): 59–65.

Bultmann, Rudolf. *Jesus Christ and Mythology*. New York, N.Y.: Charles Scribner's Sons, 1958.

Caudill, William, Frederick Redlich, Helen Gilmore, and Eugene Brody. "Social Structure and Interaction Processes on a Psychiatric Ward." *American Journal of Orthopsychiatry* 22 (1952): 314–34.

Cicourel, Aaron. *Method and Measurement in Sociology*. New York, N.Y.: The Free Press, 1964.

————. *Cognitive Sociology: Language and Meaning in Social Interaction*. Baltimore, Md.: Penguin, 1973.

Cohn, Norman. *The Pursuit of the Millennium: Revolutionary Millenarians and Mystical Anarchists of the Middle Ages*. New York, N.Y.: Oxford University Press, 1970.

Collins, Randall. *Conflict Sociology: Toward an Explanatory Science*. New York, N.Y.: Academic Press, 1975.

————. "On the Microfoundations of Macrosociology." *American Journal of Sociology* 86 (1981): 984–1014.

Coulter, Jeffrey. "Beliefs and Practical Understanding." In *Everyday Language: Studies in Ethnomethodology*, edited by George Psathas, 163–86. New York, N.Y.: Irvington Publishers, 1979.

Dahrendorf, Ralf. *Homo Sociologicus*. London: Routledge & Kegan Paul, 1973.

Daner, Francine. *The American Children of Krsna: A Study of the Hare Krsna Movement*. New York, N.Y.: Holt, Rinehart, and Winston, 1976.

Davis, Fred. "Comment on 'Initial Interaction of Newcomers in Alcoholics Anonymous.' " *Social Problems* 8 (1961): 364–65.

Dingwall, Robert. "Ethics and Ethnography." *Sociological Review* 28 (1980): 871–91.

Dodd, Charles. *The Apostolic Preaching and Its Development: Three Lectures*. London: Hodder & Stoughton, 1936.

Douglas, Mary. "The Social Control of Cognition: Some Factors in Joke Perception." *Man* 3 (1968): 361–76.

————. *Natural Symbols: Explorations in Cosmology*. New York, N.Y.: Random House, 1973.

Durkheim, Emile, and Marcel Mauss. *Primitive Classification.* Translated and edited by Rodney Needham. Chicago, Ill.: University of Chicago Press, 1963.

Erikson, Kai. *Wayward Puritans: A Study in the Sociology of Deviance.* New York, N.Y.: John Wiley & Sons, 1966.

————. "A Comment on Disguised Observation in Sociology." *Social Problems* 14(1967): 366–73.

Festinger, Leon, Henry Riecken, and Stanley Schachter. *When Prophecy Fails: A Social and Psychological Study of a Modern Group that Predicted the Destruction of the World.* New York, N.Y.: Harper & Row, 1964.

Fish, Stanley. *Is There a Text in this Class?: The Authority of Interpretive Communities.* Cambridge, Mass.: Harvard University Press, 1980.

————. "Dennis Martinez and the Uses of Theory." *Yale Law Journal* 96 (1987): 1773–800.

Garfinkel, Harold. "The Rational Properties of Scientific and Common Sense Activities." *Behavioral Science* 5 (1960): 72–83. Reprinted in *Studies in Ethnomethodology*, by Harold Garfinkel, 262–83. Englewood Cliffs, N.J.: Prentice-Hall, 1967.

————. "Studies of the Routine Grounds of Everyday Activities." *Social Problems* 11 (1964): 225–50. Reprinted in *Studies in Ethnomethodology*, by Harold Garfinkel, 35–75. Englewood Cliffs, N.J. Prentice-Hall, 1967.

————. *Studies in Ethnomethodology.* Englewood Cliffs, N.J.: Prentice-Hall, 1967.

Garfinkel, Harold, and Harvey Sacks. "On Formal Structures of Practical Actions." In *Theoretical Sociology*, edited by John McKinney and Edward Tiryakian, 337–60. New York, N.Y.: Appleton-Century-Crofts, 1970.

Geertz, Clifford. *The Interpretation of Cultures: Selected Essays.* New York, N.Y.: Basic Books, 1973.

————. *Local Knowledge: Further Essays in Interpretive Anthropology.* New York, N.Y.: Basic Books, 1983.

Geertz, Clifford. *The Religion of Java.* New York, N.Y.: The Free Press, 1960.

Gellner, Ernest. "Concepts and Society." In *Rationality*, edited by Bryan Wilson, 18–49. Oxford: Basil Blackwell, 1970.

Gerlach, Luther and Virginia Hine. *People, Power, Change: Movements of Social Transformation.* New York, N.Y: The Bobbs-Merrill Company, 1970.

Giddens, Anthony. *Central Problems in Sociological Theory: Action, Structure and Contradiction in Social Analysis.* Berkeley, Cal.: University of California Press, 1979.

Goffman, Erving. *The Presentation of Self in Everyday Life.* Middlesex: Penguin, 1959.

————. *Asylums: Essays on the Social Situation of Mental Patients and Other Inmates.* Garden City, N.Y.: Doubleday & Co., 1961a.

————. "Role Distance." In *Encounters: Two Studies in the Sociology of Interaction*, 83–152. Indianapolis, Ind.: Bobbs-Merrill Educational Books, 1961b.

————. *Behavior in Public Places: Notes on the Social Organization of Gatherings.* New York, N.Y.: The Free Press, 1963.

————. *Relations in Public: Microstudies of the Public Order.* New York, N.Y.: Harper & Row, 1971.

Goodman, Felicitas. "Phonetic Analysis of Glossolalia in Four Cultural Settings." *Journal for the Scientific Study of Religion* 8 (1969): 227–39.

Green, Michael. *Evangelism in the Early Church.* London: Hodder & Stoughton, 1973.

Grier, W. J. *The Momentous Event: A Discussion of Scripture Teaching on the Second Advent.* Edinburgh: The Banner of Truth Trust, 1945.

Habermas, Jurgen. *Knowledge and Human Interests,* translated by Jeremy Shapiro. Boston, Mass.: Beacon Press, 1971.

Hawkes, Terence. *Structuralism and Semiotics.* Berkeley, Cal.: University of California Press, 1977.

Heilman, Samuel C. *The People of the Book: Drama, Fellowship, and Religion.* Chicago, Ill.: University of Chicago Press, 1983.

Hilbert, Richard. "Covert Participant Observation." *Urban Life* 9 (1980): 51–78.

Hill, Michael. *A Sociology of Religion.* London: Heinemann Educational Books, 1973.

Hill, Samuel. *Southern Churches in Crisis.* New York, N.Y.: Holt, Rinehart, and Winston, 1967.

Homan, Roger. "The ethics of covert methods." *British Journal of Sociology* 31 (1980): 46–57.

Humphreys, Laud. *Tearoom Trade: Impersonal Sex in Public Places.* 2d ed. Chicago, Ill.: Aldine, 1975.

Husserl, Edmund. *Ideas: General Introduction to Pure Phenomenology.* Translated by W. R. Boyce Gibson. New York, N.Y.: Macmillan, 1931.

James, William. *Pragmatism and Other Essays.* New York, N.Y.: Washington Square Press, 1963.

Johnson, Gregory. "The Hare Krishna in San Francisco." In *The New Religious Consciousness,* edited by Charles Glock and Robert Bellah, 31–55. Berkeley, Cal.: University of California Press, 1976.

Jules-Rosette, Bennetta. *African Apostles: Ritual and Conversion in the Church of John Maranke.* Ithaca, N.Y.: Cornell University Press, 1975.

Kanter, Rosabeth Moss. *Commitment and Community: Communes and Utopias in Sociological Perspective.* Cambridge, Mass.: Harvard University Press, 1972.

Kituse, John, and Aaron Cicourel. "A Note on the Uses of Official Statistics." *Social Problems* 11 (1963): 131–39.

Lieberson, Jonathan. "Interpreting the Interpretor." *N.Y. Review of Books* (March 15, 1984): 39–46.

Lofland, John. "Reply to Davis." *Social Problems* 8 (1961): 365–67.

————. *Doomsday Cult: A Study of Conversion, Proselytization, and Maintenance of Faith.* New York, N.Y.: Irvington Publishers, 1966.

Lofland, John. "Becoming a World-Saver Revisited." *American Behavioral Scientist* 20 (1977): 805–13.

Lofland, John, and Robert Lejeune. "Initial Interaction of Newcomers in Alcoholics Anonymous: A Field Experiment in Class Symbols and Socialization." *Social Problems* 8 (1960): 102–11.

Lofland, John. *Analyzing Social Settings: A Guide to Qualitative Observation and Analysis.* Belmont, Cal.: Wadsworth, 1971.

Lofland, John, and Rodney Stark. "Becoming a World-Saver: A Theory of Conversion to a Deviant Perspective." *American Sociological Review* 30 (1965): 862–75. Reprinted in *Religion in Sociological Perspective: Essays in the Empirical Study of Religion*, edited by Charles Glock, 28–47. Belmont, Cal.: Wadsworth, 1973.

Long, Theodore, and Jeffrey Hadden. "Religious Conversion and the Concept of Socialization: Integrating the Brainwashing and Drift Models." *Journal for the Scientific Study of Religion* 22 (1983): 1–14.

Matza, David. *Becoming Deviant.* Englewood Cliffs, N.J.: Prentice-Hall, 1969.

McHoul, A. W. *Telling how texts talk: Essays on reading and ethnomethodology.* London: Routledge & Kegan Paul, 1982.

Merleau-Ponty, Maurice. "Indirect Language and the Voices of Silence." In *Signs*, translated and edited by Richard McCleary, 39–83. Evanston, Ill.: Northwestern University Press, 1964.

Merton, Robert. "Social Structure and Anomie." *American Sociological Review* 3 (1938): 672–82.

Milgram, Stanley. "Behavioral Study of Obedience." *Journal of Abnormal and Social Psychology* 67 (1963): 371–78.

Mills, C. Wright. "Situated Actions and Vocabularies of Motives." *American Sociological Review* 5 (1940): 904–13.

Nelsen, Hart M. "Sectarianism, World View, and Anomie." *Social Forces* 51 (1972): 226–33.

Neitz, Mary Jo. *Charisma and Community: A Study of Religious Commitment within the Charismatic Renewal.* New Brunswick, N.J.: Transaction Books, 1987.

Niebuhr, H. Richard. *The Social Sources of Denominationalism.* New York, N.Y.: World Publishing, 1957 (first published 1927).

O'Dea, Thomas. *The Mormons.* Chicago, Ill.: The University of Chicago Press, 1957.

O'Toole, Roger. "Sectarianism in Politics: Case Studies of Maoists and De Leonists." In *Sectarianism: Analyses of Religious and Non-Religious Sects*, edited by Roy Wallis, 162–89. London: Peter Owen Limited, 1975.

Parsons, Talcott. *The Structure of Social Action: A Study in Social Theory with Special Reference to a Group of Recent European Writers.* New York, N.Y.: The Free Press, 1968.

Parsons, Talcott, Edward Shils, Gordon Allport, Clyde Kluckhohn, Henry Murray, Robert Sears, Richard Sheldon, Samuel Stouffer, and Edward Tolman. "Some Fundamental Categories of the Theory of Action: A General Statement." In *Toward a General Theory of Social Action*, edited by Talcott

Parsons and Edward Shils, 3–29. Cambridge, Mass.: Harvard University Press, 1951.

Piliavin, Irving, and Scott Briar. "Police Encounters with Juveniles." In *Crime and the Legal Process*, edited by William Chambliss, 165–74. New York, N.Y.: McGraw-Hill, 1969.

Pope, Luther. *Millhands and Preachers: A Study of Gastonia*. New Haven, Conn.: Yale University Press, 1942.

Radcliffe-Brown, A. R. *Structure and Function in Primitive Society: Essays and Addresses*. New York, N.Y.: The Free Press, 1952.

Rawls, John. "Two Concepts of Rules." *The Philosophical Review* 64 (1955): 3–32.

Richards, I. A. *How to Read a Page: A Course in Effective Reading with an Introduction to a Hundred Great Works*. London: Routledge & Kegan Paul, 1943.

Richardson, James. "Financing the New Religions: Comparative and Theoretical Considerations." *Journal for the Scientific Study of Religion* 21 (1982): 255–72.

Robbins, Dick, Madeline Doncas, and Thomas Curtis. "The Last Civil Religion: Reverend Moon and the Unification Church." *Sociological Analysis* 37(1976): 111–25.

Roche, Maurice. *Phenomenology, Language and the Social Sciences*. London: Routledge & Kegan Paul, 1973.

Roth, Julius. "Comments on 'Secret Observation.' " *Social Problems* 9 (1962): 283–84.

Sacks, Harvey. "The Search for Help: No One to Turn To." in *Essays in Self-Destruction*, edited by Edwin Shneidman, 203–23. New York, N.Y.: Science House, 1967.

———. "On the Analyzability of Stories by Children." In *Directions in Sociolinguistics: The Ethnography of Communication*, edited by John Gumperz and Dell Hymes, 329–45. New York, N.Y.: Holt, Rinehart, and Winston, 1972. Reprinted in *Ethnomethodology: Selected Readings*, edited by Roy Turner, 216–32. Harmondsworth, Middlesex: Penguin, 1974.

Samarin, William. *Tongues of Men and Angels: The Religious Language of Pentecostalism*. New York, N.Y.: Macmillan, 1972.

Schegloff, Emanuel, and Harvey Sacks. "Opening Up Closings." *Semiotica* 8 (1973): 289–327. Reprinted in *Ethnomethodology: Selected Readings*, edited by Roy Turner, 233–64. Baltimore, Md.: Penguin, 1974.

Schneider, Louis, and Sanford Dornbusch. *Popular Religion: Inspirational Books in America*. Chicago, Ill.: University of Chicago Press, 1958.

Schnell, W. J. *Thirty Years a Watch Tower Slave: The Confessions of a Converted Jehovah's Witness*. Grand Rapids, Mich.: Baker Book House, 1959.

Schutz, Alfred. "The Problem of Rationality in the Social World." *Economica* 10 (1943): 130–49.

———. "Common-Sense and Scientific Interpretations of Human Action." *Philosophy & Phenomenological Research* 14 (1953): 1–38.

———. *The Phenomenology of the Social World*. Translated by George Walsh and Frederick Lehnert. London: Heinemann Educational Books, 1972.

Schwartz, Gary. *Sect Ideologies and Social Status*. Chicago, Ill.: University of Chicago Press, 1970.

Scott, Marvin, and Stanford Lyman. "Accounts." *American Sociological Review* 33 (1968): 46–62.

Shepperson, George. "The Comparative Study of Millenarian Movements." In *Millennial Dreams in Action: Studies in Revolutionary Religious Movements*, edited by Sylvia Thrupp, 44–52. New York, N.Y.: Schoken Books, 1970.

Smelser, Neil. *Theory of Collective Behavior*. London: Routledge & Kegan Paul, 1962.

Sommerfeld, Richard. "Conceptions of the Ultimate and the Social Organization of Religious Bodies." *Journal for the Scientific Study of Religion* 7 (1968): 178–96.

Stark, Rodney, and William Bainbridge. "Networks of Faith: Interpersonal Bonds and Recruitment to Cults and Sects." *American Journal of Sociology* 85 (1980): 1376–95.

———. *A Theory of Religion*. New York, N.Y.: Peter Lange, 1987.

Sullivan, Mortimer, Stuart Queen, and Ralph Patrick. "Participant Observation as Employed in the Study of a Military Training Program." *American Sociological Review* 23 (1958): 660–67.

Swanson, Guy. *The Birth of the Gods: The Origin of Primitive Beliefs*. Ann Arbor, Mich.: University of Michigan Press, 1960.

Talmon, Yvonne. "Millenarianism." In *Encyclopedia of the Social Sciences*. Vol. 10. 349–52. New York, N.Y.: Macmillan and the Free Press, 1968.

Taylor, Bryan. "Conversion and Cognition: An Area for Empirical Study in the Microsociology of Religious Knowledge." *Social Compass* 23 (1976): 5–22.

Turner, Roy. "Words, Utterance and Activities." In *Understanding Everyday Life: Toward the Reconstruction of Sociological Knowledge*, edited by Jack Douglas, 169–87. Chicago, Ill.: Aldine, 1970. Reprinted in *Ethnomethodology: Selected Readings*, edited by Roy Turner, 197–215. Harmondsworth, Middlesex: Penguin, 1974.

Van Zandt, David. "Commonsense Reasoning, Social Change, and the Law." *Northwestern Law Review* 81 (1987): 894–940.

von Hoffman, and Cassidy. "Interviewing Negro Pentecostals." *American Journal of Sociology* 52 (1956): 195–208.

Walker, Andrew, and James Atherton. "An Easter Pentecostal Convention: Successful Management of a 'Time of Blessing.' " *Sociological Review* 19 (1971): 368–87.

Wallis, Roy. *The Road to Total Freedom: A Sociological Analysis of Scientology*. New York, N.Y.: Columbia University Press, 1976b.

Weber, Max. *The Theory of Social and Economic Organization*. Edited and Translated by Talcott Parsons. New York, N.Y.: The Free Press, 1947.

———. *The Protestant Ethic and the Spirit of Capitalism*. Translated by Talcott Parsons. New York, N.Y.: Charles Scribner's Sons, 1958.

Whyte, William. *Street Corner Society: The Social Structure of an Italian Slum*. 2d ed. Chicago, Ill.: University of Chicago Press, 1961.

Wilson, Bryan. *Sects and Society: A Sociological Study of the Elim Tabernacle, Christian Science, and Christadelphians.* Berkeley, Cal.: University of California Press, 1961.

————. *Magic and the Millennium: A Sociological Study of Religious Movements of Protest among Tribal and Third-World People.* London: Heinemann, 1973.

Winch, Peter. *The Idea of a Social Science and Its Relation to Philosophy.* London: Routledge & Kegan Paul, 1958.

Wittgenstein, Ludwig. *Philosophical Investigations.* 3d ed. Translated by G.E.M. Anscombe. Oxford: Basil Blackwell & Mott, 1958.

Wuthnow, Robert. "Two Traditions in the Study of Religion." *Journal for the Scientific Study of Religion* 20 (1981): 16–32.

Zablocki, Benjamin. *The Joyful Community: An Account of the Bruderhof, A Communal Movement Now in Its Third Generation.* Chicago, Ill.: University of Chicago Press, 1980.

Zimmerman, Donald. "A Reply to Professor Coser." *The American Sociologist* 11 (1976): 4–13.

III. MO LETTERS AND OTHER COG PUBLICATIONS

The following are Mo letters (ordered by their COG number) with date of issue and distribution code (see Chapter 2, note 3):

Old Church, New Church Prophecy, A (Aug. 26, 1969) (GP).

Mountain Men, B (Dec. 5, 1969) (GP).

Faith and Healing, M (Aug. 1970) (GP).

Revolutionary Rules, S (Mar. 1972) (GP).

More on Faith, T (July 1969) (GP).

Diamonds of Dust, 3 (Oct. 20, 1970) (GP).

Let's Talk About Jesus, 20 (Dec. 5, 1970) (DFO).

Quality or Quantity?, 23 (Dec. 12, 1970) (DO).

I Gotta Split—Part I, 28 (Dec. 22, 1970) (DO).

Dumps!, 33 (Jan. 3, 1971) (GP).

Letters III, 53 (Mar. 3, 1971) (LTA).

Flatlanders (Organisation III), 57 (Mar. 13, 1971) (GP).

New Teams, 62 (Apr. 1, 1971) (DO).

Faith, 73 (May 20, 1971) (GP).

Stop-Look-Listen!, 74 (May 26, 1971) (GP).

David, 77 (June 20, 1971) (GP).

The Key of David, 78 (June 20, 1971) (GP).

The Call of David, 79 (June 20, 1971) (GP).

Personal Replies, 107 (Sept. 1971) (LTA).

Looking Unto Jesus, 126 (Nov. 12, 1971) (LTA).

The Little Book and The Time of the Gentiles, 146 (Dec. 13, 1971).

The Laws of Moses, 155 (Feb. 21, 1972) (LTA).

The 70 Years Prophecy of the End, 156 (Mar. 1, 1972) (GP)

Corrections, 156A (Mar. 12, 1972) (LTA).

Survival, 172 (June 1972) (GP).

African Nightmare, 201 (Jan. 23, 1973) (GP).

Become One, 208 (Mar. 6, 1973) (GP).

Holy Holes!, 237 (Apr. 1, 1973) (GP).

Mountin' Maid, 240 (Dec. 27, 1970) (GP).

Shiners?—Or Shamers?, 241 (June 26, 1973) (DO).

Revolutionary Women, 250 (June 20, 1973) (GP).

The Money Explodes, 294 (Jan. 24, 1974) (GP).

Prayer Power, 302 (May 29, 1972) (GP).

The Law of Love, 302C (Mar. 21, 1974) (DO).

Exorcism, 303 (Apr. 1974) (GP).

The Look of Love, 304 (Apr. 1, 1974) (GP).

Sex Works!, 306 (June 2, 1974).

Hitch Your Wagon To a Star! (MWWFNL No. 5), 311B (Sept. 8, 1974) (DFO).

Benefits of Backsliding, 312 (Aug. 9, 1972) (GP).

But if Not!, 313 (Sept. 13, 1974) (GP).

Forsaking All, 314A (Oct. 1974) (GP).

MO's Worldwide Family Newsletter No. 16, 17 and 18, 314C (Aug. 1974) (DFO).

Listening?—Or Lamenting?, 320 (Nov. 17, 1974).

Letter to a Labourer, 325 (Jan. 20, 1975) (GP).

The Word—New and Old (Mt. 13:52), 329 (Sept. 1974) (GP).

The Childcare Revolution, 330B (Apr. 1, 1975) (LO).

Eritrea!, 333B (Feb. 24, 1975) (DFO).

The Spirit of God, 337 (Aug. 28, 1974) (GP).

The Deluge!, 339 (Mar. 2, 1975).

Witnessing!, 344 (May 1975) (GP) (compiled by Apollos and Mo Ed. Dept.)

Death to the Cities, 373 (Nov. 30, 1975).

The Bait That Fell in Love with a Fish!, 552 (May 3, 1976) (DO).

The Catch!, 555 (Oct. 10, 1976) (DO).

God's Whores?, 560 (Apr. 26, 1976) (DO).

The Men Who Play God!, 564 (Oct. 10, 1976) (DO).

The FF Explosion!, 576 (Apr. 6, 1977) (DO).

Open the Door for the Children!, 588 (May 31, 1977) (GP).

God's Only Law is Love, 592 (July 29, 1977) (DFO).

Grace v. Law!, 635 (Nov. 8, 1977) (DFO).

Is Love Against the Law?, 648 (Jan. 1978) (GP).

Dear Friend or Foe, 754 (Jan. 2, 1979) (GP).

My Childhood Sex!, 779 (June 28, 1977, and Aug. 11, 1978; issued Feb. 1979) (DO).

Millions of Miles of Miracles!, 897 (Dec. 29, 1979) (DFO).

Child Brides!, 902 (Apr. 4, 1977; issued Apr. 1980) (DO).

Americans Abroad!, 905 (May 1, 1980) (DO).

Sex Jewels!, 919 (May 1980) (DO).

Tithing and the FN!, 928 (July 26, 1980) (DFO).

The Devil Hates Sex!, 999 (May 20, 1980) (DFO).

Fellowship Revolution!, 1001 (Apr. 19, 1981) (DFO).

Glorify God in the Dance, 1026 (July 24, 1981) (DO).

The New TRF!, 1051 (Oct. 1981) (DO).
PDQ Centers!, 1093 (Jan. 1, 1982) (DO).
Warning to All Sodomites!, 1110 (Oct. 22, 1981) (DFO).
Deborah & Bill Davis' Dirty Book!, 1856 (Dec. 1984) (GP).
God Hates Murmuring!, 1879 (1985 [estimated]) (DO).
Introduction to the New Heaven's Children, 2250 (June 1986) (DO).
David's Ordination!, 2347 (Jan. 1987) (DO).
The School Vision!, 2430 (Nov. 1987) (DO).
Have a School!, 2432 (May 1988) (DO).
The Appeal of the World on our Teens!, 2462 (July 1988) (DO).
When to Separate!, 2468 (Aug. 1988) (DO).
Prayers Against Our Enemies!, 2477 (Sept. 1988) (DO).
Curses Upon Our Enemies!, 2478 (Sept. 1988) (DO).
Going Home?—Go Mobile!, 2507 (Mar. 1989) (DO).

The following are miscellaneous COG publications referred to in the text:

Basic Training Manual, Zurich, Switz.: World Services, 1988.
Family Specials News Magazine!, FSM 121 (FN 230) (Feb. 1989) (DO)
Heaven's Children, Zurich, Switz.: World Services, April 1987 (including Mo
    letters from 2100 [Sept. 1985] through 2104 [Oct. 1985]).
Heaven's Girl, Zurich, Switz.: World Services, April 1987.
Latest News Flashes No. 86 (July 1986) (DFO) (prepared by World Services).
Latest News Flashes No. 120 (Apr. 1989) (DO) (prepared by World Services).
New Heaven's Children, Zurich, Switz.: World Services, April 1987 (including
    Mo letters from 2250 [June 1986] through 2293 [Oct. 1986]).
Renewing Your Mind, Mother Eve letter 27 (Dec. 1973) (DFO).
The Story of Davidito. Zurich, Switz.: The Family of Love, 1982.
"Witnessing." In *The Revolution for Jesus*. Dallas, Tex.: The Children of God,
    1972.
Witnessing Tips, [no number] (Mar. 27, 1974) (GP).

INDEX

Aaron (Family name), 31, 32
Abduction, 3
Abraham, 148
Abrahim, 21
Accounts, 96, 133–35
Actors, 14
Adultery, 161
Africa, 23
AIDS, 170
Alabama, 35
Alcoholics Anonymous, 193 n. 7
Alienation, 156–58, 159, 160, 162–64;
  commitment-threatening, 162–64; rou-
  tine, 156–58; trials and battles, 158–59
All-Things doctrine, 26 n. 10
Alternation, 150
Amsterdam, Peter, 172 n. 23
Anabaptism, 3 n. 1, 20, 23
Analogy articulation, 129–30
Antichrist, 25, 33, 58 n. 2, 152, 168 n. 11
Antinomianism, 24–25
Anti-Semitism, 23, 85 n. 3
Apocalypse, 3, 58 n. 2
Arabs, 23, 59, 189
Armstrong, Garner Ted, 185
Arnhem colony, 58–67 passim, 86 n. 5,
  114, 187, 189, 190
Artemas (Family name), 15 n. 15
Arthur (Family name), 46
Astrology, 106 n. 3, 142–43, 145
Atheism, 102 n. 2
Australia, 52
Authoritarianism, 3, 4, 40, 44–46, 173,
  196 n. 14; and Berg's extended family,
  45; and colony leaders, 44; and devia-
  tions, 56. See also Authority
Authority, 22, 146; charismatic, 30–31,
  36, 48, 52, 55; experience of, and par-
  ticipant observation, 192; and paternal-
  ism, 72–75; and the RNR, 50. See also
  Authoritarianism

Baptism in the Holy Spirit, 130–31, 174
Beam, Abraham, 141
Belgium, 8, 187, 189
Berg, David (Moses David), 4–5, 17, 166,

197; banning of Flirty Fishing, 170; and
  channels with God, 122; and charismatic authority, 30–33; claim of, to be
  God's last prophet, 162; and COG social organization, 56; death of, predictions of, 172; dissent from, 77 n. 1;
  doubts about, among members, 167;
  dreams of, 119–20 n. 2; experiences of,
  and concretization, 128; and the Fellowship Revolution, 54–55, 168; and
  Flirty Fishing, statements on, 108 n. 4;
  household of, financial support for, 68;
  in Huntington Beach, 33–34; and ideology, 18 n. 1, 19–26; and litnessing,
  43–44; and Maria, 35; and the Nationalise Re-organise Security-wise Revolution (NRS Revolution), 50–53; and
  the New Revolution, 44–46, 48–49; and
  the Obedience Revolution, 168–69;
  personal trials of, citing of, by members, 159; press secretary of, 166 n. 1;
  and religious reading, 118, 119, 121;
  and the Reorganization Nationalisation Revolution (RNR), 48–50, 53, 190;
  road travel period of, 34–36, 50; and
  supplementation, 121–22; and the
  Texas Soul Clinic (TSC), 37–40; and
  worldwide expansion, 40–43
Berg, Deborah (Deborah Davis), 31, 32,
  47, 49, 167 n. 9, 169 n. 13
Berg, Faith. See Faith (Family name)
Berg, Jane Miller. See Mother Eve (Family name)
Berg, Jonathan. See Hosea (Family name)
Berg, Linda. See Berg, Deborah (Deborah
  Davis)
Berg, Paul. See Aaron (Family name)
Berg, Virginia Brandt ("Grandmother"),
  31, 33
Berger, Peter, 149 n. 1
Bible, 5, 24, 25, 163; classes, 20, 33, 36,
  42; evangelical view of, 22; and formal
  ideology, 18; King James version, 20,
  21; literalism of, 112–13; and reading
  practices, 61, 62–63, 118–24, 150–52,

Bible (*cont.*)
  158, 182; references from, and proselytization, 26; rules of, 22
"Bible, The" (Family record album), 189
Birth control, 39, 79
Blacks, 23
Bockelson, Jan, 3 n. 1
Bradford colony, 10, 60 n. 3, 62 n. 4, 68 nn. 9, 10, 96, 177–86
Brainwashing, 3, 37, 122
Brazil, 166
Brussels, 190
Bulmer, Martin, 193 n. 8

Caleb (Family name), 33, 49
Canada, 34–35
Canary Islands, 46–48, 49, 59, 197
Canevaro, Emmanuel, 49, 190
Capitalism, 5, 23, 124, 136, 141
Catacomb Kids Clubs, 67
Catholicism, 47, 143, 159
Charismatic authority, 3, 30–31, 36, 48, 52, 55
Children, 48, 49; and the Catacomb Kids Club, 67; and litnessing, 52; and sexuality, 26, 53, 54, 170–71; and socialization, 154
Children of God, The (Davis), 47
China, 167
Christ. See Jesus
Christian and Missionary Alliance, 31
Christianity, 23, 52, 91
Church of Love, 48, 52, 63
Clarification, 123–24
Class differences, 57, 59
Colonies, 57–71; everyday life in, 59–64; and external organizational features, 69–71; field, 57; financial support for, 68–69; frontline, 57; ideological activities in, 64–67; meetings, 63–64; ratio of males to females in, 57; selah, 37, 46, 59; size of, 44–45; tithe paid by, 44; and worldwide expansion, 42. See also Homes
COMBOS, 55, 167 n. 10
Commands, 72, 73, 148
Communism, 24
Concretization, 125–27
Conversion, 3, 5–6, 27–29, 30; and authority relations, 74; brushes with, and participation observation, 16–17; and

forsaking family ties, 39; and socialization, 149–50; sociological explanations of, 103. See also Flirty Fishing; Proselytization
Creationism, 159
Criticism, of the COG, 34, 37; and Berg's direction to members to go underground, 40–41; in Germany, 186; and migration, 53; of the Tenerife colony, 47. See also Public relations
Curl, Roger, 176 n. 2

Dad. See Berg, David (Moses David)
Daily Might quotations, 158
Daniel, 152
Dating, 39, 42
Davidito, 170 n. 17
Davis, Bill, 47
Davis, Deborah. See Berg, Deborah (Deborah Davis)
Davis, Rex, 176, 186, 193 n. 8
Defections, 46, 49, 51
Deprivation, relative, sociological theories of, 103
Deprogramming, 3, 37, 80
Deviation, 156
Devil, 76, 91, 118, 139 n. 6, 140, 152, 153; and Jesus, 25; victories over, 12; views of, and the socialization process, 159–60, 161, 162, 163, 164. See also Satan
Devoids, 94
Dictatorship, 24–25
Dietrich, Arnold. See Joshua (Family name)
Dietrich, Arthur. See Caleb (Family name)
Dietrich, Lydia ("Lydia"), 33, 49
Dingwall, Robert, 195 n. 12, 196 n. 14
Dirksen, Everett, 35
Discernment, 94
District Area Fellowship (DAF), 168
Divine inspiration, 21
Divorce, 79, 102
Donations, 51; and litnessing, 29, 43–44, 49, 52, 68, 90–91, 94, 96. See also Finances
Drug use, 33, 36, 56, 91, 137, 163–64, 184
Durkheim, Emile, 7 n. 8

Egypt, 24, 33, 34, 36; spoiling, 36, 39

Emmanuel (Family name). *See* Canevero, Emmanuel
England, 38, 41, 167 n. 6, 180–82, 189; accounts of experimentation in, 46; opposition to recruiting in, 45. *See also* Bradford colony; London
Eschatology, 24
Esther (Family name), 54, 169 n. 13
Ethics, 22, 190–96. *See also* Morality
Ethiopia, 144
Ethnographic methods, 9–13, 103
Evangelism, 3, 5, 32
Eve. *See* Mother Eve (Family name)
Evidencing, 111–13, 143–44
Evolutionary theory, 113, 159

Faith (Family name), 33, 35, 172
Faith trips, 66, 69
Family News Magazine (FNM), 52, 53–54
Father Love (Family name). *See* Berg, David (Moses David)
Fellowship meetings, 54
Fellowship Revolution, 54–55, 168
Finances, and litnessing, 29, 43–44, 49, 52, 68, 90–91, 94, 96; and colonies or Homes, 51, 68–69; and membership, 39–40, 53
Fleetwood Mac, 190
Flirty Fishing, 28, 46–48, 78, 168, 189; banning of, 169–70; development of, 6; in Islamic countries, 97; justification of, 145–46; and love, 108 n. 4; Moses David on, 160 n. 6; not involving sex, 66; and the Philippine Army, 167 n. 5; and the RNR, 48, 50; and socialization, 161; and targeting individuals for conversion, 28–29; and witnessing, 98
Formal ideology, 18–26, 56, 78 n. 3, 79, 92; description of, 136; in Mo letters, 160 n. 6; and reading practices, 117, 118; and witnessing, 98, 100, 104, 114 n. 6
Forsaking all, 24, 33, 36, 42, 68, 176
France, 8, 45, 185–86, 187, 190
FREECOG, 37
Friendships, 77, 79–82
Fringe-meaning articulation, 124–25
Furloughing, 51

Garfinkel, Harold, 194 n. 9
Geertz, Clifford, 6 n. 7

Gemini, 143, 145
Geneva, 46, 59, 176
Germany, 8, 45, 186, 190
Goats, 86
God, 3, 55, 77, 124; and affirmation expressions, 120; and authority structures, 148; beliefs about, and socialization, 151–53; commitment to, 5, 24, 159–60; discussion of, and witnessing, 110–11, 112–13; as an empirical reality, 7–8; and evidencing, 144; and faith trips, 66; as a guide, 145; and litnessing, 96; and marriage, 78 n. 3; and the "Message of Jeremiah," 32; and the millennium, 25; and Moses David, 20, 21, 22–23, 30, 31, 32, 35, 162, 197; nature of, 102; new nation of, building of, 39; and the New York City blackout, 141–42; obedience to, 130; and prayer, 64–65, 119, 139; presuppositions about, 136; and proselytization, 26, 64, 135; protection by, 161; revelation from, and reading practices, 122; and sexuality, 54, 170–71; as a source of inspiration, 125; and temple time, 60; as a vengeful judge, 23; word of, 36, 45, 152
—love of, 27, 41, 47, 48, 84; and witnessing, 98, 108, 110–11, 112, 115
Gold Lion Publishing, 59, 189
Great Tribulation. *See* Tribulation
Griggs, Russell, 39 n. 2

Habbakuk (Family name), 187
Halifax, 179–80
Hare Krsna, 3
Healing, laying on of hands for, 13
Hendrix, Jimi, 85 n. 4
Hilbert, Richard, 191–92
Holland, 187, 189, 190. *See also* Arnhem colony
Holland Park (London), 59
Holy Spirit, 23, 95 n. 8, 130–31, 174
Homan, Roger, 193 n. 7
Home Area Servants, 168–69
Home Councils, 50
Homes, 5, 49, 167; and the Fellowship Revolution, 54; and the NRS, 51; number of families in, 168; and the Obedience Revolution, 168–69; posting of

Homes (cont.)
    Berg's address in, 50; and TTCs, 172.
    See also Colonies
Hosea (Family name), 32, 54, 169n.13
Houston, 35
Hoyt, David, 39n.2
Huntington Beach (California), 33–34, 50
Hypnotism, 37

Ideology, religious, 18; and education in
    the colonies, 59; and interactions in
    everyday life, 75–79; manifestations of,
    18–22; and organizational activity, rela-
    tion of, 6–8, 9; and proselytization, 18–
    29, 56; and reading practices, 117, 118,
    124, 125, 131; and socialization, 154,
    156–57, 159, 164–65; and social struc-
    ture, 173. See also Formal ideology;
    Kerygma; Practical ideology; Reason-
    ing, practical religious
Idiomatic expressions, 137–38
Imrah (Family name), 186, 189, 190
Incest, 35, 170–71
India, 167, 168, 178
Individualism, 173
Indonesia, 167
IRF program, 51, 53
Isaiah, 125
Islamic countries, 97
Israel, 23, 38, 148
Italy, 8, 190

Japan, 166, 167
Jehovah's Witnesses, 83n.1, 94, 179–80
Jesus, 95n.8, 148, 159; commitment to,
    39; the Bride of, 161; Family aphorism
    referring to, 166; and the millennium,
    24, 25; and prayer, 64, 65; reference to,
    and proselytization, 26, 27, 174, 175,
    177; revolutionary army for, 72; and
    witnessing, 102, 108, 114, 116
Jesus babies, 50
Jesus People Army, 39n.2
Jesus Revolution (Jesus People), 1, 3, 40
Jethro (John Treadwell), 32, 45, 49
Job (Family name), 187
Joela (Family name), 187
Joking, 146
Jonestown, 51, 52
Jordon, Fred, 32, 33, 34, 37
Joshua (Family name), 33, 36, 49

Judaism, 23, 85n.3
Justification, 133n.1, 144–46, 158

Kerygma, 18, 33; and Flirty Fishing, 48;
    and litnessing interactions, 83–84, 91–
    92, 94; and practical ideology, distinc-
    tion between, 19; and proselytization,
    26–27, 41; and witnessing, 99–100, 109,
    111, 112, 115
Khadafi, Moammar, 23
Kidnapping, 37, 81
Kingdom of God, 23
Knowledge, 19, 131, 173
Kohoutek, 22n.7

Language Area Fellowship (LAF), 168
Latin America, 4, 53, 168
Leaders, 11n.13, 26, 36; and access strat-
    egies, 28–29; appointment of, 30; argu-
    ing with, as forbidden, 42; as authori-
    tarian, 40; and the chain of command,
    48–49; and interpretations of events,
    140; loyalty of, to Berg, 42–43; obedi-
    ence to, 15n.15; self-aggrandizing, 74–
    75; and sense of self, 16; and socializa-
    tion, 162–63; stonewalling tactics of,
    192. See also Authoritarianism; Author-
    ity; Home Area Servants; Shepherds
Libya, 23
Light Club, 33
Literature, religious, 117–32; and group
    reading, 119–21; and interpretive pro-
    cedures in reading, 122–31; and pre-
    suppositions in reading, 121–22. See
    also Publications, COG
Litnessing, 5, 28, 83–97, 166; accounting
    for, 95–96; and categorizing prospects,
    93–95; difficulty with, 71; and every-
    day life, patterns of, 61, 63, 66; expo-
    sure to, and socialization, 155, 156,
    157, 158; from February 1973 through
    February 1975, 43–44; and giving infor-
    mation to outsiders, 81–82; income
    from, 46, 49, 68, 69; interaction, de-
    scription of, 87–93; limitations on, 96–
    97; and lit bags, 85–86, 89, 95; and Mo
    letters, 168; and nonverbal techniques,
    92–93; and the NRS Revolution, 52;
    and participant observation, 12, 14–15,
    181, 187, 191; practices, and Word
    time, 118–19; and preparation for, 84–

86; quotas, 43, 44, 45; rate of response to, statistics on, 90 n. 6; routine affirmations referring to, 138; rules governing, 84–85, 86–87; train, 145; and witnessing, comparison of, 98–99
Lofland, John, 173 n. 1, 189 n. 6, 193 n. 7
London, 16, 38, 46, 59, 173–78, 189–90
Louisiana, 35
Love, 63, 80; and Flirty Fishing, 108 n. 4; hugs, 75; and socialization, 160; and witnessing, 98, 100, 102, 107–12 passim, 115. *See also* God, love of
Love is News, 53
Luckmann, Thomas, 149 n. 1
Luxembourg, 187
Lydia (Family name). *See* Dietrich, Lydia ("Lydia")

Mail ministry, 49, 97
Malaysia, 167
Mammon, Valley of, 127, 129
Maria (Family name), 20, 21, 50, 68, 167 n. 9, 172 n. 23; Berg's move away from Europe with, 55; Berg's relationship with, beginning of, 35; Berg's trip to Israel with, 38; in the Canary Islands, 46–47; and the characterization of Moses David as a gentle lion, 197; and Davidito, 170 n. 17; as a possible successor, 172
Marriage, 53; rules regarding, removal of, 50; and sexuality, 5, 26, 39, 50, 78–79, 161
Martha (Family name), 186, 189, 190
Marx, Karl, 177 n. 2
Matthys, Jan, 3 n. 1
Meissner, Linda, 39 n. 2
Membership, 28, 29, 42, 51, 53; catacomb, 45, 126–27; formal, criteria for, 151 n. 2; and interactions with nonmembers, 79–82; statistics, 49, 54, 59, 166 n. 4; and status as a babe, 151; and transfers, 69–70. *See also* Socialization
Memorization, 152
Memphis (Egypt), 24, 33
Migration, 41, 53–54
Millennium, 5, 18, 24, 33, 84, 118, 148, 152, 171
Miller, Jane. *See* Mother Eve (Family name)
Mo. *See* Berg, David (Moses David)

Mo letters, 14, 20–22, 25, 38; and the bible, 5; and charismatic authority, 30; classification of, 21 n. 3; collection of, 189; corruption of, 48; and the *FNM* report, 52; and formal ideology, 18, 160 n. 6; and litnessing, 86; mass distribution of, vs. witnessing, 43; and mass exoduses from America, 41; production of, 58, 59; reading of, 61, 62–63, 118, 121–22, 123, 125, 182; and religious reasoning, 136, 144; selling of, 168; sensitive, 57, 82; sexuality in, 25–26; and socialization, 158, 163; and witnessing, 174
Montessori method, 59
Morality, 7–8, 107, 124, 135. *See also* Ethics
Moses (biblical figure), 36
Moses David. *See* Berg, David
Mother Eve (Family name), 31, 32
Music, 38, 56, 58, 59, 66–67, 189; and everyday life, 62
Music with Meaning (MWM), 49–50, 54, 55, 169 n. 12

Names, 5, 68, 95
Naomi (Family name), 178
Nathan (Family name), 182–84
National Broadcasting Company, 37
National Front, 94
Nationalise Re-organise Security-wise Revolution (NRS Revolution), 50–53
Neo-Pentecostals, 65 n. 6, 186
Netherlands, 8, 89, 187
New Jerusalem, 24, 125
Newlove, Rebecca, 46
New Nation News, 42, 52, 59, 71, 163
New Revolution, 44–46, 48–49, 72
Newsweek magazine, 117
New York City blackout, 141
Nuclear war, 53, 167 n. 11

Obedience Revolution, 168–69
Objectivity, 10, 124

Pakistan, 178
Paris colony, 45, 86 n. 5
Participant observation: and conversion, 16–17; covert, 177–86, 191–96; ethics of, 190–96; overt, 186–89, 193 n. 8,

Participant observation (*cont.*) 194–95; role of, and methodology, 9–13; and role stress, 14–16
Paternalism, 72–75
Patrick, Ted, 3n.2
Paul, 126, 130
Pentecostals, 130–31, 193n.7
People's Temple, 51
Philippines, 167
Plain Truth, 185
Poggio Secco, 190
Poland, 141
Police. *See* Romans
Poorboy Clubs, 43, 45, 48, 173, 175
Practical ideology, 18, 19, 93; description of, 136; and evidencing, 143–44; and proselytization, 75; and reading practices, 117; and witnessing, 113
Practical religious reasoning. *See* Reasoning, practical religious
Pragmatic imperative formulation, 130–31
Prayer, 12, 13, 20, 21, 56; and everyday life, 60, 62–63, 64–67; to God, 139; and reading practices, 119; and salvation, 27, 70; school, 35; and socialization, 157; and witnessing, 114
Procuring (provisioning), 36
Proselytization, 18–29, 58; and ideology, 75, 76; and interactions between members and nonmembers, 80–81; laws against, 38; negative responses to, 34, 38; and the NRS, 52; pleas to God regarding, 64; proclamation as the emphasis of, 54; reports on, in the *New Nation News*, 71; and the RNR, 49–50; statistics on, 59, 69, 70; and worldwide expansion, 41. *See also* Conversion; Litnessing; Witnessing
Protestantism, 20–21, 27, 56, 117
Provisioning. *See* Procuring (provisioning)
Public relations, 37–38, 47. *See also* Criticism, of the COG
Publications, COG, 55; for children, 54, 67; and formal ideology, 19; and litnessing, 91; street sale of, 5, 14; and witnessing, 41
Punishment, 24, 43, 152, 169

Quebec, 34–35

Rachel (Family name), 42, 49, 190
Racism, 23
Rationality, 8. *See also* Reasoning, practical religious
Reading, 117–32, 155, 166, 182; and analogy articulation, 129–30; and clarification, 123–24; and concretization, 125–27; and fringe-meaning articulation, 124–25; group, 119–21; interpretive procedures in, 122–31; of Mo letters, 61, 62–63, 118, 121–22, 123, 125, 182; and personal life experience, 127–28; and pragmatic imperative formulation, 130–31; presuppositions in, 121–22; product of, 131–32
Reasoning, practical religious, 113, 133–46; context-dependent nature of, 134–35; episodes of, 137–46; and evidencing, 143–44; and ideological challenges, 146–48; and instrumental utterances, 138–39; and interpreting, 140–43; and joking, 146; and justifying, 144–46; presuppositions in, 135–37; and routine affirmations, 138; and socialization, 155; and subculture idioms, 137–38
Rebecca (Family name), 178, 180
Rebuking, 73–74, 169
Recruitment, 27–28, 30, 43, 45; peak period of, 172; and socialization, 149–50
Reorganisation Nationalisation Revolution (RNR), 48–50, 53, 190
Retraining Centers, 169n.14
Revolutionary change, 30, 34, 40, 42
Role: distancing, 14, 15, 17; negotiation, 156–65; -self issue; 156; stress, 14–16
Romans (Police), 84
Routine affirmations, 120–21, 138
Royal Family, 45–46
Rules: in colonies, 36, 39, 50, 169; constitutive, 8–9; democratic, of the New Revolution, 72; on giving information to outsiders, 81–82; governing litnessing, 84–85, 86–87; regarding access strategies, absence of, 28; and socialization, 155
Russia, 147
Ruthie Rainbow (Family name), 179

Sackcloth vigil, 38
Salvation, 5, 20; and formal ideology, 23,

24; and the litnessing kerygma, 84; prayer, 70; of souls, and proselytization, 27–28, 29; and witnessing, 107–14, 116

Satan, 124, 127. See also Devil

School prayer, 35

Schutz, Alfred, 7 n. 9

Secrecy, 16, 46, 58, 74, 81–82

Self: deceptive presentation of, and participant observation, 192; role- issue, 156; and role stress, 14–16; sense of, and colony leaders, 16

Separatism, 24

Servants. See Shepherds

Service Centers, 50

Sexuality, 3, 122, 167; and children, 26, 53, 54, 170–71; and litnessing, 85, 88; and marriage, 5, 26, 39, 50, 78–79, 161; in the Mo letters, 25–26; Moses David's, 35, 36, 44; and multiple partners, 44; radicalization of, discomfort with, 49; and sexual freedom, 5, 26, 44, 50, 54; and textual analogies, 129; and visions, 21. See also Flirty Fishing

Shalom (Family name), 15 n. 15, 178, 179, 180, 182

Sheep, 85 n. 3, 94, 107

Shepherds, 40, 45, 54, 57, 118; and authority, 72–75; and colony meetings, 63–64; and everyday life, 60–66 passim; and finances, 68; and ideology, 141–42, 147–48; and litnessing, 85, 96; and participant observation, 184–85, 188, 192; and prayer, 64; and reading practices, 119; and transfers, 70; and the use of statistics, 70–71

Shillander, Vivian, 169 n. 14

Sin, 102, 110

Skid Row (Los Angeles), 37–40

Socialism, 5, 23, 24–25, 68

Socialization, 117, 149–65; into the Family, 149–55; practices, formal, 151–54; process of, 154–55; and role negotiation, 155–65

Social Science Research Council, 175

Soul Clinics, 32, 37

Souls, 25, 74; salvation of, and proselytization, 27; and socialization, 162; and witnessing, 98, 116

Soviet Union, 182

Spencer, Jeremy, 190

Spirit, 21–22, 88, 99, 136

Sterling University, 175

Subcultural idioms, 137–38

Sunflower (Family name), 15 n. 15, 180–81, 182

Sweeny, Michael. See Timothy Concerned (Family name)

Switzerland, 51

System, 5, 23–24, 41, 44, 80, 94, 136, 172, 185; activities once despised in, enjoyment of, 150; burning of bridges "back to," 151; commitment to, 106; corruption of, 33, 34, 36, 140–42; detachment from, 76; flexibility in dealing with, 45; names, 68, 95; removal of oneself from, 39

Systemites, 51, 129–30

Tax, 68

Teen Challenge, 34–35

Teen Training Camps (TTCs), 171–72

Tenerife colony, 46–48, 49, 59, 197

10:36ers, 37

Testimonies, 62

Texas Soul Clinic (TSC), 37–40

Thailand, 52, 169 n. 14

Third World, 54, 96, 174

Time magazine, 6, 117, 141, 147–48, 197

Timothy Concerned (Family name), 49, 172 n. 23

Tithe, 44, 51

Tithing Report Forms (TRFs), 51, 52, 167

Tongues, speaking in, 34, 65

Total commitment, 5–6, 24

Treadwell, John. See Jethro (John Treadwell)

Trials and battles, 158–59

Tribulation, 24–25, 171

True Komix literature, 54

Truth, 39 n. 2

Tucson (Arizona), 35

Turkey, 97

Typification, 93–95, 106–7

Uncle Dave's Teens for Christ, 34

Unification Church, 3, 173 n. 1, 189 n. 6, 193 n. 7

Utopianism, 5, 23–24

Vietnam, 31

Victory, 161

Wallis, Roy, 16, 28 n. 12, 175, 176, 183
"Warning Prophecy," 33, 35
Weber, Max, 7 nn. 8, 9, 30, 31
Wilson, Bryan, 176 n. 2
Witnessing, 5–6, 13, 27–28, 38–39, 45, 98–116, 166, 168; in bars, 146; and constitutive rules, 8; criteria of success for, 114–15; and everyday life, patterns of, 63; and evidencing, 111–13; forms, deviant, 115–16; and giving information to outsiders, 81–82; instructions on, 99 n. 1; interaction, description of, 101–7; and litnessing, comparison of, 98–99; and Mo letters, 174; and the NRS Revolution, 51, 52; and participant observation, 16–17, 187; and removing oneself from the System, 39; and road travels, 36; and salvation, 107–14, 116;

situations for, 100–101; and socialization, 155, 156, 162; and worldwide expansion, 41, 43
Witnessing Tips, 99 n. 1
Word Time, 14, 61, 95 n. 8, 118–19, 157
Wordsworth, Joel, 26 n. 11, 46
World Council for Churches, 176
World Services, 46, 50, 51, 53, 55, 167; and baby bonuses, 171; financial support of, 68; and local colonies, 58–59, 70; and posters, distribution of, 168 n. 9; "Wild Wind" unit, 59
World Wide Mail Ministry (WWMM), 51, 53

Yorkshire colony (England), 86 n. 5

Zion (Family name), 187

BP605.C38 V36 1991   c.1
Van Zandt, David E.,   100105   000
Living in the Children of G

3 9310 00088885 7
GOSHEN COLLEGE-GOOD LIBRARY